The Enigma War

The Enigma War

Józef Garliński

Charles Scribner's Sons

New York

Copyright © 1979 Józef Garliński
First U.S. edition published 1980.

Library of Congress Cataloging in Publication Data

Garliński, Józef.
   The Enigma war.

   British ed. published under title: Intercept.
   Bibliography: p. 205.
   Includes index.
   1. World War, 1939–1945—Secret service.
   2. World War, 1939–1945—Cryptography.
   I. Title.
D810.S7G32   1980   940.54′85   78-53452
ISBN 0-684-15866-3

1 3 5 7 9 11 13 15 17 19 F/C 20 18 16 14 12 10 8 6 4 2

Printed in the United States of America.

Contents

List of Plates *vi*

List of Line Drawings *viii*

Foreword by Professor R. V. Jones *ix*

Abbreviations *xi*

Acknowledgments *xvii*

Introduction *xix*

  1 The Birth of *Enigma* *1*

  2 The Breakthrough *12*

  3 The First Contribution to Alliance *28*

  4 Bletchley Park in the Shadow of the War *48*

  5 *Deutschland über Alles* *65*

  6 By Sea and in the Air *82*

  7 Secret Despatches Flow Towards Moscow *100*

  8 Uncle Sam and the Mikado *121*

  9 The Slide Towards Victory *135*

10 The Finest Hours *155*

11 In the Bunker *176*

Epilogue *188*

Appendix *192*

Select Bibliography *205*

Index *212*

List of Plates

Between pages 60 and 61
1   Primitive ciphering device
2   Ciphering machine built in Italy in 1430
3   First British ciphering device
4   Ciphering machine built in Sweden in 1786
5   Polish copy of *Enigma* made in France in 1940
6   Page from the German instructions for *Enigma*
7   Marian Rejewski in 1944
8   Jerzy Różycki in 1933
9   Henryk Zygalski in 1941
10   Lt-Col. Gwido Langer, Captain Gustave Bertrand and Captain MacFarlan at Château de Vignolles
11   Captain Henri Braquenié
12   Major Tadeusz Lisicki in 1944
13   Dillwyn Knox in 1933
14   Alan Turing in 1943
15   Commander Alastair Denniston
16   General Sir Stewart Menzies
17   Squadron Leader Frederick W. Winterbotham
18   Bletchley Park today
19   Château de Vignolles
20   Château de Fouzes

Between pages 124 and 125
21   Two surviving huts at Bletchley Park
22   British *Bombe*
23   German *Enigma* in its box
24   A typical signal deciphered and sent from Bletchley Park
25   William F. Friedman
26   Boris Hagelin
27   The reconstruction of the *Purple* machine
28   Rudolf Roessler
29   Sándor Radó
30   The Colossus at Bletchley Park in 1943

31 The *Geheimschreiber*
32 General Erich Fellgiebel
33 Admiral Wilhelm Canaris
34 Colonel Claus Schenk von Stauffenberg
35 Lieutenant Harro Schulze-Boysen
36 Captain Hans Hausamann
37 Otto Pünter
38 German B-Stellen
39 Stalin, Churchill and Roosevelt, Teheran, 1943
40 Cipher office tent at Yalta
41 MC–570, modern ciphering machine

Acknowledgments for photographs
Photographs courtesy of: Joan Bright Astley, Mavis Batey, Berto-Verlag
GMBH (Bonn), Corneille Braquenié, Bundesarchiv-Militärarchiv (Freiburg),
David and Charles (Newton Abbot), Robin Denniston, Margaret Finch,
Penelope Fitzgerald, General Sikorski Historical Institute (London), Harry
Golombek, Brian Johnson, Julliard (Paris), Hans Rudolf Kurz, Tadeusz Lisicki,
Public Record Office, Jürgen Rohwer, Secker and Warburg (London), Oskar
Stürzinger, Weidenfeld and Nicolson (London), Frederick W. Winterbotham.

List of Line Drawings

Map of Europe *xv*

Fig. 1   Diagram of inside of *Enigma* *21*

Fig. 2   Rotors *24*

Fig. 3   *Enigma*'s internal connections *31*

Fig. 4   Cyclometer *34*

Fig. 5   Polish *Bombe* *36*

Fig. 6   Perforated sheet *40*

Fig. 7   Development of German Cipher-Circles (Nets) for Radio Key M *75*

Foreword

by Professor R. V. Jones

FEW REVELATIONS concerning the Second World War have aroused so much interest as the fact that for most of the war Britain was able to read many of the secret communications of the German Armed Forces. This was largely due to the great and brilliant organization of the Government Codes and Ciphers School at Bletchley Park, whose outstanding work can at last be recognized alongside others such as the wartime developments in radar and in nuclear energy, where the achievements of our scientists and engineers have long been well known.

Perhaps one day an authoritative account of Bletchley's cryptographic achievement may become available. If so, besides paying tribute to what was done by the galaxy of British talent, it would also have to acknowledge the primary contribution of the Polish cryptographers before the outbreak of war. I was for part of the time at Bletchley, where I understood that our cryptographers were helped over one of the greatest of their initial difficulties by a gift from the Poles of a set of the cipher wheels from the type of *Enigma* machine used by the Germans to encipher their secret messages. The Poles were said to have somehow stolen the wheels; this would have been a marvellous cloak-and-dagger exploit, but the truth as told in this book is even more remarkable.

With some important help from the French regarding the nature of the *Enigma* machine which was being adopted by the German Armed Forces, a group of young Polish mathematicians set to work soon after 1930 to deduce the internal connections in its revolving wheels and their associated switching, purely from studies of the enciphered messages which it produced, and which were being transmitted by German units in the belief that they were completely secure. By 1937 the Polish cryptographers had succeeded first in working out the connections and then in deciphering German messages; they even designed a machine for the purpose. Some measure of their feat is provided by the fact that their British counterparts were still, two years later, some way from success; as I understood it, we were hampered by not realizing that although the *Enigma* machine had a keyboard with the same distribution of letters as a conventional typewriter, Q W E R T ... the keys were wired into the machine in alphabetical order, so that A and not Q went to the first connection, and B and not W to the second and so forth. This, incidentally, accounts for the fact that while the original *Enigma* machines had a typewriter keyboard, the Polish reconstructions have one that is alphabetically arranged.

With war imminent, the Poles made all their work available to the British and the French and so we were able to build upon what they had so brilliantly done. It would, of course, be wrong to give the impression that there was no more to do; the *Enigma* machine settings were changed very frequently, and each new setting had to be deduced. Moreover, the Germans introduced new wheels with different internal wiring, and each new development had painfully to be worked out. The feats of the British cryptographers in overcoming these later and greater difficulties were well worthy of the Polish act of confidence in giving us the benefit of what they had achieved.

Besides telling the story of the Polish contribution, Dr Garliński goes on to describe both the German background and the use that the Allies made of the mastery of *Enigma*. While it is probably true to say that none of the major decisions of the war was based on evidence from the *Enigma* decrypts alone, it is certainly true that this evidence entered in part into many operational decisions, and that in critical phases of the war, when forces on either side were otherwise fairly matched, *Enigma* gave the Allies a most definite and often decisive advantage.

The Poles, therefore, deserve our gratitude and admiration. Overrun within a few days of the outbreak of war, they nevertheless kept the secret of their *Enigma* work from the Germans. And we should also remember that many Poles escaped to serve, for example, with the Royal Air Force in the Battle of Britain or to re-form the Polish Army in exile, while others stayed to carry out the dangerous work of intelligence – for example actually hiding a crashed V2 and examining its components in scientific detail.

The author of this book, Dr Józef Garliński, is typical of his courageous and resilient countrymen: starting as a Cavalry Officer, he joined the underground and was attached to the headquarters of the Polish Home Army. Arrested in 1943, he was sent to Auschwitz and then to another concentration camp, Neuengamme. Triumphing over these experiences, he started a fresh life in London after the war and took the degree of Doctor of Philosophy at the London School of Economics. This is his eighth book and his fourth in English; and in recording what his Polish countrymen suffered and achieved he has performed a unique and timely service.

R. V. Jones

Abbreviations

CRYPTOLOGY AND CIPHER MACHINES

Bombe	machine composed of six *Enigmas*, powered by electricity, which worked out the *Enigma* settings.
Bruno	code name of French cryptological unit during the campaign in France, in 1940.
Cadix	code name of French cryptological unit in unoccupied France.
C-41	German cipher machine based on Hagelin's M-209.
Chi-Stelle	German Cipher Office.
Cipher	method of secret writing that replaces each character or figure of the original with a different letter or symbol, or achieving the same effect by disarranging the original order of the letters.
Clear or Plaintext	original message in ordinary language.
Code	system which substitutes certain symbols, words or groups of letters for the words or phrases or whole messages of plaintexts.
Colossus	first computer which worked out the *Geheimschreiber* settings.
Cryptanalysis	technique of deciphering or decoding secret messages without access to the code or key.
Cryptology	study of secret communications.
Cryptogram	secret message in code or cipher.
Cyclometer	machine constructed from elements of two *Enigmas* which worked out the length of cycles for the filing system.
Decipher/decode	to take a secret message and convert it into plaintext by the use of a key or a cipher.
Encipher/encode	to put a plaintext message into cipher or code.
Ekipa Z	code name of Polish cryptological team in Bruno.
Enigma	German ciphering machine.
Fish	nickname for the *Geheimschreiber*.
Geheimschreiber	German ciphering machine.
Grille	system of finding out the elements of the daily key.
Group 300	code name of Polish cryptological section in Cadix.
Grundstellung	basic encoding position of *Enigma*.
Hard-ware	main physical units making up the computer system.
HC-570	most modern computer-type cipher machine transmitter.
'Heath Robinson'	first electronic machine based on statistical systems of breaking ciphers.

Abbreviations

HX-61	electro-mechanical cipher machine.
Key	word or letters used to set the pattern of a code or cipher in such a way that the message cannot be deciphered without obtaining or discovering it.
M-209	cipher machine produced by Boris Hagelin as C-36 and sold to USA.
Net	German cipher-circle with its own key and a code name (Hydra, Triton, Thetis, etc.).
Off-line system	machine not connected to any other system, i.e., it produces a tape which can be delivered by hand or by post or transmitted by means of the machine.
On-line system	machine connected to a main installation or computer and allowing access to the information available from that computer (feed out).
'Oriental Goddess'	machine which worked out the *Enigma* settings.
Perforated sheet	piece of paper with about 1,000 holes cut according to a pre-determined pattern, which worked out the *Enigma* settings.
Purple	American name given to Japanese cipher machine.
Room 40	room at the Admiralty where, during the First World War, cryptanalysts worked.
Rotor	main enciphering component of *Enigma* in the form of a revolving wired drum creating a set of electrical paths.
'Sigaba'	slang name of the American cipher machine M-134-C.
Soft-ware	all subsidiary equipment, i.e., tapes, cassettes, reels, etc., used for feeding into or out of the computer.
Substitution	system of enciphering based on the replacement of letters by other letters, numbers or symbols.
Transposition	system of enciphering based on mixing letters and arranging them in an unusual order.
Typex	British ciphering machine.
Umkehrwalze	in English Reflector, a reversing, static drum, which caused the letters to go through all the rotors again.

GENERAL

Abwehr	German military intelligence.
A-Dienst	*Auswertdienst* (Utilization service).
Anvil	code name for the Anglo-American invasion of Southern France in 1944.
Barbarossa	code name of a secret plan for the German invasion of Russia in 1941.
B-Dienst	*Beobachtungsdienst* (radio-reconnaissance observation).
Bodyguard	code name for a deception plan to cover the Second Front in 1944.
BP	Bletchley Park.
CCS	Combined Chiefs of Staffs, the Anglo-American Supreme Command in Washington.
DAI	Director of Air Intelligence.
Deuxième Bureau	French Military Intelligence.

D/F	Direction Finder.
DMI	Director of Military Intelligence.
DNI	Director of Naval Intelligence.
E-Dienst	*Entzifferungsdienst* (cipher section).
F/A	*Funkaufklärung* (radio-reconnaissance).
FHD	*Funkhorchdienst* (radio-monitoring department of the *Abwehr* in the *Reichswehr*).
Forschungsamt	Research Office of the German Air Ministry for collecting secret information on all aspects of life in the Third *Reich*.
GCCS	Government Code and Cipher School, the pre-war British code-breaking organization moved to Bletchley Park in 1939.
Gestapo	*Geheime Staatspolizei* (secret state police).
H/F	high frequency.
HF/DF	high frequency direction finder.
Horchdienst	monitoring department of the *Abwehr* in the *Reichswehr*.
Jupiter	code name for the Western plan prepared in 1942, which envisaged the attack on Norway.
LCS	London Controlling Section, the organization within the Joint Planning Staff for the co-ordination of strategic deception.
Lucy Ring	code name for an intelligence network in Switzerland built by Rudolf Roessler.
Luftwaffe	German Air Force.
M/F	medium frequency.
MI 5	British Counter Intelligence.
MI-6	British Intelligence Service.
Mincemeat	code name for the deception operation known as 'The Man Who Never Was'.
Neptune	code name for the secret plan for landings in Normandy, in 1944.
NID	Naval Intelligence Division.
NSDAP	*National Socialistische Deutsche Arbeitspartei* (National-socialist German Workers' Party).
OIC	Operational Intelligence Centre.
OKH	*Oberkommando des Heeres* (High Command of the German Army.
OKL	*Oberkommando der Luftwaffe* (High Command of the German Air Force).
OKM	*Oberkommando der Marine* (High Command of the German Navy).
OKW	*Oberkommando der Wehrmacht* (High Command of the German Armed Forces).
OSS	Office of Strategic Services.
Overlord	code name for the plan for the invasion of north-west Europe in 1944.
Quicksilver	code name for the complex operation to convince the Germans that the main landing attack would be directed on the Pas de Calais.
Reichswehr	German Army, without Air Force, after the Treaty of Versailles.

Abbreviations

Rote Kapelle	The Red Orchestra, Soviet spy-ring in Germany.
RSHA	*Reichssicherheitshauptamt* (state security headquarters).
Schwarze Kapelle	The Black Orchestra, the name used by German security for the anti-Hitler conspiracy in the German army.
SD	*Sicherheitsdienst* (security service).
Sea-Lion	code name for the German plan to invade Great Britain in 1940.
SIS	Secret Intelligence Service.
SLU	Special Liaison Unit responsible for delivering secret messages of Ultra deciphered at Bletchley Park.
SOE	Special Operations Executive, a secret British organization set up to help the countries under German and Japanese occupation.
SS	*Schutzstaffel* (German political-military protection units).
Torch	code-name for the Anglo-American landing in North Africa in 1942.
XX–Committee	Inter-service committee responsible for strategic deception, double-agents, etc.
Ultra	code name for intelligence unit which distributed *Enigma*-deciphered messages.
VHN	*Wehrmachtnachrichtenverbindungen (Wehrmacht* Intelligence Communications).
VHF	very high frequency.
V–1	*Vergeltungswaffe I* (flying bomb).
V–2	*Vergeltungswaffe II* (rocket).
W.Board	joint inter-service board dealing with the most secret matters.
Wehrmacht	German Armed Forces.
Werwolf	secret Nazi diversionary organization.

EUROPE on 1.1.1941

GREENLAND

Denmark Strait

ICELAND

Faroe Is.

Shetland Is.

Lofoten Is.

Narvik

SWEDEN

NORWAY

FINLAND

Oslo

Stockholm

Helsinki

Leningrad

Scapa Flow

Stavanger

Marstrand

Moscow

UK

Bletchley Park

DENMARK

Gdansk

USSR

Oxford

Cambridge

Kiel

Hamburg

East Prussia

Rastenburg

London

Amsterdam

Berlin

Poznan

Warsaw

HOLLAND

Antwerp

Brussels

BELGIUM

Lux.

GERMANY

Prague

POLAND

Kiev

Paris

FRANCE

Zürich

Berchtesgaden

SLOVAKIA

Brest

Bern

Lucerne

HUNGARY

RUMANIA

Geneva

Switz.

Belgrade

Ploesti

Vichy

YUGOSLAVIA

Bucharest

Gran Sasso

Marseilles

Corsica

Rome

ALBANIA

Sofia

BULGARIA

Black Sea

Barcelona

ITALY

GREECE

PORTUGAL

SPAIN

Madrid

Sardinia

Naples

Ankara

Lisbon

Huelva

Palermo

TURKEY

Gibraltar

Algiers

Tunis

Crete

Cyprus

Casablanca

TUNISIA

MOROCCO

ALGERIA

LIBYA

EGYPT

Cairo

Acknowledgments

AT THE VERY BEGINNING I must say that this book would probably never have been written if it were not for Colonel Tadeusz Lisicki, who urged me to it. He had received a proposal from the publisher to write such a book himself, for he knew many of the details connected with *Enigma*, but being neither an historian nor a writer, he passed on the proposal to me. We were to be co-authors. Later he decided that he would not appear in this role, since in fact I did all the writing, but that in no way detracts from the part he played in gathering material and giving me every possible assistance. Thanks to him many mistakes in the text were avoided; and he also put me in touch with several people, who gave me useful information. Finally he wrote the Appendix in which he explains how *Enigma* was broken, using mathematical, cryptological and analytical methods. We began our co-operation as acquaintances; we finished as friends.

Thanks to him correspondence was kept up with Marian Rejewski in Poland, the only one of the three Polish cryptanalysts who broke the secret of *Enigma* who is still alive. Naturally what he has to say is of documentary value. In several letters he recalled the years during which they struggled with the secret of the German machine; he made clear several controversial questions; and he corrected many false, though widely accepted, conceptions. Without his help the opening chapters of the book would be much poorer.

I also received valuable help from Colonel Stefan Mayer, the one-time war Head of the Intelligence Department of the Polish General Staff and so in contact with the cryptologists.

I owe much to Professor Reginald V. Jones, who kindly agreed to write a foreword to my book. His own memoirs made many technicalities clear and demonstrated the methods used by scientific intelligence during the war. In this country valuable help was also given to me by Dr J. W. M. Chapman and Professor M. R. D. Foot, while Harry Golombek and Ruth Thompson gave me some idea of the work carried out at Bletchley Park. The personnel of the Public Record Office were also very kind.

I value highly the help of Herr Oskar Stürzinger of Switzerland, who not

Acknowledgments

only gave me much information and showed me round the modern factory of cipher machines, but also read those chapters of my script which contain technical information, and made certain essential corrections. In Switzerland I also talked to Lieutenant-Colonel Dr Hans Rudolf Kurz, Dr Xaver Schnieper and Otto Pünter who gave me valuable information.

I was also given important help by Professor Dr Jürgen Rohwer of Stuttgart, who answered my many questions and facilitated contacts with German war witnesses. Thanks to him I either talked to or exchanged letters with Captain of the Navy Heinz Bonatz, General Leo Hepp, Colonel of the Air Force Karl Otto Hoffmann, Dr Erich Hüttenhein of the Cipher Office, Captain of the Navy Johannes Möller and Captain of the Navy Hans Meckel. I am much obliged to them.

I also retain in grateful memory the help given by the following: Joan Astley, Ernest L. Bell III (USA), Mavis Batey, Miss Susan Bennet, Anthony Brooks, Peter Calvocoressi, Corneille Braquenié (France), Jerzy Budkiewicz (Germany), Robin Denniston, Margaret Finch, Penelope Fitzgerald, Lieutenant Colonel Roman Garby-Czerniawski, Richard Garnett, Peter Hennessy, Geoffrey Jacobs, Brian Johnson, Miss Diana Johnson, Dr Józef Kiermisz (Israel), Ronald Lewin, Walter Meyer (Switzerland), Józef Pawlica, Werner Rings (Switzerland), Maria Barbara Różycka (Poland), Professor J. Stengers (Belgium), J. Vanvelkenhuyzen (Belgium) and Group Captain Frederick W. Winterbotham.

J. G. London, January 1979

xviii

Introduction

LIKE SO MANY of my contemporaries, I took part in the last war and was fated to experience it from many different angles. On the basis of my own observations, I saw full well its destruction and felt that I knew a great deal about it. It was only after beginning serious historical research and examining archives that I realized how little I did know about the actual conduct of the war and that my knowledge was based mainly on a number of simplistic notions created by the propaganda machine. My eyes were only really opened when I found out about *Enigma* and about many other secrets of the last war which only now, so many years later, are coming to light. I finally accepted that for many years my views on the war had been those of the young man who had left for it on horseback and who, despite many tricks of fate, had added but little to his knowledge of the actual forces over a vast range of fronts.

Pondering the problem of *Enigma* and how to present it, I came to the conclusion that I would best achieve this in a readable book, accessible to all and not only to the expert. Thus I have tried to avoid great columns of figures or long mathematical and technical deliberations, restricting myself to the simplest of explanations and only in the appendix is there food for the specialist cryptologist. I likewise resolved not to confine myself to the actual breaking of the German machine and the circumstances surrounding this event, but to enlarge my horizons to embrace the results of this achievement and its effect on the course of the war. It was impossible to examine every area of influence, and so I have chosen only those fragments which seemed to me to be the most important and typical of the results achieved with *Enigma*. It seemed to me inadequate to examine only Polish, French and later British achievements, so I have used materials dealing with German, American, Soviet and Japanese involvement. However, in the course of my study, I have concentrated on British exploits, since it was here that the results of the original breakthrough played the greatest part, were the most widely applied and led to the most important developments. Similarly, although on a smaller scale, I have examined the German side; after all, it was here that the problem of *Enigma* arose and it was Germany who was our main adversary during the war.

I am only too conscious of the fact that my picture is incomplete, that sometimes I have had to resort to hypothesis and that I may have made mistakes of omission or fact. This has arisen because only part of the *Enigma* documents are accessible: those dealing with a number of radio signals deciphered at Bletchley Park. I have, therefore, also relied on accounts, memoirs and conversations with living participants in those events who have agreed to help.

I have had to treat all this material most carefully, since in some publications and personal accounts one comes across a great many mistakes caused by a conscious intention to mislead, which began during the war and continues even to this day.

Taking into consideration the results of the actual breaking of the German machine, I had to remember that knowledge of the enemy's secret plans was not enough: one had to have the power to resist them. Therefore, during the German attack on Poland in 1939 and the French campaign, the reading of German despatches made no impact at all or this impact was very small.

The history of *Enigma* is indeed fascinating. The decisive achievements of the Polish cryptanalysts, who managed to break the German secret by a process of mathematical deduction, only partially assisted by more traditional forms of intelligence; the Germans' unshakeable belief in the security of their own machine; the great British achievement of maintaining secrecy, even though 10,000 people worked in Bletchley Park and related establishments – all this would not jar in a work of fiction, and yet it is all true.

Oscar Wilde it was who said 'life resembles art'. In some measure the story of *Enigma* bears out this paradox.

J. G.
London

The Birth of *Enigma*

1

A GERMAN SUBMARINE was moving quietly on the surface of the Channel, off the south coast of England. It was an early morning in autumn 1939, the war was now a few weeks old and the submarine was returning to base from the Atlantic. English coastal waters were the most dangerous and submarines usually went round the north of Scotland, submerged deeply. This time, however, a fault in the batteries had caused the captain to risk the Channel route. He had brought his craft to the surface since the batteries, although still useable, were giving off gas. While his engineers worked feverishly to repair the fault, he stood on the small conning-tower with several petty officers scanning the waves, which almost blended into the horizon through his binoculars. It was still dark, a light rain was falling and the ship moved forward slowly through the silence. It seemed that the whole world was resting after the exertions of the previous day.

Suddenly the captain's keen ear caught a strange sound. He nudged the sailor nearest him and they both held their breath and listened. For a moment they seemed to be hearing the beat of their own engines, but they strained their ears and a few seconds later there could be no doubt: it was the distant throb of an approaching ship.

The captain immediately ordered 'stop engines', the submarine lost way and within a few minutes was lying motionless in perfect silence. No one spoke, no one smoked and the sailors crowded round their captain and listened intently to the growing beat. They still could not see anything, while their vessel, tossed by the waves, was barely visible. There was a possibility that they might remain undetected.

Fate, however, decided otherwise. A few minutes later the noise of engines grew louder and a long shape emerged from the dawn; those watching had no doubt that it was a destroyer and almost certainly British. The captain gave another command and two sailors uncovered a small gun. There was still a slight chance that the enemy might sail past, but, if not, they would have to fight, whatever the odds.

The dark shape drew nearer and her bridge, masts and guns could clearly be seen. Two searchlights came on and began to sweep the waves; one of them caught the submarine and held it in its beam. The German commander tried to reach the hatch, but at that very moment there was a ripple of flame along the destroyer followed by a loud detonation. The submarine reeled and the sailors were thrown from the deck into the sea. More shells exploded, machine guns opened up and bullets rang out against the armour plating. The underwater marauder had fallen prey to a stronger opponent.

The destroyer lowered her boats and a few minutes later armed sailors boarded their prize. All the Germans were ordered up and their vessel was searched thoroughly. The boats went back and forth several times, ferrying the prisoners to the British ship and only after they had been confined well below-decks did another boat set out for the submarine. It carried three men in naval uniform, who were not members of the crew. They boarded the deserted vessel and went below, where they stayed for some time. Eventually they reappeared carrying a small package wrapped in a blanket. The young sailors, for whom the capture of the enemy submarine had been a great event, paid the strangers practically no attention in their excitement. How could they know that the simple and apparently routine operation which had taken place before their very eyes, and with their help, was to be of outstanding significance for the further conduct of the war?

The three men got into their boat and made for the destroyer where they climbed aboard and disappeared below. Only then did two boat-loads of sailors cast off to take possession of the enemy ship.[1]

2

At about three o'clock on a Saturday afternoon the telephone rang in the Warsaw flat of Ludomir Danilewicz. It was the beginning of January 1929 and Europe was in the grip of one of the hardest winters of the decade. Danilewicz, a young man of twenty-five and one of the pioneers of radio in Poland, was working on the small radio transmitter which he had constructed and did not immediately answer. He let the telephone ring a few times before lifting the receiver.

The voice of the duty officer at the army General Staff came on the line. He was calling on behalf of the head of counter-intelligence and requested Danilewicz to get hold of a taxi and come over to the Staff as soon as possible on a secret and important matter.

On arrival at the General Staff, which at that time on a Saturday was almost deserted, Danilewicz met Lieutenant Maksymilian Ciężki from the Intelligence Cipher Department whom he knew well and with whom he had been working for the last few years. As an electrical engineer Danilewicz ran a wireless factory and co-operated with Intelligence, providing equipment and sometimes advice.

That afternoon a piece of interesting information had been hurriedly sent over from the Warsaw customs office. A few hours earlier the office had received from Germany a crate addressed to a German firm with offices in Warsaw. The firm's representative had immediately arrived, although no one had called him, saying that the crate contained some radio equipment which had been sent by mistake and which should be forthwith returned to Germany. The man's insistence, coupled with his Consulate's intervention, appeared suspicious and the customs office had decided to call in military intelligence.[2]

Government offices did not work on Saturday afternoons and so the Germans were told that they would have to wait until Monday. This gave the Poles several hours to examine discreetly the mysterious crate. Danilewicz, together with his closest partner, engineer Antoni Palluth, collected all the necessary equipment and tools and on the Sunday morning went to the customs office. They took all possible precautions since the Germans could well have set up some sort of surveillance. First of all they methodically examined the crate and then carefully unpacked it. It turned out that it did not contain wireless equipment; instead the engineers saw before them a machine which Palluth, an experienced cryptologist, recognized as a cipher machine. They quickly started to examine the mechanism, taking several photographs, making a diagram of its construction and measuring its dimensions. They then examined its working and the rotor mechanism and finally they played the whole machine through. The crate was repacked, all traces of their work removed and the postal labels carefully replaced.[3] Even pedantic German eyes would be unable to spot anything. The material collected, minus the name of the apparatus, since no one in Warsaw knew it, was deposited in the Intelligence Cipher Department.

3

As a result of the First World War the German *Reich* had been not only humiliated, but also considerably weakened by a multitude of restrictions and had lost much territory. She had been deprived of her colonies in East Africa, the whole Rhineland had been demilitarized, Alsace and Lorraine had been returned to France and in the east the newly reborn Polish state had taken part of Silesia, Pomerania and territory around Poznań.

All these losses hurt the Germans grievously, but above all they were angered by the thought of the provinces which they had had to relinquish to Poland. At one time the Polish state had been great and had covered an area of more than a million square kilometres in Central and East Europe. Over the years this empire had degenerated, had failed to modernize its outdated political and social system and had been unable to deal with internal troubles and the selfishness of its ruling classes. Eventually, as a result of the three partitions at the end of the eighteenth century, it had completely lost its independence, allowing itself to be divided between Russia, Prussia and Austria. Despite the Poles' own fault, this action had been plunder on a scale almost unheard of in the history of Europe.

The Poles, never reconciling themselves to their loss of independence, tried to slow down the process of forcible assimilation and resisted the partitioning countries. They suffered losses and several times started national uprisings, which ended in bloody repression. The struggle lasted for several generations and finally, in 1918, after 127 years of bondage, it brought the Poles freedom as a result of a quite exceptional series of circumstances: all the three partitioning powers were defeated in the World War.[4]

The new Polish state could exist only if some of the land previously lost in the partitions was regained. Relations with the former partitioning powers were varied. The Austro-Hungarian Empire had collapsed after the war and so the Poles encountered no problems from that direction. They waged a separate war against revolutionary Russia in 1919–1920, won it, and achieved a peace settlement in Riga in March 1921 which settled the frontiers between the two countries.[5] Aggressive Soviet communism continued to sow disorder within Poland, but the frontier issue was for some time satisfactorily concluded.

The question of the German-Polish frontier raised a number of complications. One of President Wilson's fourteen points, outlining a plan for post-war Europe, had envisioned an independent Poland with access to the sea. This could be achieved only by cutting through Pomerania to the Baltic Sea with Gdańsk (Danzig) as a port. Although this town was declared 'free', with a High Commissioner of the League of Nations, the Germans had to return a part of Pomerania to the Poles. In Poznań and the surrounding areas an anti-German uprising broke out and in Silesia there were three such uprisings. At Versailles it had been decided that in Silesia there would be a plebiscite, under the control of an Allied Commission, and consequently this province, rich in coal and industry, was divided. In the German part there were many Poles, while a number of Germans lived in the Polish part.[6]

This state of affairs continually angered German revisionists. None of them cared to remember the plunder which had taken place almost 150 years earlier; instead they used every opportunity to stress in the international arena that the Poles had taken purely German territories, to which they had no right.[7] Polish rebuttals that the Germans had attempted forcible assimilation, applied religious and economic pressures and even germanized Polish names, particularly in Bismarck's time, were ignored.

This created an atmosphere of enmity and continual tension between the two countries, fuelled by the fact that their long history had contained numerous and often very bloody wars. The Germans living in Poland ostentatiously pretended not to know Polish, while in Poznań castle, which was built in genuine Teutonic style, furniture, tapestries and pictures were frequently found to have been slashed by German tourists. In Gdańsk, where the Poles had received the right to use the port, to have their own post office and various other government departments, there were frequent incidents. The reborn Polish state felt itself to be seriously threatened from the west.

4

German revisionism, which was born the day after the Berlin parliament's acceptance of the Treaty of Versailles, by 237 votes to 138, was not directed exclusively at Poland. It had, however, no chance of success without the rebuilding of Germany's military strength. The decisions of Versailles limited the German Army, called the *Reichswehr*, to one hundred thousand soldiers, without an Air Force, without armour and with a very weak fleet, together with limitations on armament production. An Allied Control Commission operated on German soil, but the Germans used numerous means to avoid its inhibiting restrictions. From the first post-war years they began to experiment with various new weapons, which the Treaty of Versailles had not banned, since they simply had not been foreseen. German scientists argued that they were working on new inventions which were solely for peaceful purposes.[8] The whole country was undermined by post-war unrest based on class dissension; this was followed by a serious economic crisis and catastrophic inflation. The exchequer was burdened with colossal war reparations, but there was never any lack of funds for secret rearmament. Factories began to receive orders for quite innocuous products, which in time of war could be used as arms. Under the guise of mass tourism and sport youngsters were being prepared for military service. The Versailles decisions had ordered the Germans to abandon yearly conscription to avoid creating a new army, but this stipulation suited the Germans, since it built a professional force in which each private had the qualifications to be a fine NCO. These one hundred thousand soldiers could at any time become the basis for the speedy buildup of a great army, if the conditions were favourable.[9]

However all this was too little and the Germans, profiting from misunderstandings between the victorious Allies, in particular between France and Great Britain, made their own diplomatic initiative with relative freedom and, as early as 1922, came to an agreement in Rapallo with Soviet Russia. The treaty contained several clauses on military co-operation. The German government received the right to build in Russia factories producing poison gas and to send its officers for joint training with the Soviets. The training covered weapons expressly forbidden by the Versailles Treaty. This co-operation developed very successfully and the Germans carried out tests on tanks and aircraft in Russia and produced them in factories there. For their part German specialists returned the compliment by providing the Russians with technical, strategic and secret military information.[10] Notwithstanding the economic crisis, the day was approaching when the German *Reich* would be ready for a new war, with an army which would be strong and modern.

Such an army also required secure means of modern communications. During the First World War radiotelegraphy had developed rapidly, replacing all other methods of swift communication, and it was apparent that when a new war broke out, radio would be the basis for signalling between staffs and higher commands. Radio messages have the one essential virtue that they reach their destination quickly, but they also have the basic defect that they can be easily intercepted.

The Germans had had some very unhappy experiences in the First World War when, as a result of their own carelessness, signals had been intercepted and deciphered by the French. This had happened for several reasons. First of all the operators had been inadequately trained, since radio did not yet have a serious tradition, and so they had made mistakes. They requested signals to be repeated and sometimes even asked for transmissions to be sent 'in clear', because they were unable to decipher them. Furthermore the constant repetition of specific stations' call signs enabled them to be recognized more easily. Lastly, enciphering and deciphering were carried out manually and were thus very imprecise and slow.[11] If a new war was to bring some chance of success, all this had to be avoided.

It was clear that the modern German Army needed a cipher machine which would be secure and easy to operate.

5

Attempts to transmit secret information by means of signs are thousands of years old. At first pictures representing concepts were used, and later letters and numbers whose order and meaning were known only to the few people involved.

Essentially cryptography embraces only two methods of secret writing.

The first one consists of substituting columns of figures or letters for whole words or even phrases. This is called a code. In order to read a message written in this fashion the reader must have a book containing the agreed code. The second system operates with only single letters and is called a cipher. This system is now in general use and is the only one guaranteeing flexibility and accuracy while presenting great difficulty to the potential breaker.[12] It should be mentioned, however, that in business the use of coding is still popular.

Ciphers are of two basic kinds. The first one consists of mixing letters and arranging them in an unusual order: this is called transposition. For instance instead of the word *weather* one can use the ciphered, and unintelligible to the outsider, word *ewrahet*. The other system is based on the replacement of letters by other letters or numbers and even symbols: this is called substitution. Again, using our own example, let us imagine that the alphabet, consisting of twenty-six letters, can be substituted simply as follows: a=1, b=2, c=3 etc.; our word *weather* will become 23 5 1 20 8 5 18. In order to complicate the cipher and make the task of breaking it more difficult, the two systems can be combined.[13]

Any combination of letters and numbers may, of course, be used. During the last war, when almost the whole of Europe was under occupation and there were underground organizations operating everywhere, the use of various types of secret writing was widespread. This was much more complicated when it came to sending messages to London – the heart and brain of the free world at that time – and much simpler for internal communications. In resistance movements at the lower levels there was a widespread use of book ciphers, mainly for ciphering names and addresses as well as particularly important and brief messages. This cipher operated as follows: all those involved had a copy of the same book in the same edition. In the columns of figures of the agreed cipher the first one represented the page of the book, the second the line and the third one the actual letter. This primitive method could be further complicated by reading each page from the bottom, by adding to each number the date of the enciphered message and so on. A specialist would have been able to decipher it without much difficulty, but an ordinary policeman could not. It was also vital that the girl couriers, who carried messages and passed them on, meeting in the street the next girl in the chain, should not be able to read them.[14] It is probable that the same or similar methods were used in Paris, Amsterdam, Warsaw and Belgrade.

For many centuries the secret writing had been done by hand, which was a slow method and, with a greater volume of messages to deal with, particularly during wartime, it was inadequate. Various attempts were made to build a machine to do the job.

The oldest one goes back to the fifteenth century, for it was built in 1430 by an Italian, Baptista Alberti. The machine was used for transposition and for deciphering and was operated manually. It had two concentric alphabet rings and an indicator, with a window in it for each ring, to show the corresponding letters. The two rings could be turned in opposite directions to each other. The crypto letters would be located in the outer window and the corresponding plaintext letter read off in the inner window.[15]

Other devices were constructed in later centuries. One of them should be mentioned, as it was the first proper cipher machine. The inventor was a Swedish officer, Gripenstierna, who offered it to King Gustav III in 1786. It was a wooden construction in the form of a cylinder with a number of alphabet rings. The machine was operated by two people, because the inventor understood the fundamental principle of ciphering: the person setting the key should remain ignorant of the text of the message ciphered and deciphered by the other person.[16]

In later years an Englishman turned his mind to the problem of modern ciphering. He was Charles Wheatstone, a keen amateur with a lively and fertile mind. Wheatstone was one of the polymaths who, in the nineteenth century, when the great development of technology was just beginning, exercised their active minds in many diverse fields and achieved some fine results. He built an electric telegraph, published several articles on acoustics, was interested in phonetics and developed the concertina. He was fascinated by cryptology and so set about building a cipher machine. He used the case of a large clock with two circles of letters on the face and, of course, two hands. The larger circle, around which moved the large hand, had twenty-six letters and one empty space, while the smaller one, corresponding to the small hand, also had twenty-six letters, but without the empty space. The letters on the large circle were arranged alphabetically, while those on the smaller one were arranged haphazardly, according to a secret design of the constructor. The hands were linked by a system of cogs so that one complete revolution of the large hand moved the small hand only a short distance: one letter. The initial setting of the small hand was the key to the cipher. Wheatstone demonstrated his machine in Paris in 1867 and created a sensation. Even the French Army was interested. For those days the machine had great cryptographical value.[17] It was the right time to develop a fast and accurate method of ciphering, for a year before the English inventor's demonstration, the first telegraph cable had been laid between Europe and America.

Later many other men worked on similar ideas, but it was only during the First World War that serious development of better and safer cipher machines began. During the war years hundreds of inventions were built and patented. Of these only a few were of any real value, but none of them was actually used during the conflict.[18] After the war this development was not halted, in fact quite the contrary, it increased, probably in anticipation of the next world lunacy.

6

In 1919 a Dutchman, Hugo Alexander Koch, whose hobby was solving technical problems, patented an invention which, in his own words, was a secret writing machine. It was emphasized in this patent 'that steel wires on pulleys, levers, rays of light, or air, water, or oil flowing through tubes could transmit the enciphering impulse as well as electricity did'. Koch gave a number of other details of his invention, but he did not build any machine on these lines. It seemed to him that his machine had some commercial potential and so he set up a firm in whose name the patent was taken out.[19]

At the same time in the Berlin suburb of Wilmersdorf an engineer called Arthur Scherbius was carrying out various experiments and had patented a number of quite different inventions. He was also interested in cryptology and had built several cipher machines. They were large and clumsy, similar to cash registers or typewriters, were operated electrically and worked on a rotor system. There were three of these and a fourth, a reversing one, caused the letters to go through the rotors again. In German it was called *Umkerwalze*, in English Reflector. It was never altered. The machine's keys with twenty-six letters were connected to bulbs, and the connections were made by means of a permutation switch which allowed every conceivable combination. These switches were in the form of rotors which were connected by means of gearing. Scherbius also hoped that this machine might bring him some material benefits and so, in 1923, he set up a small partnership in Berlin called *Chiffrienmaschinen Aktien Gesellschaft*. He presented his invention at the congress of the International Postal Union and received extensive coverage in the *Radio News*. The scientific director of the Institute of Criminology in Vienna, Dr Siegfried Türkel, wrote at length and positively about the new machine.

During the following few years the machine went through several stages of development and several fundamental changes were made as a result of the purchase of Hugo Koch's patent. Koch himself had been stricken by a mortal illness.[20] The company started an extensive advertising campaign in the hope that the machine would interest large firms and that they would start to buy it for commercial purposes. It did not, however, meet with success; those were the years in which industry was still unwilling to incur the considerable costs connected with preserving trade secrets.

A brighter sign appeared on the horizon in 1926, when the German Navy, greatly reduced in strength under the terms of the Treaty of Versailles, yet active, began to take an interest in the machine. The Admiralty in great secrecy contacted the Berlin company, bought one machine and instructed a trusted officer, Captain Johannes Möller, to take it from Berlin to Kiel. After careful study of the complicated mechanism it was decided that the machine would be brought into use in the same year. A good number of them were ordered, on the condition that the firm would make certain modifications.[21]

The purchase made by the Navy did not impede a further sales drive, and the machine continued to be offered on the open market as a commercial proposition. It may be presumed that the German Admiralty itself demanded this, for its purchase was made in the greatest secrecy. If further advertising and sales had suddenly ceased, expert circles and foreign intelligence would have noticed this at once.

It was only in 1928 that Scherbius's machine was patented. He himself was already dead, but his successors made every effort to ensure that his invention brought the greatest possible profits for the firm.[22] Several machines were purchased by the representatives of the armed forces and telegraph companies of other countries for experimental purposes, but the sales drive did not go too well.

Suddenly, at the end of 1929, there came an order from the United States, from the eminent cryptologist, William F. Friedman.[23] This purchase would have gladdened the heart of Arthur Scherbius, had he still been alive and had he known the calibre of mind which was showing interest in his invention. His joy would have turned into euphoria had he been able to know that in the same year the secret negotiations with the *Reichswehr* were happily concluded.[24] The German Army, still small, but with great potential, followed the Navy and decided that the machine would serve its purpose well.[25]

Now it was certain that the patent would have a fine career, but it was still too early to know that history would associate it with one of the greatest secrets of the Second World War.

The machine was called *Enigma*.

NOTES

1. Johannes Möller, a recorded interview, Cologne, 27 September 1977. He worked in the cryptanalytic service of the German Navy during the last war; according to him this was the first German submarine to be captured by the British. Stephen W. Roskill, *The War at Sea, 1939–1945*, London, 1954–61, p. 599, says that in 1939 the Germans lost two submarines in the Straits of Dover, but this was because of mines.
2. Leonard Stanisław Danilewicz, 'AVA', description of the operations of the firm set up in Warsaw by his brother Ludomir, Penrhos, 28 February 1975.
3. Ibid.
4. A. Polonsky, *Politics in Independent Poland, 1921–39*, London, 1972, pp. 1–2.
5. An important role was played by Polish cryptanalysts, who managed to break Soviet ciphers and thus Polish command knew the enemy's orders (M. Ścieżyński, *Radiotelegrafia jako źródło wiadomości o nieprzyjacielu*, Przemyśl, 1928, pp. 16–26).
6. T. Piszczkowski, *Plebiscyt i powstania na Górnym Śląsku*, London, 1972, pp. 20–1.
7. J. Joll, *Europe since 1870*, London, 1973, p. 278.
8. J. Garliński, *Hitler's Last Weapons*, London, 1978, pp. 2–3.

9. Joll, op. cit., p. 281.
10. W. Schellenberg, *The Schellenberg Memoirs*, London, 1956, pp. 42–3.
11. Ścieżyński, op. cit., pp. 8–10.
12. D. Khan, *The Codebreakers*, New York, 1967, pp. 71–105. Also: B. Norman, *Secret Warfare*, London, 1973, pp. 13–14.
13. Norman, op. cit., p. 14.
14. Based on the author's personal experience.
15. O. Stürzinger, 'Cipher Technique Today', 1976, p. 3.
16. Ibid, pp. 4–5.
17. Kahn, op. cit., pp. 196–8.
18. Stürzinger, 'Machinelle Chiffrierverfahren', 1960, p. 2.
19. Kahn, op. cit., p. 420.
20. Ibid.
21. Möller, op. cit.
22. Stürzinger, 'Cipher Technique Today', op. cit., p. 8, says that Scherbius died in 1920, but other evidence shows that he died later.
23. R. W. Clark, *The Man who broke Purple*, London, 1977, p. 79.
24. General L. Hepp, recorded interview, Ulm, 19 September 1977.
25. The German Air Force did not order the machine because, according to conditions laid down at Versailles, it did not exist at that time.

2
The Breakthrough

1

FROM VERY EARLY MORNING the Berlin barracks of every section of the armed forces were filled with confusion and rang with the shouts of NCOs, the clatter of weapons and the crashing of studded boots. Everyone was unusually excited and, for the thousandth time, checked his rifle, adjusted his uniform and polished his boots to bring out the brightest shine. In the streets nearby large columns of para-military organizations, delegations of guilds, Bavarian farmers, fishermen and miners were forming up. Adolf Hitler, the leader of the National Socialist party, had become Chancellor and today, 1 May 1933, the first parade before him was to take place on the great Tempelhof field in Berlin. It was planned for eight o'clock in the evening, but preparations had begun early.

At the edge of the huge field a great stand had been constructed for the diplomatic corps, party leaders, generals and invited guests. The dense ranks of the *Reichswehr* formed up around it, while beyond them stretched a seemingly endless ocean of people: a crowd a million strong.[1]

During the last few months the new leader, embroiled in a whirl of political meetings, bargaining and discussions, had usually appeared in civilian clothes and he had even on several occasions been seen wearing a top hat and tails; today, however, when he and his followers were celebrating a great victory, he had decided to appear in party uniform. He wore high leather boots, brown breeches, a trench coat of a lighter colour, without any insignia except for an Iron Cross, and a belt with a shoulder strap. A tall peaked cap, adorned with the German eagle and a swastika badge, completed his outfit. Dressed thus he appeared in an open car and the deafening roar from a million throats and the vast forest of upstretched arms were the best proof that his instinct had not failed him.

He appeared at the front of the stand and, surrounded by a huge suite, assumed the place of honour. A march started up. He stood with his arm outstretched, from time to time lowering it to rest. Below him soldiers' boots marched past, colours were lowered and the steel of unsheathed swords glinted. The magnificent regiments of the *Reichswehr*, composed of professionals, passed; dense columns of cavalry clattered by, heavy artillery trundled along, vehicles roared and the white and blue of naval uniforms stood out against the rest.

Hitler looked closely at the marching columns and noticed the faithful glances turned in their thousands in his direction, but it was only when the huge columns of *SA, SS* and party uniforms appeared that a gentle smile hovered on his lips. The leader's face, which had so far been set in motionless severity, relaxed and became more cheerful. He continued to betray little emotion, but his arm straightened even more. It was clear that now not only was he looking, but that he was also drinking in every step of the marching columns. His mood was shared by the vast crowd, which once again raised a deafening roar and stretched out hundreds of thousands of arms.

Enthusiasm was universal, the mood of the moment was contagious; everyone realized that it was an exceptional day, that a turning-point had been reached and that this man who had come to power would halt the German nation's decline, would jolt it, awaken it and lead it back onto the path of its former might.

2

Amidst the excited crowds there were a few people who remained calm and refused to allow themselves to be seized by the mood of the moment, although adapting perfectly to their surroundings. One of these was a small, stout man with a strong, energetic face, who stood not far away from the main stand and intently observed all the dignitaries assembled on it and the marching columns. This was an officer of the Second Bureau of the French General Staff, Captain Gustave Bertrand, who had come to Berlin completely incognito on false documents, especially to observe this first Nazi parade.

Of all European countries France had suffered most grievously in the First World War. Part of her territory had been occupied, she had lost several million of her youngest men and thus she was the most sensitive to the rebirth of German militarism. The building of the Maginot Line had certainly allayed all sense of danger and had created an illusion of complete security. The French nation was exhausted from the great wartime effort. Nevertheless, the General Staff worked as in its best years and the feelers of its intelligence service reached deep into German political, military and industrial life. The politicians somehow could not raise any energy, but the military continually warned that the Germans were evading the conditions of Versailles, that they were rebuilding their industry and were secretly arming and training their forces in Soviet Russia.

Captain Bertrand was involved in radio intelligence on the Staff, and so field work and the intelligence network within Germany were not in his sphere of responsibilities. He had, however, visited Germany several times, for he was interested in the internal changes taking place there. He knew German well and he listened and keenly observed everything around him. For some years past, from 1926 to be precise, his interest in the secret changes within Germany had taken on a special significance, for intelligence reports were saying that the Germans had introduced a cipher machine into their Navy, and that they felt it to be impossible to break.[2] This information was extremely important for radio intelligence, since it was now reasonable to assume that enciphered messages would soon be travelling the air waves, that monitoring stations would pick them up and that incomprehensible columns of letters would soon be appearing on intelligence officers' desks.

Work began on breaking the German secret, but several years passed and nothing was achieved. Meanwhile Intelligence reported from Germany that the cipher machine which had been introduced into the Navy had also been accepted by the *Reichswehr*. This took place in mid-1929 and Captain Bertrand, together with many of his colleagues, redoubled their efforts so as to break through the steel wall of German secrecy.

The introduction of a cipher machine into the Navy and the *Reichswehr* was, naturally, a great secret and an elementary task was to establish what sort of machine it actually was. The intelligence network in Germany managed to accomplish this and reported that it was the *Enigma*. This news was at first greeted with some scepticism, since the machine was on sale and was being bought by large companies, but Intelligence repeated the information, which was then believed. Since this machine was being sold on the open market and the German Navy and Army had accepted it into service for secret purposes, it had to contain additional secret devices. These had to be discovered.

Captain Bertrand, who was the most interested in this problem, had from 1930 been head of Section D of French Intelligence (the Scientific, Technological, Intelligence and Decoding Service) and was in the closest contact with his colleagues, who were collecting information inside Germany. It was early autumn in 1931,[3] when one of them, Captain Henri Navarre, told him that he had been contacted by a young German, who worked in the cipher bureau of the *Reichswehr* and could therefore supply information interesting to Bertrand. He was called Hans-Thilo Schmidt, the younger brother of a General in the German Army. All the details of his identity and position, which guaranteed the value of the information he could supply, had already been checked. Bertrand was very interested and asked to be put in contact with him as soon as possible.[4]

From the very beginning the German wanted to take every precaution and demanded that all contacts with him had to be made on neutral ground and not too far away, since he had only the weekend and had to return to work for Monday morning. For the first meeting Captain Bertrand chose a good hotel in the Belgian Town of Verviers. On the French side, in addition to himself, there was the head of Section E (Germany) and an intelligence officer named Lemoine who was responsible for the recruitment of new agents. He was a German by descent, called Stelmann, a former officer in the German Army, who had been living in France for a number of years and become a French citizen. He was a rather shady entrepreneur, but useful for he had many interesting contacts and was excellently informed on every aspect of German life. He chose the codename *König*; the French called him *Rex*.[5]

Their first meeting went unexpectedly well. Through secret channels Bertrand requested a sample of documents from the cipher office and he received them. Everything had to be photographed on the spot, for the German had to take them back. He was between twenty-eight and thirty years old and made a good impression; he appeared to be brave, resolute and to know what he wanted. The meeting had to take place in conditions of great secrecy and yet, for both casual and professional observers, it had to give the impression of a cheerful gathering of friends. The German was well suited to this role and at table and in the bar was an easy and urbane companion.

The first meeting was followed by others at which various officers from Section E were present in turn: Guy Schlesser, Henri Navarre, Manier and Perruche.[6] Bertrand and Lemoine were always there. The limitations of a weekend forced them to use places within a certain radius, so after Verviers they went to Liège in Belgium, Copenhagen in Denmark, Bern, Basel, Caux, Lucerne, Montreux, Mürren and Zürich in Switzerland, Prague, Turnow and Spondlemühle in Czechoslovakia and once to Paris. On that occasion the young German had more time and had already accomplished a great deal so, as a reward, the French showed him the night life of the great city. Each meeting kept up the appearance of a sophisticated reunion, good hotels were always used and a great deal was spent on food and drink. The programme also included visits to night clubs, beaches and sightseeing in beautiful mountain country.[7]

The French observed the young German who was alone in their midst and wondered what motives forced him to betray his own country and run great risks into the bargain. At their first meetings they were above all concerned to establish whether he was an agent provocateur and was being followed by German Intelligence. Various precautions were taken and very close surveillance revealed that this was not the case, while the materials which he brought were of the highest quality. It was recognized that, by all intelligence criteria, he was trustworthy, but before they included him on the list of regular informers, they had to establish who he really was and what sort of a person he was from the point of view of intelligence work. Captain Bertrand, *Rex* and the officers of Section E were experienced men and knew that there are essentially two main motives for this kind of work: money, or idealistic beliefs due to membership of a very aggressive and radical political party, or of a religion, or of a group with a specific philosophical outlook. Force or blackmail did not come into it, since the German had come forward voluntarily. Experience had taught them that idealistic motives, on the face of it the best, did not make a good informer. Such people were usually naïve, over-sensitive, one-sided, stubborn and impractical. It was fairly soon apparent that the new man did not belong to this category. It was for this very reason that the meetings had been arranged in big hotels so as to observe his disposition. In these conditions, in the midst of strangers, in new surroundings and constantly in danger, he remained unusually calm, displayed great courage, self-control and an ability to adapt to the situation.[8] At the same time it was clear that he felt at home at a well laden table in a luxurious hotel. The financial motive seemed to be uppermost. Yet it was not the sole driving force behind the young German. As his co-operation increased, he often went beyond what was required and showed great energy and conscientiousness, which are not common in the normal run of agents.[9] The reasons for his actions had, therefore, to be deeper and more complex than a cynical desire to get rich quickly.

It was realized that his work was of great value and that he could be trusted, so he was put on the list of regular informers, given a substantial advance payment and the codename *Asché*.

The very first meetings had provided some quite extraordinary information.[10] The new agent produced not only documents confirming that the *Reichswehr* really had introduced *Enigma*, but he also provided instructions for its use, some details of its construction and the keys by which it was set. These were of particular importance to the specialists, for every cryptanalyst knows that the secret of a cipher machine lies in its setting. Whoever could discover this secret and recreate a copy of the machine would be able to read the enciphered message.

Captain Bertrand's thoughts immediately turned towards Poland. He knew that Polish Intelligence had for some years past been trying to break the Germans' secret. The Poles had been co-operating and exchanging information with him and now he could present them with a discovery of incalculable value.

On 7 December 1931 he found himself on the platform of the Central Station in Warsaw.[11]

3

In 1920 the reborn Polish state, in existence for less than two years, found itself at war with revolutionary Russia and was again threatened with a loss of independence. The Polish Army was short of weapons, ammunition, uniforms and boots. Polish diplomatic sources abroad tried to procure these items in many places, including Britain, where the problem was aggravated by the dockers' purely political strike. The 'workers' and peasants' state', born out of revolution, had a certain attraction from afar and the strike was led by Ernest Bevin.[12] It was the same man who in 1945, as Foreign Secretary and a politician of great experience, protected Polish soldiers from pressure by members of his own government to send them back, against their will, to their towns and villages, which had fallen under the control of the army and police of the same Soviet Russia.

The one country, apart from the United States, which honestly wanted to help the young Polish state, was France.[13] Poland and France were linked by a centuries-old friendship, born out of political co-operation and cultural influences; the time of Napoleon conjured up warm memories which were close to Polish hearts. During the partitions underground activists and soldiers, on the run from the Russian or German police, headed for France; for many Poles free France was a second homeland. Now, in addition to equipment which was sent to Poland and which had been purchased under a credit agreement, a French military mission, under the command of General Paul Henrys, came to Warsaw. Amongst its four hundred officer-instructors was Captain Charles de Gaulle. General Maxime Weygand also came, with the task of advising the Polish High Command.[14]

Fortunately, the war with Soviet Russia was won, and the Polish state could begin the hard and slow unification of the lands seized by the partitioning countries and the rebuilding of the destruction caused by seven years of war. In many fields of Polish life there were very strong French influences. This was evident in the new Polish constitution; the reformed Polish Army learnt from French experience; French customs were adopted in various organizations and French became compulsory in Polish schools.

Naturally political co-operation sprang up immediately between the two countries, as seen in the official alliance, while military co-operation was also apparent in close intelligence links. Captain Bertrand had for some years been in close contact with the Poles, and he knew that they were working on the breaking of the German ciphers and now, when he arrived in Warsaw with these revelationary documents received from *Asché*, he knew that he would be doing his Polish friends a great favour.

4

Polish cryptanalysis, despite great achievements during the war with Soviet Russia, was at a pretty low ebb during the first few post-war years. It employed only a few people in the radio intelligence and cryptography sections of the Second Bureau of the General Staff in Warsaw, and the pressure of current work, relating to the organization of the newly reborn state and its armed forces, was so great that there was no time and energy for creative thinking about the future.[15] This state of affairs was soon changed and Intelligence was instructed to examine the present situation and begin the methodical organization of a competent professional section.

Both neighbours, Russia to the east and Germany to the west, were enemies of Poland, but while the war with Russia had been won and a peace treaty concluded, only an arbitration pact had been signed with the Germans, whose aggressive revisionism was becoming more strident every day.[16] Furthermore, Intelligence reported that the Germans, in defiance of the stipulations of the Versailles Treaty, were rearming, training their specialists in Russia and rebuilding their industry. The greater threat came from them, and so it was decided to watch carefully developments in that direction.

Monitoring stations had already been built in Poznań, in Krzesławicc near Cracow and in Starogard in Pomerania.[17] These stations intercepted German radio traffic and sent it to the General Staff in Warsaw. After some preliminary difficulties, the Poles managed to solve the German ciphers and began to read their secret transmissions, but, towards the end of 1926, this ceased to be possible.[18] The Germans had been using a manual cipher, called 'double cassette', which was based on the concept of double transposition; now fresh columns of letters showed that a completely new method had been devised, which was incomprehensible. The Germans must have changed their earlier methods of enciphering; the solution of its secret demanded a greater effort on the part of the Poles and greater professionalism.

The Polish intelligence net in Germany was given the urgent task of finding out about the German cipher changes. While monitoring stations were still picking up incomprehensible columns of letters, a course in cryptology was started in Poznań for twenty of the most advanced mathematics students at the University. Poznań was chosen because in 1929 nearly every local student knew German well, having started school during the partitions, when not only was Polish not taught, but its use was completely forbidden. The course was set up on the initiative of the radio intelligence department whose head, Major Franciszek Pokorny, and his closest colleague, Captain Maksymilian Ciężki, both attended. It was decided that specialist officers would come from Warsaw to lecture, and that they would aim to select the most gifted students who later would volunteer to continue their studies and work in this very secret branch of military intelligence.[19]

On 15 January 1930 there was a change of personnel caused by a decision to reorganize the department. Major Pokorny left and was replaced by Major (later Lieutenant-Colonel) Gwido Langer.[20] He was a short, corpulent and jovial-looking man, of forty-five, who came from southern Poland, was a former officer in the Austrian Army and so spoke excellent German. There was an amalgamation of the radio intelligence and cryptography sections and midway through 1931 a cipher department was formed within the Second Bureau under the command of Gwido Langer. As well as the monitoring stations, the department embraced the following sections; BS.1 – own ciphers; BS.2 – radio intelligence East; BS.3 – Russian ciphers and, most important of all, BS.4 – radio intelligence and German ciphers, under the command of Captain (later Major) Ciężki. The department was also responsible for the radio network, which maintained contact with the monitoring stations and internal and foreign intelligence posts, as well as radio counter-intelligence.[21]

At the same time as this reorganization and the formation of a cipher department in Warsaw, the cryptology course in Poznań was coming to an end. The three young men who had shown the greatest ability and enthusiasm for the subject were Marian Rejewski, Jerzy Różycki and Henryk Zygalski. Of the three Rejewski was the most advanced, since he had just obtained his degree in mathematics and had spent a year studying the subject in greater depth at the famous German university of Göttingen. All three of them had frequently managed to solve the German ciphers, which they had been set on the course, and they had decided to dedicate themselves completely to cryptology. A small section of the cipher department was set up for them in Poznań.

5

When, on 7 December 1931, the representative of the cipher department greeted Captain Bertrand on the Central Station in Warsaw, the Poles already knew that the Germans had introduced a cipher machine into the Navy and the *Reichswehr* and that it was called *Enigma*.[22] This information had been supplied by Intelligence and had been corroborated by the crypt-analysts, who for several years had been vainly trying to read intercepted German signals.

As soon as it was confirmed that the Germans were really using a cipher machine, the Poles turned to examine the files in the radio intelligence section and found the reports from January 1929. These described a cipher machine and the experts had to ascertain whether they had any connection with the machine which the German Army was now using. Captain Ciężki knew that a cipher machine, also called *Enigma*, was available to large firms on the open market in Germany. One of these had to be purchased and compared with the 1929 details. Antoni Palluth was singled out for this job.

He was a partner in an electrical firm, AVA, and no one knew that he had links with Intelligence. For complete security the purchase was arranged through a German industrialist.[23]

A machine was duly bought and it became immediately clear that it was almost an exact copy of the model which had been secretly examined and described in 1929. It had a keyboard with twenty-six letters, which was connected electrically to three rotors with rings and from these led further connections to twenty-six electrically illuminated letters (see Chapter 1, pp. 10–11). By pressing a key an electric current, supplied by a battery, passed through the machine and rotors with the rings turned mechanically but not in unison. At the same time a light came on behind a letter, which was always different from the original one. When a plaintext letter of a message was depressed, the ciphertext letter appeared in the illuminated window, and when someone else, using the *Enigma* with the same setting, depressed the ciphertext letter, the letter of the original message lit up. This was the basic principle of *Enigma*, the principle of reciprocity, from which it was evident that, in order to read messages enciphered on it, one needed a similar machine with an identical setting. *Enigma*'s second principle was that the original plaintext letter could never appear in the lighted window. This was the principle of exclusivity. Furthermore each of the three rotors could be taken out and replaced in a different order.[24]

However the commercial machine did not answer the question of whether there was any connection between it and the machine used by the Navy and *Reichswehr*. Greater attention was paid to radio monitoring; once again the intelligence net was faced with a great many questions and yet this difficult problem could not be solved. Monitoring alone could not specify on what sort of machine the new cipher was being made and Intelligence was unable to break through the German security screen. It was established that, although there was a great similarity between the commercial *Enigma* and the *Enigma* which was used in the Navy and *Reichswehr*, there were some additional complications to the system.

The arrival of Captain Bertrand was vital in this respect, since he brought a document which helped to solve the problem. This was an operational instruction for *Enigma* (*Gebrauchanleitung für die Chiffriermaschine Enigma*), which contained at the end four drawings of the machine.[25] It was now possible to establish that the military *Enigma* was, to all intents and purposes, based on Arthur Scherbius's design, which relied on the principle of substitution and was in some respect similar to the one secretly examined in Warsaw in 1929 and which was sold on the open market. The difference, and an essential one, lay in the addition of a kind of switchboard, which complicated matters greatly. This took the form of a plug board with plugs. Also the rotors had different inner connections.[26]

Captain Bertrand also brought a second document (*Schlüsselanleitung*)

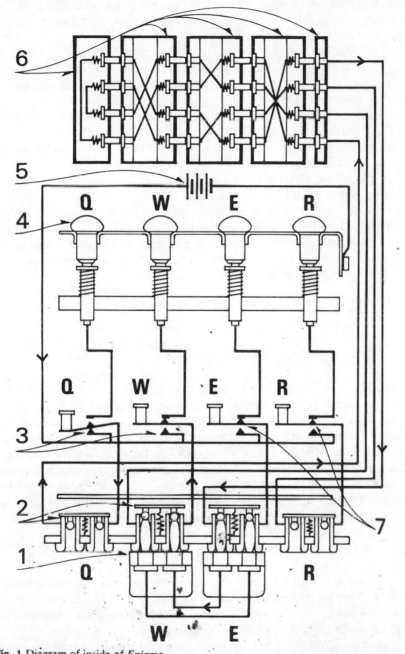

Fig. 1 Diagram of inside of *Enigma*
1 – Plug; 2 – Sockets; 3 – Keys Q and W; 4 – Electric lamps; 5 – Battery; 6 – Reflector, three rotors and entry rotor; 7 – Keys E and R

which revealed how frequently the machine's settings had to be reset. The three rotors were shuffled every three months, while their ring settings and plug connections were changed every day. Likewise the setting of the basic position (*Grundstellung*), from which the enciphering of the telegram key began, was changed each day. Also in this instruction an example was given of a message in clear, together with its enciphered equivalent and relevant keys.[27] These were top secret documents, which, nevertheless, had found their way into the hands of the potential enemies of the German *Reich*. These additional elements, which made the *Enigma* cipher even more secure, explained why the German military authorities introduced a cipher machine, whose basic model was available commercially.

This was not all. Bertrand came to Warsaw for the second time,[28] in 1932, and brought two tables of telegram keys for September and October 1932 which showed how all operational *Enigmas* were set for those two months.[29]

All this information, added to the results of the work done by Polish cryptanalysts, enabled them to solve in a comparatively short time the two major problems: how to reconstruct the machine and how to work out methods of finding out the keys.

6

Before the three young cryptanalysts could set about solving these final problems, they had to appreciate the difficulties posed by the *Enigma*'s military version. This they very quickly did, since they had been working in the field for some months. For outsiders all this appeared to be black magic and needed very simple examples in order to become comprehensible.

Each of three rotors contained 26 inner connections, corresponding to 26 letters, but if each one had only one single connection, there would then be only three encoding positions. Since, however, each rotor had 26 letters, the number of encoding positions increased to 17,576 ($26 \times 26 \times 26$). It has to be borne in mind, however, that the rotors could be taken out and re-arranged. This increased the number of combinations to 105,456 (17,576 $\times$ 6).

These are quite high figures, but the machine had also *Umkehrwalze* (Reflector) which could have as many as 7,905,853,580,625 connections.

This was not all, since there were also six electric plug connections which could be set in 100,391,791,600 different ways.

To all this should be added the inner electrical connections of the rotors. Each of them had 26 contacts on one side and 26 contacts on the other side, so it had as many as 403,291,461,126,605,635,584,000,000[30] different connections. If we would like to get the number of connections for all three rotors, we should multiply the above figure by three.

The final number of encoding positions of any ordinary *Enigma* with only three rotors, *Eintrittwalze*, reflector and six plug connections is represented by the figure:

$$5\ 172\ 165\ 503\ 971\ 832\ 752\ 302\ 775\ 832$$
$$450\ 732\ 675\ 000\ 000\ 000\ 000\ 000\ 000\ 000$$
$$000\ 000\ 000\ 000\ 000\ 000\ 000\ 000\ 000\ 000$$

Only a mathematician can look at such a figure without fear, but he knows that the discovery of the secret of these billions cannot be done by simple mechanical means and that for this exists advanced mathematics which, sooner or later, will permit the correct solution to be found. It was, of course, now of prime importance to discover this secret and the Polish cryptanalysts were faced with it. It was clear that both French and British experts were simultaneously working on the same task, for Bertrand had also shown them the documents received from *Asché*.

The most important and most immediate objective was to discover the inner connections of the rotors so as to give these details forthwith to the AVA firm which was only waiting for specifications to convert the commercial *Enigma* to a military one. The *Enigma* cipher was based on substitution so Rejewski used a similar mathematical theory. This was a lengthy process involving a whole series of calculations, since each rotor had to be considered separately. There arose equations with a great many unknowns and great columns of letters and numbers appeared in most unusual sequences. The document giving the keys for two months was extremely useful.[31] The concept of permutation was constantly used; mathematics alone, however, was not enough. High intelligence, intuition, an inquiring mind, powers of precise analysis and patience were also needed. The work required complete dedication to the problem's solution and every ounce of mental and physical energy had to be expended. This could lead to complete exhaustion. William F. Friedman, after breaking the Japanese cipher machine, called *Purple*, was so exhausted that he had to spend several months in hospital.

The first step in breaking a cipher always stems from the study of a large number of long signals sent on the same day and which are thus based on the same machine setting and the same keys. This presented great difficulties, since the monitoring stations were not always able to oblige. Furthermore, Saturday and Sunday were usually of little value, for then there was less radio traffic. The cryptanalysts pored for whole days and nights over columns of letters in groups of five (that was how *Enigma* enciphered) and looked for letters which were frequently repeated. They also hoped to hit on an error which might give them some sort of start. It was a question of looking for an irregularity, for some repetition of various elements. They all

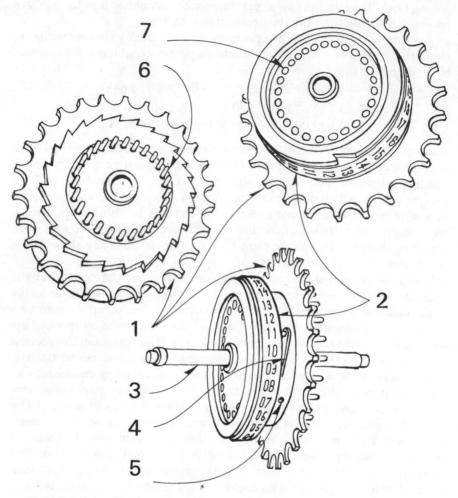

Fig. 2 Rotors
1 – Indent for setting; 2 – Cipher rings; 3 – Spring knob; 4 – Button; 5 – Datum for the position of the ring; 6 – Spring-loaded contacts; 7 – Ordinary contacts

worked along the same lines, and often exchanged views and analysed the progress made.

Certain useful changes were made in the organization of their work, for on 1 September 1932 the Poznań section was closed down and the three cryptanalysts were transferred to Warsaw to the cipher department of the General Staff. There they were provided with good conditions of work and with only one task: the speedy breaking of *Enigma*.

Only the use of mathematical examples allows us to explain how the secret of *Enigma*'s internal connections was eventually discovered (see Appendix). The cryptanalysts had brilliant mathematical minds, in fact Rejewski even formulated a new theory in this field. Suffice it to say that by November 1932 the internal connections of the rotors were known. All this information was immediately turned over to the AVA firm where feverish work began. A working model of the military *Enigma* had to be produced as speedily as possible. Without it, it was impossible to read the German cipher.[32]

After the rotors it was the turn of the plug connections. This was also a difficult problem and was solved thanks to observation of the cycles of specific letters and various examples of permutation. At first the methods used were rather slow and not yet very practical, but then there was a breakthrough which gave rise to the hope that in the future there would be discoveries permitting much faster progress. The secret of the daily keys was also quite rapidly discovered.[33]

The final stage was being tackled from two directions. AVA was building a model of *Enigma* at top speed, while the cryptanalysts were getting down to understanding the final secret which separated them from reading German messages. The key to each individual signal had to be deducted.

The technique of enciphering on *Enigma* was as follows: the two soldiers operating the machine first set it according to standing orders. (There had to be two of them, since *Enigma* did not print out the deciphered text.) They did not touch the three rotors, unless the three-month period was up, however they daily had to set the rings, the plug connections and the position of the machine to encipher the signal's key. So far these tasks had been automatically prescribed in the operators' instructions, but now they had to use some initiative and make up a telegram key for the signal. This key consisted of three letters and, theoretically, from these three letters, could have 17,576 combinations, but the German cipher clerks were simple people, and they had a tendency to use easy combinations such as AAA, ABC, XYZ. All of them repeated this key a second time, so that the receivers might make no mistake and set their machines accordingly.

The Polish experts were waiting for just this kind of slip. If on the same day there were two signals with the same first letter, then in each case the fourth one would be identical. This applied also to the second and fifth, the third and sixth. Using the methods of characteristic keys, statistics and the theory of unequal letters (see Appendix) they finally managed to discover the secret of these keys and the way to reading German secret messages was wide open.

It was during the last days of December 1932, over Christmas, when parties and celebrations were taking place, that the three young cryptanalysts, sleepy, unshaven, exhausted, but very content, put on their superior's desk the first completely deciphered secret *Reichswehr* signal which had gone through *Enigma*.[34]

NOTES

1. Joachim C. Fest, *Hitler*, pp. 422–3.
2. Möller, op. cit.
3. Gustave Bertrand, *Enigma*, p. 23. Also: Henri Navarre, *Le Service Renseignements, 1871–1944*, pp. 54–5. Both authors say that this took place in 1932, but from further pages of their books and from other sources it would appear that it was 1931.
4. Bertrand, p. 23. Also: Paul Paillole, *Services Spéciaux (1935–1945)*, p. 63.
5. Bertrand, pp. 24–5. Also: Navarre, p. 72. Also: P. Renauld, 'La machine à chiffrer "Enigma"'.
6. Bertrand, p. 29.
7. Ibid, pp. 25–9.
8. Paillole, p. 64.
9. Bertrand, pp. 28–9. Also: Navarre, pp. 54–6. In his opinion the young German, as well as being in constant need of money – for he was a gambler and lost large sums – also felt a need for revenge on the German nation as a whole, which did not appreciate him sufficiently.
10. During the period from autumn 1931 to mid-1939 there were 19 meetings with *Asché*, the last one in Basel in June. During the war contact was broken off due to the fall of France. In all Bertrand received 303 documents, some of which concerned the cipher office and some monitoring office (*Forschungsamt*) to which *Asché* was transferred in 1934 (Bertrand, p. 29). In 1943 he was arrested, sentenced to death and shot in Berlin in July of that year. He was betrayed to the *Gestapo* by *Rex*, who had been under observation by the Germans for a long time and who was arrested in the south of France in November 1942, immediately after the German divisions had marched in, and interrogated. By revealing all the secrets he knew he saved his life and survived the war. He died in 1946 in a French prison (Navarre, pp. 54–6 and 72–3. Also: Paillole, p. 64).
11. Bertrand, op. cit., p. 37.
12. He was at the head of the *Council of Action*, which was formed to organize a general strike should the British Government wish to intervene militarily on behalf of Poland. There was no chance of such action (Norman Davies, *White Eagle, Red Star*, London, 1972, pp. 178–9).
13. The US Government decided to equip ten Polish infantry divisions, but the decision to do this came too late. In the Polish Air Force there were native-born Americans serving alongside Americans of Polish descent (the Kościuszko squadron). In Poland there was also the *American Relief Administration*, run by ex-president Herbert Hoover, which came to Europe after the First World War. It had, however, a purely charitable rôle.
14. Davies, op. cit., pp. 94–5, 171 and 191–3.
15. The organization of the Polish General Staff was based on the French model. The Second Bureau was Intelligence.
16. Joll, op. cit., p. 289.
17. In addition to the monitoring stations directed towards Germany there were also four stations directed eastwards: Warsaw, Lida, Równe i Kołomyja (Gwido Langer, 'Report', Paris, 1940, p. 5, typewritten copy in the author's possession).
18. Marian Rejewski, 'Reminiscences of my work in the cipher office of the Second Bureau of the General Staff in 1930–1945', Bydgoszcz, 1967, p. 3 (typewritten copy in Polish in the author's possession).
19. Ibid, pp. 3–4.
20. Langer, op. cit., p. 1.
21. Ibid, pp. 1–5.
22. Stefan Mayer, 'The breaking up (sic) of the German ciphering (sic) machine *Enigma* by the cryptological section in the 2nd Department (sic) of the Polish Armed Forces General Staff', London, 1974, p. 1 (typewritten copy in the author's possession).

23. Ibid.
24. Rejewski, 'Reminiscences . . .', op. cit., pp. 21–2.
25. Rejewski, letter to T. Lisicki dated 25 May 1976 (a copy in the author's possession). The author also has a copy of the original German instructions of 1937, which are almost identical to those of 1932.
26. Rejewski, 'Reminiscences . . . ', op. cit., pp. 26–30.
27. Rejewski, 'Appendix to a memorandum by G. Langer drawn up in France in 1941' (a copy in the author's possession).
28. Rejewski, 'Reminiscences . . . ', op. cit., pp. 26–30.
29. Tadeusz Lisicki, 'Polish methods for the reconstruction of the *Enigma*, setting the daily keys and German efforts to combat these methods', London, 1973, p. 3 (a copy in the author's possession).
30. Rejewski, 'Appendix . . . ', op. cit., p. 14.
31. Ibid, pp. 8–15.
32. Rejewski, 'Reminiscences . . . ', op. cit., p. 51.
33. Rejewski, 'Appendix . . . ', op. cit., p. 18.
34. Rejewski, 'Reminiscences . . . '. op. cit., p. 51.

3

The First Contribution to Alliance

1

COLONEL ERICH FELLGIEBEL, the head of Signals in the *Reichswehr*, a man of about forty-five with an open, honest face and attentive eyes hidden behind thick glasses, paced his office for several minutes.[1] He had been a professional officer for all his adult life. He had entered the Army in 1905 as a very young volunteer, had gone through the First World War and had always served in Signals. He had climbed through the ranks to reach the highest position that the German Army, limited by the decisions of Versailles, could offer an officer in his field.

During the years 1926 to 1929 he had had to take a very difficult decision on the modernization of radio communications, of which ciphers were an integral part. Hitherto encipherment had been done by hand, but the development of machines to simplify this task had, since the war, become so rapid, that they had had to be introduced so as not to fall behind the armies of other countries and even behind some of the great industrial companies. The machine invented by the German engineer Scherbius, called *Enigma*, was known commercially. The Colonel became interested in it, but before he had made up his mind the German Navy bought it (see Chapter 1, pp. 9–10). This was a very important decision and one which quite clearly showed the path to be followed. For the Navy the only means of communication in the modern world was radio, and since its experts had decided that *Enigma* would provide complete security for their ciphers, what was the point of puzzling over this problem?

And yet the Colonel had hesitated for a few years. He was a signals expert and knew that no security, however excessive, is ever unnecessary. The *Enigma* had for some years past been sold openly on the market, had been bought by several countries and was being used by some companies; it was therefore well known. Naturally one could introduce all sorts of technical improvements and complications, but this did not alter the fact that the machine's essentials were the same. It would be much better to construct secretly one's own machine which would be quite different. However, how could this be done, who would do it? A completely new design, based on a different concept, would require a new invention and several years' development work, and time was pressing. Furthermore, the Navy's decision had to be taken into account. Every arm of the forces could have its own secrets and ciphers, but it would be better if everyone were to use the same basic machine. *Enigma* was based on the concept of reciprocity: a message enciphered on it could be read only by another *Enigma*, which was of fundamental importance for the central authorities. These considerations finally prevailed and in 1929 the Army followed in the Navy's footsteps.

That decision had been hard, but it had had only one side to it: namely the technical. Now the Colonel prowled around his office torn over a decision which might determine his whole future. Hitler had come to power and a shock wave, foretelling a surge of changes, had hit the country. It was widely known that the new Chancellor had far-reaching political plans, that he was opposed to the present state of affairs and that he would strive to eradicate the results of defeat in the war. His gaze was turned above all on the armed forces, which would have to undergo fundamental change. Hitler's closest friend and colleague, the famous First World War fighter ace, Hermann Göring, had already started to create an Air Force; the shipyards were beginning to build new warships and submarines. The *Reichswehr* was to cease to exist and in its place there were to be the new countless ranks of the *Wehrmacht*.

Here lay the Colonel's problem and internal drama. He had, of course, been a soldier for all his professional life and could quite well show no interest in politics, but he had been brought up not only on a code of discipline, but also on a patriotism which led to a concern for all aspects of the country's and nation's life. The defeat of 1918 had touched the innermost chords of his heart and had there left a scar. He had been upset and worried by the post-war years and he had seen the country tottering towards economic and moral chaos. Together with millions of other Germans he had waited for some change, for upheaval, for the arrival of a man, a new leader who would halt the ceaseless decline and would lead the nation in a fresh direction. Many people pinned their hopes on Adolf Hitler, but from the very beginning the Colonel belonged to his secret opponents. He held a senior military post and thus secret reports concerning events throughout the country reached him. He knew by what methods the National Socialists were making their way to power, he knew their various secrets, while the brutality of their methods aroused grave doubts within him. He could not understand their hatred for the Jews and now, when they had attained power and had shown openly what kind of people they really were, he was quite simply filled with dismay. He was already receiving information on the creation of the first concentration camps in which people were being imprisoned without trial; outrages were increasing, censorship of the press was introduced, trade unions were dissolved and with every month the terror increased.

The *Reichswehr* contained many officers with a long family military tradition; there were many Junkers who held right-wing views but who reacted to political excesses with repugnance. They all anxiously observed the changing situation and wondered what would happen. The plans for the reorganization of the armed forces concerned them directly; there was no doubt that they would be needed, although the new Chancellor would certainly have preferred to rely on people coming from his own ranks. It was, however, too early for that, the changes within the Army had already begun and officers, particularly senior ones, were faced with the problem of what to do.

Colonel Fellgiebel had had this on his mind for many months. His first reaction was to resign from the Army and find some more peaceful occupation, but his closest friends tried to dissuade him from this. Very difficult years were approaching, years which would bring events whose shock waves would be felt throughout the nation and by every social group, that would reach everywhere and miss no one. There would almost certainly be a new war in which experienced, professional and idealistic officers would be very much in demand. Times were bad, the Government had fallen into the hands of quite unsuitable people, but withdrawal from the scene would improve nothing. The thing to do was to stay and to carry out one's responsibilities, while keeping one's eyes open as widely as possible. There might come a time when one might be needed.

The Colonel stopped and looked out of the window. On the street two floors below an army unit was marching past. The young soldiers, only recently mobilized, passed in tight formation, their studded boots beating a steady rhythm, their helmets shining cheerfully in the spring sun. The Colonel felt a warmth in his heart and, despite himself, smiled. He immediately relaxed inside and the long months of anguish came to an end. He realized that there was only one decision for him: to stay.

2

All the experts were agreed that, after several modifications and improvements, *Enigma* would be one hundred per cent secure and that there was no fear of it being broken.[2] Nevertheless, their habitual German thoroughness warned them to be prepared for any eventuality. After all, what human ingenuity can devise, human ingenuity can also counter. Furthermore they had to expect foreign intelligence services to make a great effort to break it and they could not even discount treachery on their own side. It was thus necessary to employ every possible means of security to prevent enemies from breaking through the barriers around this great secret.

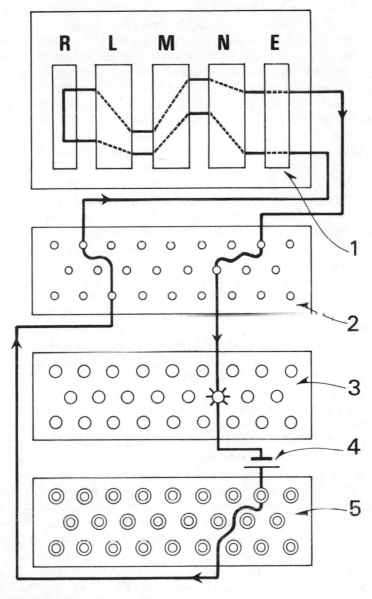

Fig. 3 *Enigma*'s internal connections
1 – Rotors (E entry rotor, L M N operational rotors, R reflector); 2 – Plugboard and plug connections; 3 – Bulbs; 4 – Battery; 5 – Keyboard

Above all, the different arms and para-military formations began to introduce their own modifications to the *Enigmas* which they had accepted into service. From the very beginning the Navy had used five and not three rotors, although only three were in use at one time.[3] This greatly increased the number of possible permutations and the machine was called *Enigma M*. The Navy had also differentiated between the various types of key in use, introducing separate ones for the low-grade traffic (*Marinenschlüssel*), others at staff level (*Stabsschlüssel*) and further ones at Admiralty level (*Admiralschlüssel*).[4] The higher the level, the more complex the key. Thus, in addition to the separate nets for each arm and formation, each one of them had also introduced an additional internal net, each with its own keys.

In 1935 the *Reichswehr* ceased to exist and was replaced by the *Wehrmacht*, which took over all the departments of the 'Versailles army' and, therefore, *Enigma*. Unlike the Navy the Army could also use telegraph cable, which could not be overheard, but some important and urgent messages were also sent by radio. The Army began to grow dramatically, new districts were formed and each one had its own radio station. In 1936 the *Wehrmacht* was approaching 850,000 soldiers and that figure was constantly increasing. The Army enciphered with its own keys, but they were easier to read.

The German Air Force (*Luftwaffe*) began to form immediately after Hitler came to power and by the turn of 1934/35 it had introduced *Enigma*, using the model in service with the Army.[5] Six Air Force districts had their own radio stations, which they used intensively. Naturally the *Luftwaffe*, like the Army and Navy, had its own keys.

The Party security service (*Sicherheitsdienst – SD*) also introduced *Enigma* and used it in a most sophisticated manner. Independently of its own keys, the *SD* first encoded each message and only then handed it over to *Enigma* cipher clerks. Units of the *SS* also used the same machine, although in a somewhat less complicated way.

At the turn of 1933/34 the Germans introduced for a short while a new *Enigma* which printed out the deciphered signal and which had as many as eight interchangeable rotors. It was intended for use at all levels of command, but it had soon to be withdrawn, owing to frequent breakdowns.[6]

Despite the different branches of the armed forces and their various nets, which later reached sixty, further modifications were made to all *Enigmas*. At first the arrangement of the rotors was changed every three months, later, from February 1936, once a month, and from October of the same year, daily. Eventually during the war, from the summer of 1942, they were changed every eight hours.[7] The same applied to the rings, which at first were set every month and in time were changed once a day. They did not forget the plugs which were constantly being made more complex. From October 1936 the number of these plugs varied between five and eight, from

January 1939 between seven and ten, and was never constant. Towards the end of 1937 the *Umkehrwalze* was also changed and replaced by a new model called *Umkehrwalze B.*[8] The German experts constantly paid attention to details, so as to avoid creating situations which could provide an analyst with an opening, and so the letter Y was introduced instead of a full stop. The letter Y is rarely used in the German language and their aim was to ensure that its absence did not make it easier to break the cipher.

This was all taking place at the same time as a great expansion in every branch of the German armed forces and security organizations. This expansion was accompanied by an increase in the number of operational *Enigma*s. In the Army each division had to have one,[9] in the Air Force each unit operating independently, and each flight, while in the Navy it was each ship and submarine.[10] There are no details of the exact numbers in service with the German armed forces, but on the basis of fragmentary information one can suggest a figure of over thirty thousand. The Navy alone used about six thousand and the Air Force over twenty thousand.[11]

It is not hard to imagine how many problems were caused by the frequent changes which affected every *Enigma*, nevertheless the Germans, with determined consistency, continued to make them. According to the experts' deep convictions *Enigma* was unbreakable, so what then were the reasons for these constant alternations, adjustments and modifications? Did German Counter-Intelligence have any information leading it to suppose that the Third *Reich*'s neighbours were already on the machine's trail? Did they have information that some Germans were prepared to go so far as co-operate with foreign intelligence services to betray the most closely guarded of secrets?

3

The breaking of the first German signals was an outstanding event, but it did not solve the problem once and for all. The Polish cryptanalysts had become familiar with German methods and they realized that they were dealing with very serious opponents and so prepared for a further struggle.

Above all they had to improve their efficiency and make discoveries which would allow them to read monitored signals very much faster. Slowness on their part could cancel out the practical value of the Polish achievement.

The first step forward in discovering the daily keys from the intercepted signals was the *grille* method. It solved the problem of the plug connections and was based on the fact that the plugs changed only six pairs of letters, thus leaving fourteen letters unchanged. The method looked as follows: on a sheet of paper with slots in it a series of letters was written according to a specific pattern related to the internal connections of the right-hand rotor and then this sheet was placed over another sheet on which letters related to the signal key (telegram key) were written. In a certain position of these two sheets letters showing the plug connections appeared. It was a good method but apparently the Germans intuitively felt that *Enigma* was threatened, for they increased the number of connections and the *grille* system lost a great deal of value.[12]

Fortunately the Polish cryptanalysts also hit on another idea, which achieved the same result. They built a so-called *cyclometer* (see Appendix and picture below). This was a machine constructed from elements of two *Enigma*s and based on the principle of the length of cycles. It was already known that the rotors had a maximum of 105,456 positions and the *cyclometer* allowed their arrangement to be rapidly calculated. To increase efficiency a card index of these cycles was also introduced and, after a few years, it contained about 80,000 different *Enigma* settings. It was hard work, but using these aids it was possible to discover within a few minutes the sequence and position of the rotors as well as that of the plugs.[13] The Germans, however, again came to life and behaved as if they knew what line the Polish

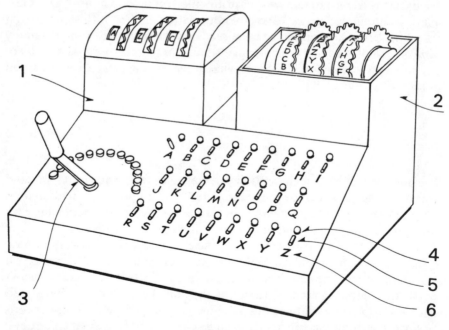

Fig. 4 Cyclometer
1 – Enigma rotors cover closed; 2 – Enigma rotors cover opened; 3 – Rheostat; 4 – Bulbs; 5 – Switches; 6 – Alphabet

efforts were taking. In November 1937 they changed the *Umkehrwalze* and the whole work had to be begun afresh. After a year's strenuous efforts, a new card index was compiled.

It was already 1938, Hitler had repudiated the decisions of Versailles, had built up an Army, Air Force and Navy, had occupied the Rhineland, had annexed Austria and was marching on. War could be felt in the air and all the intelligence services were working feverishly to obtain as much information as possible about their potential adversary. Captain Bertrand continued to maintain secret contact with *Asché*, who no longer supplied information on *Enigma*, but on German monitoring stations, since in 1934 he had been transferred to the *Forschungsamt*.[14] These reports were also important, since they showed what the Germans were picking up and what particularly interested them. Their aim also was to discover and break British, French and Polish ciphers and to find out what their enemies knew of their own cipher system.

In the first half of 1938 the Polish Cipher Department reached the height of its achievements. Only naval ciphers still caused trouble, since they used five rotors on their *Enigmas*, while *Wehrmacht* and *Luftwaffe* traffic was being read almost daily and very rapidly. Suddenly, half-way through September 1938, everything came to a standstill. They began to intercept messages which were quite incomprehensible. The cryptanalysts worked feverishly, while Intelligence in Germany tried to find out what had happened. It turned out that a further change had been introduced into the cipher system. This could have had something to do with the Munich conference at which the Allied leaders had tried to find some way of resolving the Czech crisis in discussions with Hitler and Mussolini.[15] It was unclear how these discussions would end and war could suddenly become very real, so the Germans preferred to make their radio messages even more secure.

The new problems were fairly speedily recognized. They consisted of a change of the *Grundstellung*, that is the position of the machine when the signal key was enciphered. Hitherto the position had been the same for the whole day, but now it was changed for each message, which continued to have its own key, which was repeated twice.[16]

This change ruined all the previous methods of unravelling the order of the rotors and the plugs, since they had been based on cycles, which were no longer viable, as the Germans had ceased enciphering all signals on one day on the same *Enigma* setting. A new method of solving this problem had to be found. Rejewski set about it.

His mind, always practical, turned to the idea of developing equipment which could in some way work out the *Enigma* settings, that is the position of the three rotors and the plugs. He designed a machine which would consist of six *Enigmas* connected together and called it the *Bombe*. The principle of it was that the rotors of these six machines revolved, powered by electricity,

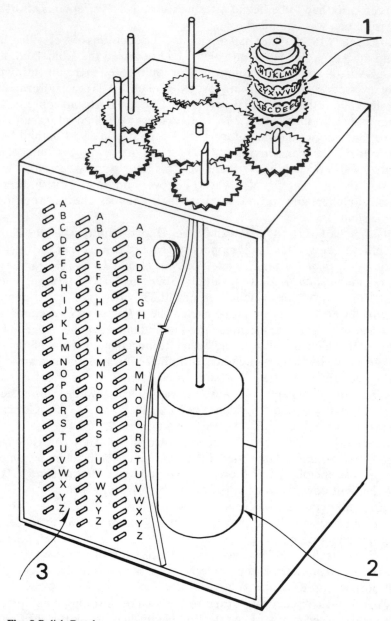

Fig. 5 Polish Bombe
1 – Six *Enigma* rotors (only one shown); 2 – Electric motor; 3 – Three rows of switches

and in two hours tested every possible position. Speed was of the essence and so it was planned to use six *Bombes*: one for each rotor position. When they reached the right solution, a light came on and the motor stopped automatically. This was the first primitive computer, without electronics or memory. The design, together with plans, was sent to the AVA firm to be built as quickly as possible. By November 1938 the *Bombes* were ready and again the process of reading German signals began.[17]

Alongside this solution Henryk Zygalski devised another method, which was manual and not mechanical, called the *perforated sheet*. About one thousand holes were cut in a piece of paper according to a predetermined pattern. Twenty-six of the sheets were required, one for each of the rotor positions. When they were laid on top of each other one by one, after some time, usually around the tenth sheet, in one place a hole appeared through all of them. This was the secret setting of the machine. Six complete sets of twenty-six sheets were needed, just like six *Bombes*. The use of the sheets and the *Bombes* was a practical and mechanical application of mathematical permutations. Unfortunately, the production of these sheets could not be entrusted to AVA and the cryptanalysts had to make them themselves, not only calculating their layout, but also cutting out these holes to the last millimetre with a razor blade, which was an endless task. The first two sets of sheets were completed about the same time as the *Bombes*: towards the end of 1938. The sheets had the advantage over the *Bombes* that changes in the number of plugs in the machine did not affect their value.[18] (See Appendix.)

Nevertheless, pleasure at having both *Bombes* and sheets was short-lived. By December 1938 a new complication arose. The Germans once again made an alteration to *Enigma* and again their signal became long lists of jumbled letters. The Cipher Department equipment, which had been developed with such ingenuity and cost, was now very slow in use.

4

Lieutenant-Colonel Langer, although feeling a certain satisfaction with the results already achieved, was worried. Despite the general air of optimism and the strident propaganda proclaiming that Poland was a great power, he knew that the country was poor and that both technically and economically it was a long way behind the West. Despite the Polish cryptanalysts' great achievements, the obvious lack of material resources prevented the Poles from completely mastering German secrets and especially from keeping up with the frequent modifications. The *Bombes*, which had been constructed at the great cost of one hundred thousand zlotys, which for Poland at that time was a great deal of money, had become of little worth and there were no resources to continue producing the *perforated sheets*, which likewise, as a result of German alterations, had become far less effective.

Fortunately, a new impasse was averted by Captain Bertrand who at that very moment sent Warsaw an invitation to the first secret cryptology conference. He had been in the Polish capital in May 1938 and *Enigma* had been the main topic of conversation and debate. With Langer he had also discussed the problems of co-operation with the Czechoslovak Intelligence. They were both in contact with the head of it, Colonel František Moravec (*Raoul*), but were forced to take great precautions since it was very probable that, after the Sudeten crisis, the Germans had penetrated the Czechoslovak General Staff.[19] Now Bertrand wanted to arrange a meeting for French, British and Polish cryptologists. The charged atmosphere of the approaching storm could be felt ever more clearly and action had to be taken.

The conference took place in Paris between 9 and 10 January in the French Intelligence building. The French side was represented by Bertrand himself and a specialist cryptologist from the Air Force, while on the Polish side were Lieutenant-Colonel Langer and Major Ciężki. The Poles very carefully observed the British delegation, with which they had had no previous contact. It was led by the head of the Government Code and Cipher School, Commander Alastair Denniston. He was a man of medium height, about fifty years old, very experienced and with a fine mind; during the First World War he had been one of the cryptanalysts in the famous 'Room 40' at the Admiralty.[20] For complete security codenames were used: Denniston was called *Crypto*, Bertrand *Bolek* and Langer *Luc*.

The aim of the conference was to share progress made so far in breaking the secret of *Enigma*, particularly in view of the Germans' constant changes. In this respect the personal contact of the representatives of the three nations produced minimal results, since none of them was really frank. The British arrived in a rather sceptical frame of mind, for hitherto they had been unable to break the German machine, despite having great experience and far more technical resources than their partners. The French had already earlier released to the British and the Poles documents received from *Asché* and now they had nothing new to add. The Poles stayed silent and mentioned not a word of their own ability to read German messages, for they had come with instructions to reveal nothing, unless they were convinced that their partners had made considerable advances in this direction.[21]

The conference ended in a minor key. It appeared that all three partners were at an impasse and that they had at all costs to seize an *Enigma* intact, or at least some of its more important parts, in order to move forward. Mere instructions and descriptions were not enough.[22]

5

At the beginning of July every European capital was deserted, since the inhabitants, as happened every summer, had left town to go to the seaside, to the lakes or the countryside; but military and intelligence staffs stayed behind. Poland had already received the British and French guarantees and in May had carried out partial mobilization. Her western frontiers were straining under the weight of massed German divisions, and only a few weeks separated the world from a new round of insane slaughter. Feverish diplomatic activity continued, but Hitler did not intend to be diverted from his chosen path.

Morale in Poland was high, for it was widely expected that, immediately after a German attack, British and French bombers would appear in the skies over the cities of the Third *Reich*. Such views were even held on the Staff, although intelligence reports contained worrying information on the slowness of preparations in France and on a general reluctance to make any effort or sacrifices there.

The approach of the war meant that essential and rapid decisions had to be made about *Enigma*. Polish intelligence post No. 3, which had had a *Luftwaffe* radio NCO working for it for the past few months, transmitted the news that the Germans had introduced two new rotors: IV and V.[23] The cryptanalysts confirmed this on the basis of intercepted signals and, thanks to some mistakes made by the *Sicherheitsdienst* (*SD*), they managed to duplicate the connections of these two additional rotors. This was possible since the *SD*, although introducing the rotors, did not use the new system

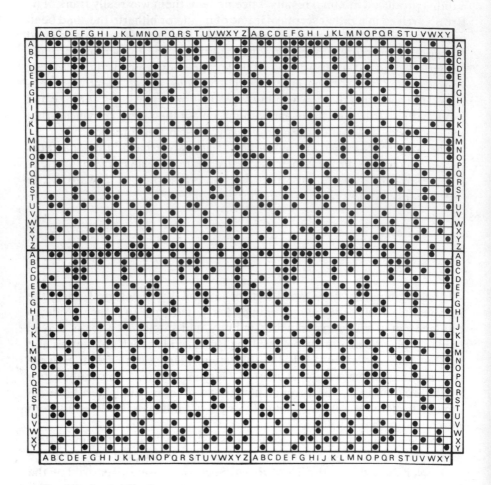

Fig. 6 Perforated Sheet

immediately. The Poles could, therefore, continue to read German signals, but mainly ones from the *SD* and *SS*; furthermore, decipherment was extremely slow, taking ten times longer than previously. The only solution would be to build sixty *Bombes* or sixty sets of the *perforated sheets*.[24]

The rapid change of events and the lack of national resources to pursue further improvements to the equipment already devised, caused the Chief of the Polish General Staff, General Wacław Stachiewicz, to decide that the Western Allies must be let into the Polish secret and that, while there was still time, they must be told of everything that had been achieved.[25]

Everything had to be kept in the greatest secrecy, since spying German eyes could be expected everywhere. They had probably not succeeded in catching up with Polish achievements and now, just before hostilities, this secret had to be kept at all costs. It was decided to organize a conference in Poland between 25 and 27 July and to invite both French and British specialists.[26]

6

About ten kilometres to the south of Warsaw lie the Kabacki woods and in their midst is the little town of Pyry. Before the war it really was a village, although it did have a small railway station.

To the east of Pyry the wood is mixed and especially beautiful, with thick undergrowth. There, in a clearing, much of which had been carved out of the woods, and not more than a kilometre from the village, the General Staff Second Bureau had in 1936 begun to build a special transmitting station and cipher centre. Work was completed a year later and the building handed over. It was in the shape of a square, with sides of about two hundred metres, entirely surrounded by a high wall, while inside there were two solid brick buildings. The first was a large single-story structure and garages, while the second, smaller, one was an air-raid shelter containing the radio station. It was estimated that it could withstand the impact of a fifty-kilogram bomb. It was a communication centre maintaining permanent contact with Paris and with Czech Intelligence. Its power output was twenty kilowatts and its aerials were thirty metres high. They could be lowered and hidden, and would then be impossible to find amidst the trees. The centre was continuously manned by several dozen young officers and other ranks, all of whom were highly qualified signallers. Their work was important and secret and so they wore civilian clothes. The analysts came in from Warsaw every day. In a camouflaged villa nearby lived a dozen or so civilian guards who were responsible for security.[27]

This was the place in which it had been decided to hold the planned conference and acquaint the Western guests with the results of the Polish experts' work. Relations with the French had for a long time been very cordial and so a telegram was sent to Captain Bertrand asking him to get in touch with the British and to invite them on behalf of the Poles. Part of the secret was revealed in the cable when it mentioned that, during the conference, Polish methods of breaking German ciphers would be demonstrated.[28]

The invited guests appeared in Warsaw on 24 July. The British arrived by air, while the French travelled by the northern express which linked Paris and Moscow via Warsaw. The French were given rooms in the Hotel Polonia, while the British were accommodated in the Bristol, which was the best hotel in the city. It was there, over lunch, in a private room on the first floor, that the first meeting of all the participants in the conference took place on 24 July. The Bristol was often used for such meetings and the two waiters serving were specially screened.

In addition to Commander Denniston, the British were represented by Alfred Dillwyn Knox, a slim, tall, dark-haired and balding man of fifty-six, wearing glasses and with tired, ill eyes.[29] He had a fine mathematical mind and wide cryptanalytical experience, but little stamina and poor health. They were accompanied by a third man, who was tall and about fifty, with light reddish hair and very pale blue eyes. He remained silent and said little; he was introduced as Professor Sandwich from Oxford, who, although not himself a cryptologist, worked closely with the experts in this field. It so happened that at the table the Professor was seated opposite Lieutenant-Colonel Stefan Mayer, head of the Intelligence Department, who was acting as host. The Colonel was not surprised by the Professor's presence, for during the First World War and the Russo-Polish war of 1920, he had encountered close co-operation between academics and cryptologists. However, he had the impression that the Oxford man was in fact the most important member of the British delegation.[30]

The French sent two officers, Captain Bertrand, naturally, and Captain Henri Bracquenié. Bertrand dominated his colleague and he alas has remained in the memory of the conference participants.

The Polish delegation was led by Lieutenant-Colonel Langer, with Major Ciężki at his side. They were accompanied by the three young cryptanalysts, who were unknown to any of the guests. Only when the conference began would it transpire that they were its most important participants, since they were to show the foreign experts just how much they had achieved. They had an excellent knowledge of German, which became the basic language of the conference, since all the three Britons and Bertrand spoke it. In addition Zygalski communicated with them in English. The lunch passed in a pleasant and relaxed atmosphere, with the conversation touching only on neutral matters, but the thoughts of all the participants were turning to the immediate future, to the next day.[31]

7

Only ten people travelled out to Pyry, for Colonel Mayer remained in Warsaw. He was extremely busy and cryptology was not his field.

Colonel Langer, after a very short tour of the centre, led them all into the analysts' office where several medium-sized cases under covers stood on tables. The Colonel gathered everyone round and, without a word, quickly uncovered one of the cases. The guests saw a typewriter of a slightly unusual shape, supplemented by a few electrical connections and lights and with three drums fixed above the keyboard.

The visitors immediately showed great interest. They all knew already what *Enigma* looked like in principle.

'Where did you get this from?' asked Captain Bertrand quickly.

'We made it ourselves,' answered Langer.

The British group at once came to life. All three of them bent over the machine and began to examine it with the greatest interest. Knox concentrated on the drums and their arrangement. 'Professor Sandwich' for a moment abandoned his reserve and threw Langer a swift, inquiring glance.

'Yes,' repeated the Colonel, 'this is an exact copy of the German machine built by our cryptanalysts.'[32]

Zygalski stepped forward and began to explain. He outlined the machine's construction and all its connections, he touched a few keys and showed how each time a different letter lit up, and explained how the Polish analysts had managed to break the machine's secrets. He emphasized that buying a commercial *Enigma* had been a great help in reconstructing the military version. The documents supplied by Captain Bertrand had been invaluable.

His listeners caught every word with the greatest attention and began to ask questions. The most lively of them was Knox who felt quite at ease in this complex field. He was primarily interested in the rotors and the order in which the electrical current travelled from the keys to them, particularly to the third one (C). He knew that *Enigma*'s basic feature was reciprocity and so the Germans already had to have thousands of these machines. Perhaps it would have been simpler if Intelligence had managed to steal a machine from a German ship or military unit;[33] in practice, however, the Polish analysts had broken its secret using mathematics and cryptanalysis with the aid of the priceless documents brought from France.

Commander Denniston, very excited, wanted to rush to the telephone and call the embassy in Warsaw to request London immediately to send specialists and electricians, but Colonel Langer restrained him. This was not all: there was more to come.

They all went through to the next room and there were shown six small cupboards, each about 120 centimetres high and looking just like washing machines. A switch was thrown and all the machines started up with a discreet hum: drums began to revolve and little lights to flicker. This time Rejewski supplied the commentary, since the machine had been built to his design.

These were the *Bombes* whose task was to mechanize the reading of *Enigma*'s daily key. If one ran all six *Bombes* simultaneously, the required answer would be calculated within two hours.[34]

There was silence in the room when Langer stopped the machines and showed his astounded guests a deciphered signal sent that morning from the *SS* High Command. Denniston and Knox asked to see the *Bombes* working again and followed their operation with great attention. Rejewski answered questions. The 'Oxford professor' remained calm, but it was clear that the demonstration of Polish achievements had visibly affected him. The Frenchmen, gesticulating wildly, showered Rejewski and Langer with questions.

Denniston once again wanted to go to the telephone to call London, but Langer once more restrained him. A whole second day of the conference lay before them and it might bring further surprises.

8

After the great success of the first day, when the Poles were able to show their guests their achievements, the second day began on a quite different note. Langer said that hitherto they had shown only one side of the problem, the Polish one, and the interception and reading of German signals. Now they had to discuss the German side, not only from the point of view of *Enigma* operations, but also taking into account that the Germans realized that their enemies were trying to wrest their secret from them. For some years the actual encipherment and the machine itself had been continually modified by the Germans, and this their enemies had always managed to detect and overcome, but now the situation had changed. That was what needed to be discussed.

Until mid-December of the previous year *Enigma* had had only three rotors and the Polish analysts had managed to read most signals, but from then onwards the Germans had introduced a further two rotors and decipherment had become more difficult. It was still possible to decipher, but now the process lasted ten times longer and had ceased to be practical. Furthermore the number of plugs had been increased to between seven and ten, which had decreased the effectiveness of the *Bombes* even more drastically. Finally the Germans had begun to set up more and more separate radio nets,[35] all with their own keys. These changes had produced yet another invention, which would be demonstrated in a moment. This was the *perforated sheet*, which had been designed by Zygalski, and so it fell to him to explain their principles and mode of operation. They had replaced the *Bombes* which, in order to be effective, would now have to number not six, but sixty; but there were also not enough sheets.[36]

The moment arrived when Colonel Langer came to the most important point of the whole conference. He saw that what he had demonstrated to his guests had greatly interested and even impressed them, but that was not all. He now has to reveal Polish worries and intentions. War was inevitably approaching and Poland almost certainly would be the first object of a German attack. She had allies in the West and so the decision had been taken to turn over to them all the Polish cryptanalysts' achievements. They were well advanced, but needed constant improvement so as to keep pace with the Germans who were continually introducing changes into their *Enigma* system. In order to read German signals enciphered on five-drum machines, both *Bombes* and the sheets had to be built up, and Polish resources had already turned out to be inadequate for this. There might also not be enough time. It had been decided to hand everything over to the Western Allies, who were so much wealthier and possessed so many more technical resources. Both delegations, the British and the French, would receive a copy of an *Enigma*, built in Poland, together with drawings and plans of the *Bombes* and *perforated sheets*. This gift would be Poland's first contribution to the common victory.[37]

The guests were all moved. Commander Denniston warmly grasped the Colonel's hand, Knox quickly went into the other room and began to examine the machines again, Captain Bertrand loudly expressed his joy. Alcohol was forbidden in the centre, but a few bottles of beer were found, as it was a hot summer. They were brought and drunk to joint success. The British promised to produce immediately more *Bombes* and *perforated sheets*.[38]

Two weeks passed and the French diplomatic bag brought two *Enigmas* to Paris. On 16 August Captain Bertrand, accompanied by a French diplomatic courier[39] and Commander Wilfred Dunderdale, the British Intelligence 'resident' in Paris, arrived at Victoria Station in London. They had brought with them a largish suitcase containing an *Enigma* which they handed to the 'Oxford professor', who was anxiously awaiting them. He was on the way to some reception and was wearing a dinner-jacket with the ribbon of the Legion d'Honneur in his button-hole.[40] Only a few select people knew that it had taken just a few minutes for one of the most important and far-reaching acts of the impending war to take place.

Several days later German tanks crossed the Polish frontier.

NOTES

1. Hepp, op. cit.
2. Möller, op. cit. Also: Heinz Bonatz, *Die Deutsche Marine-Funkaufklärung, 1914–1945*, Darmstadt, 1970, p. 87.
3. Rejewski, 'Reminiscences . . .', op. cit., p. 65. Also: Möller, op. cit.
4. Ibid.
5. Karl Otto Hoffmann (a former officer of the *Luftwaffe*) a letter to the author, 8 September 1977.
6. Rejewski, 'Reminiscences . . . ', op. cit., p. 65.
7. Werther, 'Die Entwicklung der Deutschen Funkschlüsselmaschinen: die Enigma'. Also: Rejewski, 'Appendix', p. 23.
8. Ibid.
9. Hepp, op. cit.
10. Möller, op. cit.
11. Jürgen Rohwer, a conversation in London on 5 July 1977 in the presence of Tadeusz Lisicki.
12. Rejewski, 'Appendix . . . ', op. cit., pp. 19–20.
13. Ibid, p. 22.
14. Bertrand, op. cit., p. 29.
15. On 30 September 1938 the meeting between the British and French Prime Ministers, Neville Chamberlain and Edouard Daladier, and Hitler and Mussolini took place in Munich. As a result of this meeting an agreement was signed giving part of Sudetenland to Germany.
16. Rejewski, 'Appendix . . .', op. cit., p. 26.
17. Rejewski, 'Reminiscences . . . ', op. cit., p. 66.
18. Rejewski, 'Appendix . . . ', pp. 30–2.
19. P. Renauld, 'La machine a chiffrer "Enigma" ', p. 45.
20. This room had been the scene of the decipherment of German signals. One of these, sent on 16 January 1917 by the German Minister of Foreign Affairs, Arthur Zimmermann, to the German ambassador in Washington, concerned the increase of German U-boat activity in the Atlantic and the involvement of the United States in war with Mexico. The publication of this telegram caused the United States to enter the war (B. Norman op. cit., pp. 47–60).
21. Mayer, 'Supplement to the paper of May 1974 (Enigma)', London, December, 1974, p. 3.
22. Bertrand, op. cit., p. 58.
23. Mayer, 'Supplement . . . ', op. cit., p. 3.
24. Rejewski, letter to T. Lisicki, 25 May 1976.
25. Mayer, 'Supplement . . . ', op. cit., p. 2.
26. Mayer, 'The breaking up of . . . ', op. cit., pp. 3–4.
27. Mayer, an authorized conversation with the author on 9 May 1977.
28. Ibid. Also: Bertrand, op. cit., p. 59.
29. Frederick W. Winterbotham, *The Ultra Secret*, London, 1975, p. 32. Also: Penelope Fitzgerald, *The Knox Brothers*, London, 1977, p. 280.
30. The riddle was cleared up only after the war when, in 1945, in London, Colonel Mayer met Major-General Stewart Menzies, head of intelligence (M.I.6) and recognized him as the 'Oxford professor'. At that time, in July 1939, Menzies, as a colonel was the deputy head of M.I.6 (Mayer, 'Supplement . . .', p. 3.).
31. Mayer, an authorized conversation . . ., op. cit.
32. Rejewski, 'Appendix . . . ', op. cit., pp. 10 and 32.
33. Möller, op. cit.
34. Rejewski, 'Reminiscences . . . ', op. cit., p. 66.
35. During the war the number of these nets increased to sixty.
36. Rejewski, 'Appendix . . . ', op. cit., p. 4.
37. Mayer, 'The breaking up of . . . ', op. cit., p. 4.

38. Rejewski, 'Reminiscences . . . ', op. cit., p. 67.
39. P. Renault, 'La machine a chiffrer "Enigma" ', he states that it was not a courier, but Tom Greene from M.I.6.
40. Bertrand, op. cit., pp. 60–1 (France was used as an intermediary, since the Poles had long intelligence links with the French which at that time they did not have with the British).

4

Bletchley Park
in the Shadow of War

1

THE UNITED KINGDOM is a rather small country, with a population which even today does not reach sixty million, and yet it succeeded in building a huge empire and governing it for many years. Furthermore, the task was made harder since the Empire spanned vast distances throughout the world, and embraced a multitude of exotic peoples, often numbering many millions, with varied religions, traditions and cultures.

This was all made possible by the exceptional ability of the British to select the right people. This is a rare talent, the lack of which has caused other intelligent, populous and enterprising nations to fail to attain the sort of success which they apparently deserve.

During the last war this ability to pick out the right person was clearly evident. It was this that ensured that the Government Code and Cipher School had the most suitable people before the war even began. They were recruited from two sources. First of all there were the specialist crypt-analysts, who had been working in this field since the First World War. The most eminent of these was Alfred Dillwyn Knox, who had been in Pyry at the *Enigma* demonstration.

Knox was descended from a family which had settled in Northern Ireland in the eighteenth century; his ancestors had also sought their fortune in India, and his father had been an Anglican bishop. In addition to two sisters, he also had three brothers, all of whom had been successful in different fields. 'Dilly' (that was his nickname) was exceptionally talented. At Eton he had shown great mathematical aptitude, while at Cambridge the wide range of his talents and interests had attracted attention. He was a quite extraordin-ary character combining the highest academic qualities with a penchant for useless schemes, and a sharp and penetrating intellect with extreme absent-mindedness. Properly employed he could get results worthy of a genius, on the other hand he could also be completely wasted.[1]

During the First World War it was just this kind of sensible recruitment which plucked him from Cambridge and, at the beginning of 1915, brought him into naval intelligence and to the famous 'Room 40' where the first cryptanalytical work began. He distinguished himself there by his great powers of intuition and by the extravagance of some of his ideas, which usually gave good results. In the summer of 1917, while lying in the bath, he hit on the code used by the commander of the German Navy to issue orders to his U-boat flotillas.[2]

At the end of the war he was persuaded to remain in 'Room 40' which, after reorganization, became the Government Code and Cipher School attached to the Foreign Office. It was there that the *Enigma* problem found him in the thirties. Like the analysts in Poland, he was able to use the German commercial model and also the documents which Captain Bertrand received from *Asché*, but he had been unable to make the final breakthrough, although he had been very close.

In addition to Knox, other outstanding cryptanalysts had worked in 'Room 40', such as Travis de Grey, who had also helped to decipher the Zimmermann telegram, and 'Nobby' Clarke, who was on duty during the Battle of Jutland.[3]

The second source of new recruits consisted of academics, not necessarily mathematicians, with sharp analytical minds and a restless inquiring imagination, who were invited down from the leading universities, mainly Oxford and Cambridge. Commander Alastair Denniston, head of the school, already sensing the approaching storm, as early as 1938 began to seek outstanding minds for his work. Some of them joined the school before the war; some later, during the struggle, transferred from the Army, Navy and the Air Force. There were mathematicians: C. H. Alexander, Charles Babbage, Peter Twinn and Gordon Welchman; writers and historians: Dr Frank Adcock, Desmond McCarthy and Angus Wilson; the chess master, Harry Golombek; great individualists who loved music, 'Josh' Cooper and Oliver Strachey; the eventual inventor of the computer, Alan Turing; the eccentric, Frank Birch; Peter Calvocoressi, Edward Crankshaw, Dr I. J. Good, Roy Jenkins, Stuart Milner Barry, J. H. Tiltman and many others.[4] It is an intriguing fact that many of the mathematicians, whom one would imagine to be dry and practical people, were also interested in music and knew a great deal about it. There is a relationship between the attraction for numbers and musical sounds, both of which stimulate the imagination. Denniston was building a team which, when the time came, would strain every mental and physical sinew in the common cause.

2

At the very time as Captain Bertrand was handing over the copy of the Polish *Enigma* to the British at Victoria Station, in the same area of London the Government Code and Cipher School was beginning its move into the heart of England. War was now inevitable and it was essential to move as much as possible out of London, which could well become a target for aerial attack. Every institution which was vital to the war effort and which could be moved, was sent out to country houses and to small villages hidden deep in the countryside.

Commander Denniston's school was transferred to Bletchley Park, about seventy or so kilometres to the north-west of London in Buckinghamshire. This site was selected since it lay almost mid-way between Oxford and Cambridge. In a great park running down to the railway line stood a large Victorian Tudor-Gothic mansion in red brick. Today it houses the Post Office Training Centre, but then the large building had a rather grand appearance as a result of the not inconsiderable sums of money spent on it by its owner, the wealthy businessman Sir Herbert Leon. The numerous rooms were all panelled and the electricity and plumbing were of the highest order. The whole estate was surrounded by barbed wire and patrolled by men of the RAF Regiment; everyone either leaving or entering the park had to produce identification papers. The house immediately turned out to be too small and so they began to build huts, sheds and cafeterias in the park, among the cedars. Only a few specialists, like Dillwyn Knox, who were constantly needed and who had no interest in personal comfort anyway, decided to sleep in their offices; the vast majority of those working there had to be found accommodation in local inns and houses. Suddenly, amidst the country people, the shopkeepers, drivers, farmworkers and craftsmen there appeared dozens of strange, unusually dressed and rather dishevelled eccentrics, speaking in drawling Oxford accents, looking for copies of *The Times* and expensive pipe tobacco, sometimes playing chess and bridge. Every day the numbers working at Bletchley Park increased and these people had to be found housing in towns and villages further and further afield. Local hotels and country houses were filled up.[5] Right until the end of the war a whole community of government departments, special housing and various other services grew up around the tightly guarded and isolated centre, officially known as *Station X*. About ten thousand people worked there.[6] A number of cover stories were devised to justify the large influx of unusual people who suddenly descended on the quiet and peaceful rural area, but this was quite unnecessary. The local inhabitants belonged to a great race which values its personal freedom above everything else, but which, in times of difficulty, has a strong sense of unity and of the need for sacrifice and discipline. The keeping of this secret was all the more astonishing as practical considerations caused the secrets of Bletchley Park to be revealed to a number of people, who even had the right to visit this camouflaged centre.

One of these was Dr Reginald Jones, an eminent young scientist, only twenty-eight, who was working on the German secret weapons. When at the very beginning of the war, Hitler in his speech at Gdańsk (Danzig) on 19

September 1939, revealed that the Germans had secret weapons, Jones went for the first time to Bletchley Park, to dig into the archives of the Intelligence (M.I.6) which had been taken there. The co-operation then established became closer as the war went on, with ever better results, for Jones received the full advantage of the cryptanalysts' work.

The first important achievement, which may be taken as an example of the value of this co-operation, concerned the German device which corresponded to the British radar. During the period of the fall of France, when the British Isles were threatened by invasion, a German dispatch was read in Bletchley Park, which touched on the problem of the secret device, *Knickebein*. Jones, with the aid of information from conventional intelligence, was able to work out that this was the codename of a device to make night bombing easier. It was a type of radio-beam bombing system with which the Germans managed to find their targets. The matter was so important that Churchill arranged a special secret conference in Downing Street on 21 June 1940. Jones's report was listened to, the fact of the German achievement was accepted as was also the opinion of the young scientist that the best counter-action would be jamming and putting in a false cross-beam to make the German airmen drop their bombs early.[7]

The most important, the most closely guarded and relatively the smallest focal point of the whole centre was the small team of cryptanalysts, whose task was to break *Enigma*. Only about five hundred or so people in Great Britain knew what they were doing. Many very highly placed persons had to be satisfied with information reaching them by secret channels, but without any indication as to its source. At the beginning, the team consisted of at the most ten people, with Knox and Twinn in charge, and assisted by two young and extremely talented girls, Margaret Rock and Mavis Lever. They all worked in a small whitewashed hut opposite the stable yard.

This small group's efforts had hitherto met with little success, since they had concentrated on the arrangement of the letters on *Enigma*'s keyboard, which was of lesser significance.[8] All this changed when the machine sent from Poland was delivered to the hut, together with details of how to produce *Bombes* and *perforated sheets*. Now they could begin real creative work which was aimed at developing aids for quickly discoving the German keys and breaking down the secrets of the signals enciphered on *Enigma*.

The discovery of the principle of the German machine, although of great importance, was barely the first cog in the great structure called Bletchley Park. The deciphered signal had to be translated into English then interpreted and assessed by a quite different set of people. Each section of the German armed forces used a different sort of jargon in its signals, with abbreviations and very concise prose, which was both difficult to understand and technical, demanding from the translator an excellent knowledge of the subject from every point of view. A number of new teams and departments had to be created, taking into account the tri-service structure. They had to have good, fast communications, yet they could not meet the others working in this field nor even knew what they were doing. Those who were translating and interpreting the German signals could not be told the origin of their material. Everyone was bound by the Official Secrets Act, which they had signed in the presence of their commanding officer, and which is binding to this day.[9]

Examining the internal structure and organization of Bletchley Park and assessing the value of the work done there, one must not forget that it was one hundred per cent dependent on the monitoring stations which intercepted German signals. There were a great many of these stations all over Britain, reporting to three centres: for signals from the German Navy in Flowerdown and Scarborough; for the *Luftwaffe* in Chicksands in Bedfordshire and for the Army in Chatham.[10] Later they were on British Mediterranean bases and in the Near East, ringing Germany and her ally Italy. Thousands of people worked round the clock in three shifts on these stations and all of them were highly trained and well prepared for their work. The radio waves were cluttered with traffic in a multitude of languages, which, to the average listener, were just so many Morse dots and dashes. They had to be intercepted, identified, sorted out and immediately forwarded by teleprinter to the cryptanalysis centre. There were various *Enigma* nets, using different techniques and even different machines; mistakes were made, and even subtle tricks were played to make monitoring that much more difficult and sometimes even impossible. The radio operators had to handle all this, but after several long months of hard work they became so experienced that, by the sound, they could recognize the sender and faultlessly classify a message. This was difficult, important and never-ending work demanding complete dedication and all their time.

The final task which had to be carried out with the greatest speed and precision, so as not to squander the analysts' efforts, was to deliver the information to the people who needed it. These were a small number of politicians and military commanders, who for the most part were unaware of the information's source. A special secret network had to be set up which would compromise between the general political line and the requirements of the three services.

3

Squadron-Leader Frederick W. Winterbotham, a tall, very handsome man of about forty, had spent several years before the war in Germany as an RAF intelligence officer. He had met many famous people there, including Hitler, but in 1938 his real job had been discovered and he had had to return to England. At the beginning of 1939 he set up the first scientific intelligence team in the Air Force section of the SIS (Secret Intelligence Service). It had its offices on Broadway near Victoria Station. Two floors below it was the Government Code and Cipher School headed by Commander Denniston.

In August Station X was set up at Bletchley Park with Denniston in charge and with his School as the hub of a great expanding organization. In September, after the outbreak of war, the whole of SIS together with Squadron-Leader Winterbotham and his scientific intelligence team, also found itself there.

The Polish campaign ended; Hitler divided that country between himself and Stalin and the Polish cryptanalysts tried to reach the West via Romania. Meanwhile in France, behind the Maginot Line, soldiers waited for the German attack. The nervous months of the war's first winter had begun.

It was during the warmer days of early April 1940 that Colonel Menzies summoned Winterbotham and handed him four thin strips of paper. They were short, unimportant personal *Luftwaffe* messages, but when Menzies explained where they came from, Winterbotham trembled with excitement. He knew in very general terms that the cryptanalysts were trying to break the *Enigma* machine and that they had received some extremely important information from the continent, but it was only now that he realized that the long awaited miracle had become reality.[11]

Several days later, after a sleepless night, Winterbotham once again reported to Menzies, but this time at his own request. He had devised a plan, which he wanted to lay before his superior as quickly as possible and to try to get him to accept it.

The decipherment of the first German signals at Bletchley Park had been an achievement, but its value could only be assessed on the basis of the practical use of the information. There was need for a secret, extensive organization whose task would be the preparation and delivery by the fastest route of the intercepted material so that it could be acted upon with the minimum delay. This work had to be centralized as much as possible and it would be ideal if all three services could agree to a joint department. The information gleaned in this way would have to be sent great distances to reach the right people quickly, and so it would be essential to use radio. Without any central co-ordinating department the volume of radio traffic alone might alert the Germans. There might also be mistakes made by untrained operators which the German specialists would use to read these top-secret signals. If the enemy found out that *Enigma* had been broken, the whole huge effort would be wasted.[12]

Colonel Menzies was immediately interested in this idea whose practicality appealed to his imagination and professional experience, but he foresaw certain difficulties. The first of these would be the resistance of the individual services who might not agree to a joint department. The second and even greater one would be created by the officers on the receiving end of the information taken from deciphered German signals. They would not want to believe the information, if they were not told its source, and that was out of the question. Maintaining the secret was the basic condition of success. Winterbotham could also see these difficulties, but he had some prepared answers which his superior behind the desk found convincing. After some thought, Menzies agreed. His agreement was conditional on the Directors of Intelligence of all three services doing the same.[13]

The Squadron-Leader ran out of the room and set to work. He headed first for Charles Medhurst, the Director of Air Intelligence (DAL) at the Air Ministry, who was his direct superior and a good friend. He had no trouble in convincing him and the next day three young RAF officers, all fluent German-speakers, reported to Bletchley Park. They had already been given full security clearance and were eager to start work. Winterbotham put them in hut No. 3, which he was already occupying and he added one of his own officers armed with a map of Germany, with every *Luftwaffe* base marked and with every possible detail about the German Air Force and its commanders.

By lucky chance the next deciphered signal was from the *Wehrmacht*, which provided a splendid opportunity to convince the Director of Military Intelligence (DMI), General Davidson. When he heard that the Air Force had already agreed to the idea, he gave the order for two officers and a sergeant to report to Bletchley Park the very next day with all available information on the German Army. After several weeks' work, which was aimed at co-ordinating all the different elements involved, Winterbotham received one more RAF officer, a reservist called Humphreys, who for many years had been a salesman in Germany and knew both the country and its language, with its many regional accents and slang.[14]

It was, however, not quite so easy with the Navy. Unlike the War Office and the Air Ministry, the Admiralty had its own operational Headquarters, which sometimes even took independent tactical decisions. Furthermore, the Admiralty wanted to examine the *Enigma* material itself together with other intelligence information and only then send it to the right place. Finally, despite the fact that Bletchley Park took extreme care over security, the admirals felt that anything which was to be sent to the Navy's units should go through its own Operational Intelligence Centre (OIC). Despite these reservations, the Navy finally agreed to send Commander Malcolm Saunders to Bletchley Park. He arrived in July 1940 and became the head of hut No. 3. Later he shared this function with Wing Commander Humphreys and another officer, and finally this duty was taken over by Group Captain Eric Jones who remained there till the end of the war. The Admiralty insisted that all the deciphered signals must be sent to it in the original German.[15]

There remained one further problem which had to be solved as speedily as possible, for the phoney war could suddenly burst into flame on the Western front. They had to devise a secure and rapid form of communication so that the cryptanalysts' results were not held up for technical reasons.

Winterbotham selected a certain number of highly qualified RAF signal officers and set up for them a completely new course. They were to be seconded to the senior commanders in the field to relay to them intelligence information received from Bletchley Park. The small unit which served these officers consisted of one truck, manned by some NCOs trained in ciphers and working round-the-clock, where the messages were decoded. The commander who received it could not be told how it had been obtained, and were not to do anything which might lead the Germans to suspect that their most secret messages were being read. It was not surprising that the selection of candidates for this job was extremely difficult: they were required to have a knowledge of their subject, absolute discretion and great tact. Every time they delivered a copy of a secret message to the commanding officer, it had to be taken back and destroyed. Frontline generals are not easy people and regularly become enraged when an intelligence officer brings important information without giving a source.[16]

The need to transmit such information over great distances required radio and this created the need to introduce ciphers which could not be broken. The widely known one-time pad system was used. The essence of this system is that the agreed key, which is known only to the sender and the receiver, is used only once. It is not a popular technique, since it is not very suitable for widespread use; the key is known only to the sender and the receiver, and so they cannot be replaced. But the cipher cannot be broken. With time even more German signals were being read, but only the most important were sent on, and so this cipher system could be used. Winterbotham trained his airmen and called them the Special Liaison Unit (SLU).[17] The Navy did not make use of it preferring to employ its own ciphers in communication with its ships, unless it shared joint base facilities with the Army and Air Force.

The first person to get the intercepted and deciphered German signals was Winston Churchill, who waited for them very impatiently. Winterbotham always delivered them personally, carrying them in a small red box.

The new organization needed a name to distinguish it easily from the other intelligence nets. Winterbotham got in touch with the intelligence chiefs of all the three services and accepted their suggestions.

The name 'Ultra Secret' was adopted; 'Ultra' for short.[18]

4

After the German attack on Poland on 1 September 1939 and the break-through of their armoured columns near Warsaw, the Cipher Department received orders to leave the capital and its centre in Pyry as soon as possible, to take its essential equipment and to make for Brześć on the river Bug. The Polish High Command was meant to establish itself there, but the advance of the Red Army into Poland on 17 September changed these plans dramatically. The cryptologists were forced to destroy their equipment and documents, retaining just a couple of *Enigma*s, and cross the frontier into Romania. There the Cipher Department was split up, with the military section being sent in one direction and the civilian in another.[19]

The three young cryptanalysts did not heed Romanian suggestions and instead of going to an internment camp, they headed for Bucharest. There, in collusion with the Polish military attaché, they tried to get in touch with the British authorities. Romania was under strong German pressure to apply internment rigorously and so there was not a moment to be lost. It so happened that when the three cryptanalysts reached the British embassy, cars bringing the staff of the Warsaw embassy were just arriving. Everyone was thus too busy to pay any attention to the young Poles. Since they could not wait, they went to the French embassy, using the name of Captain Bertrand as a reference. Their case was dealt with immediately; they received all the necessary documents, money and railway tickets and French Intelligence did everything it could so that, on 25 September, the young men reached Paris. Then the British intervened and proposed that the crypt-analysts come to London, but the French refused. On 1 October Lieutenant-Colonel Langer, together with some others, also arrived. Several more specialists joined them later.[20]

After the outbreak of war, the French Staff reorganized its intelligence service and from its various parts formed the fifth Bureau.[21] The new department moved from Paris to the little town of Gretz-Armainvillers, about forty kilometres to the north-east of Paris. It took up quarters in the surrounding country houses and châteaux and adopted the codename *Victor*. Bertrand, now promoted to Lieutenant-Colonel, was responsible to the fifth Bureau; he was in charge of the radio intelligence and deciphering centre, located in the château at Vignolles in the same area and carrying the codename *Bruno*. By 20 October officers and specialists of the Polish Cipher Department were there.[22]

Colonel Bertrand's centre had about 70 people working for it; everyone in uniform. Among them there were 48 Frenchmen, fifteen Poles and seven Spaniards. Lieutenant-Colonel Langer headed the Polish team, which received the codename *Ekipa Z*. Everyone in it was a professional, who knew his job well, and they were all used to working as a team. The knowledge that it was they who had led to the breaking of *Enigma* gave them a certain feeling of confidence and a sense of pride. They were growing impatient that organizational matters were preventing them from getting down to their real job.

The seven Spaniards, with five young officers and two political commissars, were formed into a group codenamed *Team D*; all were expert cryptanalysts. Bertrand had found the officers in the Pyrenees after Republican resistance had been destroyed in the Spanish Civil War; the commissars had joined later. They had been accepted on the decision of the Head of National Defence, General Maurice Gamelin, and they worked on Italian and Spanish ciphers.[23]

The centre *Bruno* was, like Bletchley Park, a top-secret unit and so a high degree of camouflage and security was required. No one was allowed to leave without a pass, and entry into the grounds of the château at Vignolles was absolutely forbidden. The seventy people working there formed a sort of rather strict monastic community. Whether they liked it or not, everyone was thrown together; friendships began to develop, little groups of new friends formed and likes and dislikes were born. The Poles were a close-knit little group, which willingly mixed with the French, but avoided the Spaniards. Perhaps they really were republicans, but they were taken to be Communists, which aroused the worst fears amongst the Poles. Hitler was the Spanish left's enemy for having helped France, but at this time he was also Stalin's ally, and so it was difficult to foresee how the Spanish Communists would react. Moreover it was quite possible that the two dictators would find Europe too small for both of them and reach for each other's throats. What would happen then? Would not the great secret of the breaking of *Enigma* then be revealed to the Soviet Union?

The *Bruno* centre also had a British liaison officer, Captain MacFarlan, *Pinky* for short because of his rosy complexion; he was directly responsible to London, but was also in contact with the high command of the British Expeditionary Force in Arras. He knew all about the centre's secrets, including *Enigma*; he also had direct teleprinter communications with London and through London with Bletchley Park. This was the most that the French agreed to, for they had rejected the British suggestion to create a joint cryptology centre in France.[24]

Colonel Bertrand energetically set about organizing the centre. His duties also included receiving intercepted signals straight from three monitoring stations in Metz, Strasbourg and Mulhouse; he therefore required a special team, which worked round the clock, operated teleprinters and passed on the intercepted signal traffic. The same routine applied to the cryptanalyst who also had to work round the clock and had to pay particular attention around midnight, when the Germans changed the machines' settings according to the new keys. Unfortunately the lack of sufficient *Enigma*s was a great handicap. The Poles had brought two, and the French had the one they had received from Warsaw; people from the AVA firm were on the spot preparing designs, but the production of new machines was going exceptionally slowly. In fact one of the *Enigma*s had to be dismantled so as to facilitate the production of new ones, and so the analysts had only two working machines left.

This state of affairs worried Colonel Langer greatly, and so in December he travelled to London, thence to Bletchley Park, where, in consultation with the British, he arranged detailed co-operation. *Bruno*, which had far fewer resources, was to carry out research work, while Bletchley Park was to manage the technical side and the exploitation of the results.[25]

5

Alan Turing, a strongly built young man in his late twenties and Knox's colleague at Bletchley Park, combined all the features of a classic cryptologist. He had a precise, analytical and visionary mathematical mind, which permitted him to calculate faultlessly immensely long sums, and yet he was so absent-minded that anyone casually meeting him might have thought that the young genius was incapable of adding two and two. For many years the following story of his legendary absent-mindedness was told. Fearing that the war would cause the pound's value to drop considerably, Turing had collected a great deal of silver money, melted it down into bars and buried it in the grounds of Bletchley Park. The war ended and it was time to retrieve the silver; unfortunately the great mathematical mind was unable to remember where he had buried it.[26] His long hair, rumpled and dirty clothes, strangely coloured and cut shirts, his shoestring tie, all this completed the picture of the real eccentric.

As early as 1937 Turing had been thinking about constructing the first computer; now, when Poland had sent the designs and details of the *Bombes*, which were an early but successful attempt at building just such a machine, he energetically set about examining them.[27] The *Bombes* did not possess one basic feature of the invention which now runs our life; they did not have a memory and were unable to recreate and use information which they had received earlier. However, in principle they were very similar: their task was to carry out difficult calculations far faster than the human brain. Electronics were then unknown and so the *Bombes* were based on electro-mechanical principles.

Turing had not the slightest difficulty in understanding the *Bombes*, which were a combination of six *Enigma*s all joined together (see Chapter 3, p. 36).

Their object was to discover as quickly as possible the settings of *Enigma*'s rotors and plugs. The more elements a *Bombe* possessed, the more effectively it worked. The Germans increased the number of rotors from three to five and also the number of plugs, and machines had to be built to keep up with these developments.

Barely a few months passed and it was the beginning of 1940 when in the most closely guarded 'shrine' at Bletchley Park, to which only a few people had access, there appeared a large copper-coloured cupboard, almost two and a half metres high and of similar depth, which on first glance looked like an oriental goddess. It contained a complicated network of rotors, lights, plugs and a wide array of wires and connections, which would have been incomprehensible to the layman. This was a new improved *Bombe*, which was meant to deal with any new German idea.[28]

In addition to this they had started producing *perforated sheets*, not in the primitive way used in Warsaw, but from specially printed sheets on which a large number of girls were working. The promises made at Pyry were not forgotten and several copies of these sheets were sent from England to *Bruno*. It was impossible to send a replica of the 'oriental goddess', but it has to be admitted that co-operation between the two centres was extremely good. By air the distance from Bletchley Park to the château at Vignolles was about 250 kilometres, but it seemed as if the two places were next to each other. The war was now raging and practical British common sense managed to deal with every sort of personal complex, ambition, lack of co-operation and envy. Captain MacFarlan was invaluable; his tact, good will and knowledge of the tasks involved were of the highest order.[29]

The mental energies of the Polish cryptanalysts at *Bruno* were above all directed at breaking the new German keys, by which, at this stage of the war, *Enigma*s were set once every twenty-four hours. Bletchley Park found out that the Germans did this around midnight and accordingly told *Bruno*, and it was then therefore that the cryptanalysts were busiest. The first few weeks passed in feverish work which produced no results. There developed a suspicion that the Germans had introduced some new changes; this turned out to be true. It was confirmed by Alan Turing who arrived at the French centre on 17 January 1940, bringing with him sixty complete sets of the *perforated sheets* and the extremely confidential information that a damaged and drifting German U-boat, with a dead crew, had fallen into the Navy's hands a few weeks earlier.[30] An *Enigma* with a sixth and seventh rotor had been found aboard. Additional important information brought by the Englishman, together with an indication of the direction that investigation should take, gave the work an immediate impetus. The very same day they managed to break the Germans' key of 28 October of the previous year and this opened the door to further successes.[31] The secret of the key to each individual message was easily solved, for some of the German cipher clerks, after setting the machine and closing it, selected for the key the three letters which were visible in the windows on the lid. The analysts knew that these usually coincided with the setting of the rings. This was all they needed and within a few minutes of midnight they were reading German signals almost as quickly as the addressees.[32]

From the breakthrough of 17 January *Wehrmacht* signals were regularly deciphered and their contents sent to Bletchley Park on Captain Mac-Farlan's teleprinter. The teamwork of the two centres was excellent. Every day they exchanged the deciphered general and daily *Enigma* keys, views, additional information and ideas. Unfortunately, the information thus obtained could not always be acted upon effectively. In the early spring of 1940 *Bruno* deciphered a *Luftwaffe* signal dealing with plans for an air attack on the Renault car factory near Paris. The plan, which was part of an overall operation (*Unternehmen Paula*), gave the exact numbers of bombers and fighters taking part as well as details of the height they would be flying at, their exact routes and the precise date and time of the action. The Allies had eight days to prepare some sort of defence, and yet the cryptanalysts watched in impotent anger as the tight German formation flew high over the centre heading for its target.[33]

6

Bletchley Park was expanding on a large scale, but it was only at the beginning of April 1940 that they managed to break a German signal for the first time (see Chapter 4, p. 53). This happened just at the time when Hitler unexpectedly attacked Denmark and Norway. The Norwegian campaign greatly increased the activity at both centres, and their continued, faultless co-operation produced some excellent results. The British figures are unknown, but it has been confirmed that during the Norwegian campaign *Bruno* deciphered 1,151 German signals.[34] Unfortunately, this did not change anything, and the Allied forces had to withdraw. This led to a political crisis in Britain and the Prime Minister, Neville Chamberlain, resigned to be replaced by Winston Churchill who formed a coalition government.

The German attack in the west could come at any time and intercepting and reading their messages assumed even greater importance; but it was just at this time that German radio became rather reticent. This did not mean that the Germans suspected that *Enigma* had been broken, it was merely a question of not increasing the volume of normal radio traffic, which would arouse suspicions that something big was about to happen.[35] There was nothing to stop the Germans operating in this way, for they could also

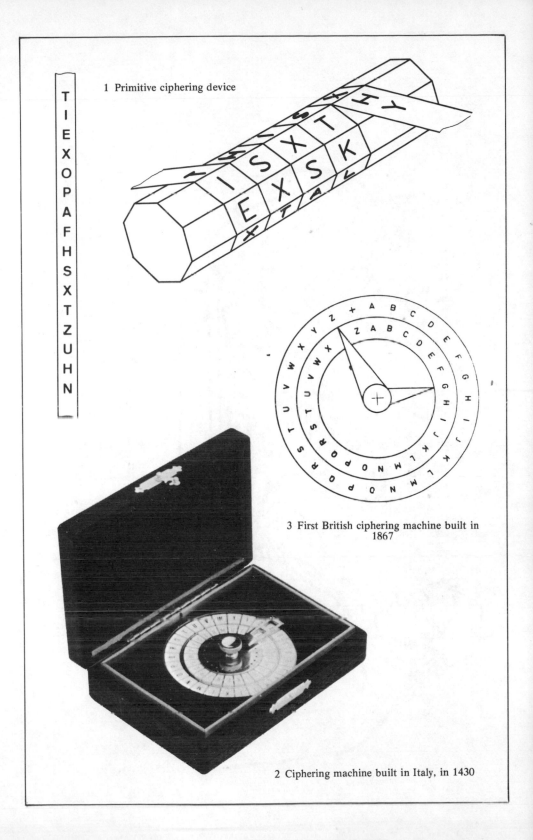

T I E X O P A F H S X T Z U H N

1 Primitive ciphering device

3 First British ciphering machine built in 1867

2 Ciphering machine built in Italy, in 1430

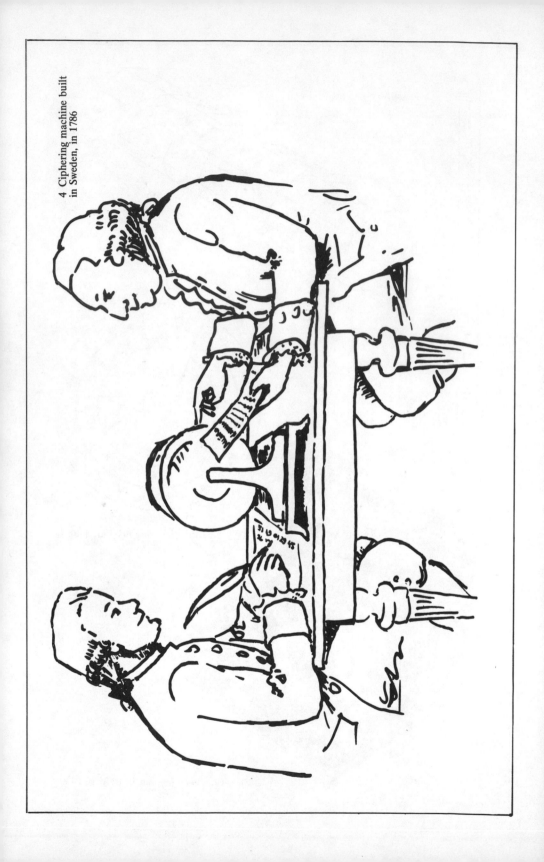

4 Ciphering machine built in Sweden, in 1786

5 Polish copy of *Enigma* made in France, in 1940, with the electric plugs above the rotors (now in the Polish Institute and Sikorski Museum in London). 1-Letter keys; 2-Bulbs; 3-Spare rotors; 4-Entry rotor; 5-Three operational rotors with rings (note the letters on the rings; the German military *Enigmas* had figures); 6-Reflector; 7-Plugs

VIII. Beifpiel.

17. Gültiger Tagesschlüssel:

(Ausschnitt aus der für die Verschlüsselung des Klartextes in Betracht kommenden Schlüsseltafel, z. B. »..........· Maschinenschlüssel für Monat Mai«)

Datum	Walzenlage	Ringstellung	Grundstellung
4.	I III II	16 11 13	01 12 22

Steckerverbindung	Kenngruppen-Einsatzstelle ...... Gruppe	Kenngruppen
CO DI FR HU JW LS TX	2	adq nuz opw vxz

Nach diesem Tagesschlüssel ist die Chiffriermaschine einzustellen (vgl. Ziff. 4 und 5).

Der im nachfolgenden Beispiel eingesetzte Schlüsseltext ist aus Geheimhaltungsgründen nicht mit der Chiffriermaschine getastet, sondern willkürlich gewählt worden.

6 Page from the German instructions as to how *Enigma* should be set
7 Marian Rejewski in 1944
8 Jerzy Różycki in 1933
9 Henryk Zygalski in 1941

10 Lt-Col. Gwido Langer,
Captain Gustave Bertrand
and Captain McFarlane
(Pinky) at Château de
Vignolles

11 Captain Henri
Braquenié

12 Major Tadeusz Lisicki
in 1944

13 Dillwyn Knox in
1933

15 *Right:* Commander
Alastair Denniston

14 Alan Turing in
1943

17 Squadron Leader
Frederick W.
Winterbotham in 1942

16 General Sir Stewart
Menzies

18 Bletchley Park today

19 Château de Vignolles (Bruno)
20 Château de Foozes (Cadix)

use field telephones, teleprinters and other landline communication systems.

On 10 May the great German offensive began, heading for Holland and Belgium, which were not protected by the Maginot Line. Hitler's promised *Blitzkrieg* came true. The Allied armies were unable to withstand the massed panzer attacks, the dive-bombers and the paratroops who were dropped on bridges, crossroads and important strategic points.

The Allied monitoring stations worked ceaselessly, intercepting German signals which now filled the air waves. Bletchley Park received a great many such signals and deciphered most of them. They provided information about the orders of the German High Command which *Ultra* relayed to the appropriate quarters. On 14 May they deciphered a signal from General Walter von Brauchitsch, head of the Army High Command (*Oberkommando der Wehrmacht – OKW*), to General Walther von Reichenau, Commander of the 6th Army attacking in the north; the following day another deciphered signal revealed that the German panzer attack at Sedan had broken through the front.[36] This sort of information, together with reports from the front line and aerial reconnaissance clearly showed that, after a few days, Allied resistance was weakening. An anxious Churchill climbed aboard an aircraft and on 16 May landed in Paris to see the situation for himself.[*] The attitude of the French Government and High Command was such that the British premier immediately returned to the airfield and flew back to London the same day. At exactly the same time Bletchley Park was reading a new German signal which said that an armoured corps on the Belgian front was to move south immediately to strengthen the forces which had broken through at Sedan. This at once caught the eye of the British staff officers: the front at Sedan had already been broken and the new panzer units were not needed there, whereas their withdrawal from the Belgian front reduced pressure on the British-held sector. London's surprise intensified when yet another signal was deciphered, this time from General Franz Halder, the German Army's Chief of Staff, to General Fedor von Bock, Commander of the army group attacking the British sector of the front. Halder ordered von Bock to exercise restraint when pursuing the retreating British.[37]

In England work could continue peacefully, but in France things looked different and, after a few days, *Bruno* was threatened. Evacuation was ordered and the whole centre was transferred to Paris, to the Second Bureau's building on the rue Tourville. The hitherto feverish tempo of work increased. The staff worked day and night and each deciphered signal was awaited by French liaison officers, some of whom even slept in the building

---

[*] Being in a hurry, he took with him an officer who spoke Hindustani, leaving another in England. He used them for communication by telephone with London (Deighton, p. 72).

in order to receive the necessary information as soon as possible. Naturally no one revealed to them the source of these intelligence reports. They were typed out in five or six copies on yellow paper (*feuillets jaunes*). The volume of radio traffic was enormous and every day several dozen and even more signals were deciphered. Unfortunately, after a few days the French capital was threatened and once again the specialists had to be evacuated. All the cryptanalysts were loaded onto Paris buses and taken south. They stayed for a short time at la Ferté, then at Bon Encontre and finally at Toulouse.[38] At each stop they got out the equipment and carried on working; the number of deciphered signals was now in the thousands. Constant communication was maintained with Bletchley Park, which provided invaluable assistance by sending the deciphered keys of the various *Enigma* nets.[39]

To the north the battle of France was entering the decisive phase. On 14 May the Dutch Army capitulated and on the 19th the Commander-in-Chief of the Allied armies, General Gamelin, resigned and was replaced by the First World War veteran, General Maxime Weygand.

On 23 May Bletchley Park deciphered a new German signal which finally convinced Lord Gort, the Commander of the British Expeditionary Force, supported by Churchill, that it was time to withdraw from the continent of Europe. The signal was sent by General Von Brauchitsch to the Commanders of Army Groups A and B, ordering them to turn north immediately. This order left no one in any doubt that the Germans wanted to cut off the British from the French, push them up to the Channel and force them to capitulate. This eventuality had already been foreseen and Admiral Sir Bertram Ramsey, in Dover, had on 19 May received the order to prepare 'Operation Dynamo', which was to consist of collecting every available craft, right down to the smallest private launch, in order to evacuate the British Army from France.[40]

London was once again amazed that von Brauchitsch's order was not carried out by the Commander of Army Group A, General Gerd von Runstedt, with typical German efficiency. It only transpired later that Hitler was at the time at von Runstedt's Headquarters and that it was he who had restrained the panzer divisions around the British Army positions at Dunkirk.[41]

The monitoring stations were now working at fever pitch to intercept every available German signal, but this effort brought no success. Hitler did not reveal his intentions in any radio message, which was hardly surprising. He had his own personal vision of the future which he discussed only in the company of his closest colleagues. On the outside it only showed itself in his orders, and in this case it was his wish that von Rundstedt's armoured divisions should not attack at Dunkirk. By doing this and giving the British the opportunity to rescue their Army, he moved logically to one of his main political objectives, namely that of coming to some compromise with Great

Britain to divide up the world, giving him a free hand on the European mainland.

This goal was not attained. Although France, under the leadership of Marshal Pétain, signed an armistice with the Germans and the Western Front ceased to exist, the free world was not yet on its knees. The words of Winston Churchill rang out around the world and Great Britain stood alone prepared to fight to the last.

NOTES

1. Fitzgerald, op. cit., p. 170.
2. Ibid, pp. 144–5.
3. P. Beesly, *Very Special Intelligence*, London, 1977, p. 10. Also: R. V. Jones, letter to the author, 10 January 1979.
4. Winterbotham, op. cit., pp. 31–2. Also: Kahn, op. cit., p. 275. Also: Fitzgerald, op. cit., p. 239.
5. Fitzgerald, op. cit., pp. 234–6. Also: H. Golombek, recorded interview, London, 21 December 1977.
6. Beesly, op. cit., p. 70.
7. R. V. Jones, *Most Secret War,* London, 1978, pp. 59–61, 92–105.
8. Fitzgerald, op. cit., p. 234.
9. C. Fitzgibbon, *Secret Intelligence in the 20th Century*, London, 1976, p. 228.
10. W. Woolard, Post-production script of *The Secret War*, BBC London, 1977, p. 13. Also: R. Lewin, *Ultra Goes To War*, London, 1978, p. 115.
11. Winterbotham, op. cit., pp. 24–5, 30–4.
12. Ibid, p. 36.
13. Ibid, p. 40.
14. Ibid, pp. 41–2.
15. Beesly, op. cit., pp. 68–9. Also: Winterbotham, op. cit., p. 42. Also: P. Calvocoressi, interview, London, 8 February 1979. Also: Jones, letters to the author, 10 and 18 January 1979.
16. Fitzgibbon, op. cit., pp. 283–4. Also: Winterbotham, op. cit., p. 39.
17. Winterbotham, op. cit., pp. 39–40.
18. Ibid, p. 42.
19. Rejewski, 'Reminiscences', op. cit., p. 68.
20. G. Langer, 'Report for 1939–40, appendix: France', 1940, p. 2. Also: Rejewski, 'Reminiscences', op. cit., pp. 69–70. Also: Bertrand, op. cit., pp. 69–70.
21. Second Bureau (reconnaissance and studios) kept its separate identity.
22. Langer, op. cit., p. 2. Also: Bertrand, op. cit., p. 70.
23. Bertrand, op. cit., p. 71.
24. Bertrand, op. cit., p. 72. Also: Langer, op. cit., p. 11.
25. Langer, op. cit., p. 11.
26. Fitzgerald, op. cit., p. 239.
27. Ibid.
28. Brian Randell, 'The Colossus', University of Newcastle upon Tyne, 1976, p. 6.
29. Rejewski, 'Reminiscences . . . ', op. cit., p. 70.
30. Brian Johnson, *The Secret War*, London, 1978, p. 320. Also: Langer, op. cit., p. 2. Also: Möller, op. cit. (See Chapter III, p. 55).
31. Ibid.
32. Rejewski, 'Reminiscences . . . ', op. cit., pp. 70–1.

33. Ibid, p. 72.
34. Langer, op. cit., p. 4.
35. Winterbotham, op. cit., p. 51.
36. Ibid, p. 53. Also: Guy Chapman, *Why France Collapsed,* London, 1968, p. 164.
37. Ibid.
38. Rejewski, 'Reminiscences . . . ', op. cit., pp. 72–3.
39. Langer, op. cit., pp. 4–8. He states that during the Battle of France, 5,084 signals were deciphered and 126 keys were broken. Bletchley Park's contribution was very great and, according to Langer, more than eighty per cent of the success was due to them.
40. Chapman, op. cit., p. 212.
41. Winterbotham, op. cit., p. 54.

Deutschland über Alles

1

THE FIRST WORLD WAR ended in Germany with a revolution and a change in the form of government. The overthrow of the old order almost led to the country becoming communist, while the decisions of the Versailles conference hampered the working of the war-weary state.

The main aim of the Versailles decisions was to deprive the Germans of any opportunity to start a new war. It was thus decided that their new armed forces, called the *Reichswehr*, would consist of two services: the Army (*Reichsheer*) and the Navy (*Reichsmarine*), without any air element, and not exceeding one hundred thousand men in strength. In overall command of these forces was the President of the new republic, under whom came the *Reichswehr* minister with, under him, two separate service chiefs, one for the Army and one for the Navy, each with his own staff. The *Abwehr*, which had at first been formed for counter-intelligence, but was in fact military intelligence, likewise was responsible to the President. The Second Section of the *Abwehr* handled ciphers and radio monitoring. At that time the monitoring department was called *Horchdienst*.[1]

This arrangement continued, with small variations, for a number of years until 1933 when Hitler came to power and great changes began. The Nazis were planning a new war, which was to be a war of revenge and of great territorial conquest. They therefore rejected the decisions of Versailles and the *Reichswehr* was renamed the *Wehrmacht*, without any restrictions on its numbers. The *Wehrmacht* High Command (Oberkommando der Wehrmacht – *OKW*) stood at the head of the German armed forces: the Army (*Heer*), the Navy (*Kriegsmarine*) and the Air Force (*Luftwaffe*). The *Abwehr* naturally also came under its control, and in 1935 Admiral Wilhelm Canaris, a man of Italian descent, assumed command of it. At that time he was not an opponent of Nazism; only later, in 1937, did he change his mind when he realized that Hitler was steering a course towards a new war. The *Reich*'s main security office, the *RSHA*, commanded by the aggressively ambitious Reinhard Heydrich, was also involved in intelligence work. A certain duplication of effort arose, which was only eliminated with great difficulty: *Abwehr* retained control in military matters, while the *RSHA* dealt with everything else.

In 1929 the *Abwehr* also adopted *Enigma* and had its own nets with its own keys, as well as its own radio-reconnaissance with six important monitoring stations in the large towns of Königsberg, Munich, Münster and others. Despite this service's efficiency, it remained a sore spot for the Party leadership, which, moreover, suspected Canaris of disloyalty, and thus in 1937 he was forced to hand over his entire radio-reconnaissance to a new department of the *Wehrmacht* which covered communications in all three services and had the very long name, *Wehrmachtnachrichtenverbindungen – WNV* (*Wehrmacht* Intelligence Communications). Towards the end of August 1939, just before the attack on Poland, Erich Fellgiebel, who meanwhile had been promoted general, was appointed head of this department and was directly responsible to the head of *OKW*, Field Marshal Wilhelm Keitel, above whom stood only Hitler. As a result of this he had an insight into the radio communications of all three services; but this was really something of an illusion, for both the Navy and the Air Force had a great deal of independence. He did, however, have an inside view of the Army's communications, since he was in charge of them.[2] It was ironical that the *Abwehr's* radio-reconnaissance, which it had lost since Canaris was suspected of a negative attitude towards Nazism, passed into the hands of Fellgiebel, who was already known not to be sympathetic towards Hitler.

2

The German defeat in the First World War hit its Navy most severely. The damage to world shipping which it had caused had been so great that the Allies decided to destroy it once and for all. In June 1919 all its surface vessels and submarines were ordered to Scapa Flow, where they were sunk. After such a complete humiliation, it was difficult to imagine that the German ensign could soon reappear on the world's oceans or that there could be men ready to rebuild a navy from scratch; and yet things turned out differently. Before the German delegation even arrived at the Versailles conference, the first steps on the long road to naval recovery were already being taken.

Amidst many other activities work was begun on reforming Naval Intelligence and within it radio-reconnaissance (*Funkaufklärung*). The Admiralty staff in Berlin set up a small unit with a single official in the observation section (*B-Dienst*), with another man in the cipher section (*E-Dienst*), helped by six assistants. They also, on a small scale, began to prepare monitoring stations.[3]

Progress was slow but steady and when Hitler came to power the naval leadership in Berlin already possessed a fairly widely developed Information Section (A III) containing three departments: the collection and distribution of information (A III a), radio-reconnaissance and cipher machines (A III b) and foreign fleets (FM). This last-named department collected information on the fleets of other countries from a variety of sources: from the *Abwehr*, from military attachés, from the press and, naturally, from its own radio-reconnaissance department. Fortunately, the director of *Funkaufklärung* was simultaneously the director of the *Abwehr*'s Department IV and thus had easy access to the other departments of Intelligence. Although this 'personal contact' later ceased to exist, good relations, once made, remained.[4]

The rapid development of radio at that time resulted in the radio-reconnaissance branch expanding on a large scale. *B-Dienst* had a wide network of monitoring stations, while in 1926 *E-Dienst* received *Enigma* and worked on complicating it so as to make it unbreakable. The Germans regularly intercepted signals from the British, French, Russian, Polish and Italian navies and usually read them.[5] At that time the British Admiralty continued conservatively to use hand ciphers and thus its messages were easy to decipher. During the Abyssinian war, which began with the Italian attack of 1935, basic security procedures were ignored to such an extent that German cryptanalysts succeeded in reading the main British operational and administrative ciphers.[6] They achieved this by using mathematics and without recourse to classic intelligence methods, such as either stealing or buying someone else's secrets. This did happen a number of times, but against the French. In 1935 the German naval attaché in Stockholm secretly purchased two parts from two cipher machines made by the Hagelin firm for the French Army. They were then used to help reconstruct these machines and read their keys. In the same year radio-reconnaissance, through the agencies of the *Abwehr*, bought the French Admiralty's emergency code from a French officer. It turned out to be of little use, since the officer quickly betrayed himself by carelessly spending money, was arrested and tried and the code was changed.[7]

On the outbreak of the Second World War German naval radio-reconnaissance was already a highly developed department employing hundreds, while at the height of its activities this figure exceeded five thousand. The whole department was divided into a number of sections, amongst which were three devoted entirely to cryptanalysis: West I devoted to Great Britain, West II to the United States and East to the Soviet Union. Later the two western sections were amalgamated to form one large unit. As the war progressed and the Germans gained more victories, new monitoring stations were set up in the occupied countries and moved nearer to the Allied sea lanes. They were situated in Denmark, Norway, Belgium, France, Greece and North Africa, where Erwin Rommel's corps had landed, and eventually, after the invasion of Soviet Russia, on the Black Sea in Estonia and Finland. They already had stations in Italy and Spain. (See map, pp. 124–5, Bonatz, op. cit., p. 102.) All these establishments employed thousands of specialists working round the clock in three shifts.

3

After the cessation of hostilities in November 1918 the huge German Army of millions of men demobilized very slowly. It withdrew quite quickly from the Western front, but in the east, on the huge conquered territories, the situation looked different. New states were appearing, while old ones, like Poland, regained their independence and their hastily formed armies were engaged with the Germans who were reluctant to withdraw in some areas. Eventually, however, their starving, war-weary homeland, shaken by revolutionary currents, drew them all back and civilian life began.

Despite the defeat, German militarism was so strong that, as in the Navy, there were men who immediately set about rebuilding the Army, although its 'Versailles' dimensions were rather limited. During the war the Army had used radio, had sent signals enciphered by hand, using its own stations, and intercepted enemy signals, and so in 1919 it began the reconstruction of its own radio-intelligence section. At that time it consisted of just twelve people and its main task was obtaining information on the military manoeuvres of the neighbouring countries. A few cryptanalysts, who had worked in this field during the war, began rebuilding the section analysing the intercepted radio traffic, but on a small scale, for the *Abwehr* Second Section (ciphers and monitoring) was already doing this for the whole army.[8]

In 1929 Colonel Fellgiebel, who had been in charge of Army communications, and was thus responsible for radio-reconnaissance, the Cipher Office *(Chiffrierabteilung)* introduced the *Enigma* into service (See Chapter 3, pp. 28–9.) Then all those activities, which after 1933 would gain even greater momentum, picked up speed. The greatest problem was caused by the lack of specialists, who had been recruited by the other services and various ministries, particularly by the Ministries of Foreign Affairs and Propaganda.

When Erich Fellgiebel (promoted to general) assumed command of communications for the entire *Wehrmacht* in August 1939, everything connected with its radio-reconnaissance was so similar to that in the Army that it was difficult to talk in terms of two separate sections. A department called *Amtsgruppe WNV*, commanded by a friend of Fellgiebel's, General Fritz

Thiele, was formed to maintain communications between the three services. This department also took over the Cipher Office which had been removed from Canaris in 1937. With every day it grew and in 1944 contained eight groups. Group I handled monitoring stations as far apart as Madrid and Seville in the west and a number in the east. Group III's task was to provide cipher equipment (*Enigmas*), ciphers and keys. Group IV, the most important, led by Dr Erich Hüttenhein, carried out some cryptanalytical work. The Cipher Office also maintained contact with all the services and government departments, which possessed their own ciphering units, the Navy, the Air Force, the *RSHA*, the *Forschungsamt*, the Ministry of Foreign Affairs, the Propaganda Ministry, the Ministry of Production, the Post Office, the Party and the *SS*. Only seven of them had their own deciphering units: *OKW/Chi, OKH, OKM, Luftwaffe, Forschungsamt*, the Ministry of Foreign Affairs and *RSHA*.[9]

4

One of the first actions of Hitler's new government was to set up an Air Ministry *(Reichsluftministerium)* headed by the Chancellor's closest associate, Hermann Göring. The Ministry was not yet a clear rejection of the Versailles dictates, but it did signify the beginning of an era of great German achievement in the air. In 1935 the Germans showed their hand and formed the *Luftwaffe*, which, as a result of its chief's explosive energy, grew rapidly. It had its own communications network, which initially was the Sixth, and later the Seventh, Department of the Air Staff and had the long name: *Generalstabsabteilung der Luftnachrichtentruppe – GAF* (Signal Corps). Responsible to it was the Cipher Office (*Chi-Stelle*) of the *Luftwaffe* High Command. During the years 1935 to 1939 it was located in Berlin; after the outbreak of the war it was moved to Potsdam-Marstall, right next to the Air Force High Command. After the capture of Paris, it went there for a few months, together with the Command, to be followed by a return to its former site where it stayed until almost the end of the war. It was only in 1945 that it was moved to Oberndorf and Wasserburg in Bavaria. The Office was in fact busy setting up its own radio-reconnaissance, which in the Air Force was called *Funkhorchdienst – FHD*.[10] It had nothing to do with the *Forschungsamt* (Research Office) which had been operating in the Air Ministry since 1933 and which was used to garner as much secret information as possible on everyday life in the Third *Reich* in order to provide Göring with material to be used in such power struggles as the Röhm putsch.

The *Chi-Stelle*'s initial task was to develop a network of monitoring stations. Before the war it had been possible to install them only on German territory directed towards Poland, Great Britain and France; after the German victories, it was possible to extend them onto Danish, Norwegian, Belgian, Dutch and French soil and later, in 1941, to install them in the Mediterranean Basin, in Greece, Crete, the Dodecanese and North Africa. They also had facilities in allied Italy and in neutral, but friendly, Bulgaria and Spain.

These stations had more than 4,500 specialists working on them, whose task was to intercept Allied radio signals dealing with bomber, fighter and transport aircraft and all air operations in Western Europe. A special unit of one thousand people dealt exclusively with heavy bombers. An unknown number of people worked on the stations grouped around the Mediterranean, while an unknown number also intercepted Russian signals, working on the newly established stations in the occupied territories in the east and using materials supplied by Finland.[11]

Parallel to the development of the monitoring stations, hurried efforts were made to create a cryptanalytical department (*Entzifferungsdienst*). This department was located at Potsdam-Marstall near Berlin, remaining there throughout almost the whole war and employing more than eight hundred specialists at the height of its activities. It was subordinated to the *Chi-Stelle* and, in addition to its main centre, also possessed special trains which during the fighting in France and later in Sicily and the Italian peninsula, accompanied the fighting units so as to be able to read intercepted signals as soon as possible on the spot. During the war more than ten thousand people worked at any one time in monitoring and deciphering.[12]

Before the official formation of the *Luftwaffe*, at the end of 1933 and the beginning of 1934, the Air Force followed the Navy and the Army by accepting *Enigma* into service.[13] At the outbreak of the war each German Air Force unit, down to the flight level, had a machine and the number of *Enigma*s in use was in the thousands, reaching a figure of twenty thousand at the height of the struggle (see Chapter 3, p. 33).

5

Also in 1919 the German Ministry of Foreign Affairs began preliminary work on setting up a radio-reconnaissance unit. Over a number of years it was expanded and two departments were created: cryptology, or a cipher office, and cryptanalysis. This department was subdivided into a cipher group with a great number of mathematicians working for it, and a code group containing many linguists. Overall the unit was small and employed about three hundred people, amongst whom were one hundred or so cryptologists and cryptanalysts. It was possible to operate with such a small number of personnel because the Ministry did not have its own monitoring facilities and used material provided by military and post-office stations. The Cipher Office sent its messages mainly using the one-time pad system, which had been devised by its own people, while the analysts used special machines, somewhat similar to the Polish *Bombes*, which speeded up their work (see Chapter 3, p. 37).

The Ministry dealt with a great number of countries and different languages, thereby increasing its difficulties, yet it managed to achieve significant results. Its experts were reading messages from the following countries: Argentina, Belgium, Bolivia, Brazil, the British Empire, Bulgaria, Chile, China, Colombia, Dominican Republic, Egypt, Ecuador, Ethiopia, France, Greece, Ireland, Japan, Manchu Kuo, Mexico, Peru, Persia, Poland, Portugal, Romania, Siam, Spain, Switzerland, the United States, Turkey, Uruguay, the Vatican, Venezuela and Yugoslavia.

From 1933, when the Ministry of Propaganda was created, Joseph Goebbels also had some cryptological ambitions and thus had his own unit. Naturally the *Reich* security office, *RSHA*, also had to have one as did the Ministry of War Production under Dr Fritz Todt, which in February 1942 was taken over by Albert Speer. Even the Post Office had to become involved, while the Party also could not afford to fall behind.[14] Each of these departments, as well as using various codes, also employed *Enigma*. There was a great demand for the machines, since the armed forces alone had more than thirty thousand of them in service. They were manufactured in two factories in Berlin: the first was set up in the twenties and was called *Chiffriermaschinen A.G.*, and the second dated from the thirties and was called *Chiffriermaschinen Geselschaft Heimpold und Rinke*. Both factories depended on other plants throughout Germany producing many parts of the *Enigma* machines.[15]

Examining this incredible duplication of German cryptological effort with the advantage of hindsight, it is simply hard to believe that such a thing was possible in the Third *Reich*, which was under the iron will of one man. Despite his complete authority he was unable to control the unrestrained ambition of his closest associates, who, in their struggle for power in the national hierarchy, missed not a trick. Certainly co-operation was the ultimate aim and this co-operation did exist, but personal animosities and dislikes frequently were stronger than reason. Effort was duplicated, time was wasted, and rival services bid for the same specialists. In comparison with Bletchley Park and logical British centralization, this all sometimes looked almost amateurish.

There is a further point which should be emphasized. Despite having such a widely developed monitoring and cryptanalysis apparatus, none of the German units in this field discovered during the course of the war that the secret of *Enigma* had been unravelled and that the Allies were regularly reading their most sensitive signals. Several times they managed to come across some of their messages which had been deciphered, but each time they assumed that their secrets had been betrayed. The first time this happened was in France when, after the collapse of the front, part of the French Staff's Second Bureau archives in Paris fell into German hands. One of their top analysts received the German text of a signal which had been enciphered on *Enigma* and which had been read by the French. However, he came to the conclusion that this had been achieved by help obtained from a German NCO from East Prussia, who had sold the French the arrangement of the rotors and daily keys for a specific period.[16] A similar conclusion was reached when they began to suffer the first reverse at sea. The Germans did not want to believe that their ciphers were being read and sought culprits amidst the French and Norwegians working in the ports, particularly Brest and Kristiansand. They also had great respect for British Intelligence and believed that it had obtained their most important secrets and passed them over to the Admiralty. 'The possibility of the enemy's being able to read signals by deciphering them has been universally discounted by all the experts.'[17] In several other similar incidents the Germans came to the same conclusion.

6

The British Admiralty was aware that the Germans had succeeded in penetrating its secret radio communications and, after the outbreak of war, began to make its ciphers more complicated, particularly those used to call ships at sea. Ciphers and individual codes were introduced, with a different one for each ship, and the Germans began to find themselves in difficulties. They deciphered only a small proportion of intercepted signals and that very slowly. This had little value in swift operations at sea, but it did permit them to obtain an impression of British tactics and strategy, in addition to providing information on actual ships. Towards the end of 1939 it was from this source that the German Admiralty received a great deal of information on the movements of capital ships, such as the aircraft carrier *Eagle*, the battleships *Renown* and *Repulse*, the battle cruiser *Hood* and others. At the beginning of 1940 two signals were read, which indicated that in November and December of the previous year the cruiser *Belfast* and the battleship *Nelson* had both been seriously damaged by mines.[18]

The changes in the British codes and keys were, however, broken by the Germans whose naval radio-reconnaissance achieved great success before and during the Norwegian campaign from April to June 1940. Already after Hitler's decision to occupy Norway, the Germans managed to intercept and read British signals on the mining and occupation of Narvik in order to cut off the Germans from the Swedish iron-ore mines at Gällivere. The German Admiralty then decided to deceive the British by waiting until the British ships were on their way to northern Norway and then feign an attack on them, thus drawing off the bulk of the Home Fleet in this direction. The manoeuvre succeeded and the Germans, without any great difficulty, transported their ships, loaded with troops, along the Danish coast. During the following few days, 13, 14 and 18 April, when the landing's fate was in the balance, the Germans deciphered a series of important signals and knew the position of many British capital ships, such as the *Repulse*, the *Renown*, the *Warspite*, the *Ark Royal*, as well as the French battleships *Dunkerque* and *Strasbourg*, together with the cruiser *Emile Bertin*. Thanks to radio-reconnaissance, Admiral Raeder received such precise information about British moves that Admiral Alfred Saalwächter, commander of the German Navy's Western group, remarked ironically that 'Churchill is also a German agent'.[19]

The Norwegian experience shook the Admiralty, in addition to which the British themselves could not benefit from their own analysts, since Bletchley Park had been as yet unable to handle the German naval ciphers. In August 1940 the British further complicated their own ciphers, particularly those dealing with capital ships, and the Germans were thus no longer able to discover the Home Fleet's position on the basis of British signals; the *B-Dienst*, however, continued to deal with the easier convoy ciphers. The great majority of these were deciphered and the submarines knew where to wait for the convoys. Losses of Allied shipping in the Atlantic increased immediately, helped also by the fact that the Germans increased the number of submarines operating in the area.[20]

In addition to mathematical methods of breaking British ciphers, the Germans tried also to obtain the necessary information by capturing ships and their tables of keys and other secret information. They managed to do this several times. Once they captured an MTB (Motor Torpedo Boat) sailing from Sweden and found aboard a whole table of keys, but these dealt only with communications for this one vessel and were thus useless.[21] A real and unusually important success was achieved on 10 July 1940 when, in the Indian Ocean, a German armed merchant ship, the *Atlantis*, captured the British vessel, *City of Baghdad*, and seized all her secret papers, together with Allied code tables for merchant shipping, British Admiralty codes and several tables of keys, which, although, no longer in use, were a valuable model. Aboard the *Atlantis* was a specialist cryptanalyst, who, from the captured papers and newly intercepted signals, was able to reconstruct the actual tables of keys. When their validity expired, Q–ship captured another vessel, the *Benarty*, obtained some more papers and, with the help of the *B-Dienst* in Berlin, with which she was in radio contact, established that they had got hold of the exceptionally important *BAMS* (Broadcasting for Allied Shipping) code. The ability to read Allied signals for merchant shipping not only increased the *Atlantis*'s effectiveness, for she now knew where to lie in wait for solitary vessels, but it also put an important card in the hand of the U–boat 'wolf packs' which operated in the Atlantic and attacked convoys carrying supplies from the United States. Losses soared dramatically. In March, April and May 1941,142 Allied ships were sunk, which was one every sixteen hours.[22]

The Army's radio-reconnaissance was making similar achievements. Its analysts were also reading British signals and thus the High Command could reap some tactical benefit from them. During the operations against Yugoslavia in April 1941 German specialists, dressed in civilian clothes, operated monitoring stations in Sofia (Bulgaria), intercepting radio signals sent by the defending Yugoslavs which they forwarded to the analysts. Thanks to their work, the German command knew where to deploy its tanks, which in difficult, mountainous terrain was extremely important. Later, after Yugoslav resistance had been broken, this same monitoring operation intercepted the signals of the two guerilla armies: the Royalist under General Draza Mihailovic and the Communist under Josif Bros 'Tito'.[23]

Luftwaffe cryptanalysis also achieved some notable successes. Even before the war it had succeeded in breaking several British ciphers by reading their keys and later, after the beginning of the war, managed to break the following codes: Air-Rep, Ac-Mov (used mainly in Africa), NERO, SYKO and UKO. As early as 4 September 1939, while the Germans were dealing with Poland, they managed to shoot down a *Blenheim* bomber in the west, which fell into the port of Wilhelmshaven. In the aircraft were found the keys of the ciphers of the Second Bomber Group, which enabled the Germans to read the Group's signals for a whole month. Later *Luftwaffe* radio-reconnaissance was able to read RAF traffic dealing with communications with the United States, Africa, Murmansk and in the Mediterranean. When, in 1943, the British complicated their naval ciphers and Admiral Dönitz left the U–boat Command, it was mainly thanks to German Air Force radio-reconnaissance that further accurate attacks on convoys were possible.[24] Probably *Luftwaffe* cryptanalysis's greatest achievement was the decipherment of an Allied signal concerning the great attack on the Ploesti oil fields in Romania, which was to take place on 1 August 1943. The fields' anti-aircraft defences, the strongest in Europe (after all, they were protecting the last huge German oil deposits) were warned in time and greeted the American *Liberators* with such a concentration of fire that out of 178 aircraft 53 were shot down.[25]

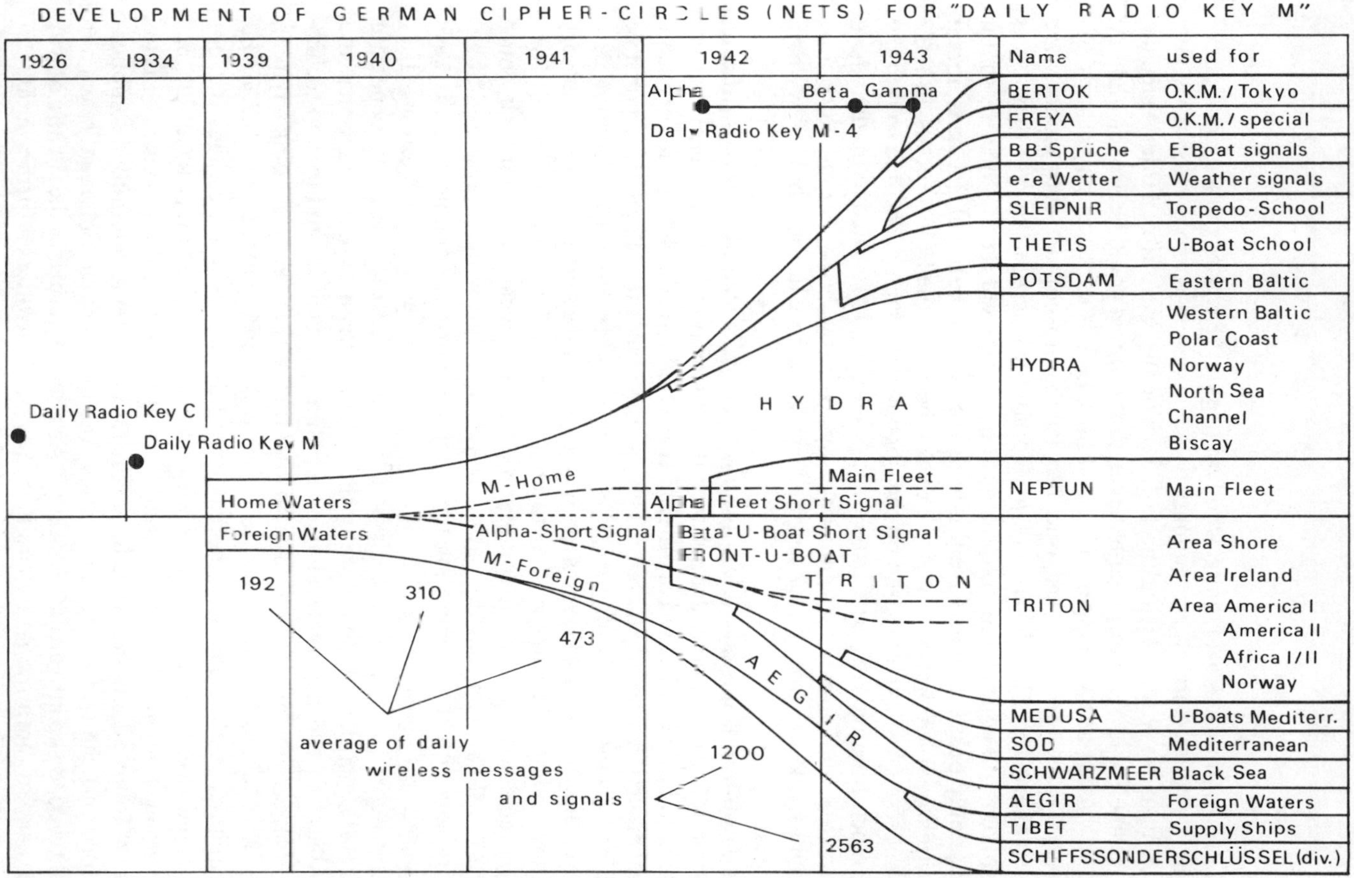
DEVELOPMENT OF GERMAN CIPHER-CIRCLES (NETS) FOR "DAILY RADIO KEY M"
1926
1934
1939
1940
1941
1942
1943
Name
used for
Alpha
Beta
Gamma
Daily Radio Key M-4
Daily Radio Key C
Daily Radio Key M
Home Waters
Foreign Waters
M-Home
Alpha-Short Signal
M-Foreign
H Y D R A
Main Fleet
Alpha
Fleet Short Signal
Beta-U-Boat Short Signal
FRONT-U-BOAT
T R I T O N
A E G I R
192
310
473
1200
2563
average of daily
wireless messages
and signals
BERTOK
O.K.M. / Tokyo
FREYA
O.K.M. / special
BB-Sprüche
E-Boat signals
e-e Wetter
Weather signals
SLEIPNIR
Torpedo-School
THETIS
U-Boat School
POTSDAM
Eastern Baltic
HYDRA
Western Baltic
Polar Coast
Norway
North Sea
Channel
Biscay
NEPTUN
Main Fleet
TRITON
Area Shore
Area Ireland
Area America I
America II
Africa I/II
Norway
MEDUSA
U-Boats Mediterr.
SOD
Mediterranean
SCHWARZMEER
Black Sea
AEGIR
Foreign Waters
TIBET
Supply Ships
SCHIFFSSONDERSCHLÜSSEL (div.)

Fig. 7 Development of German Cipher-Circles (Nets) for Radio Key M (diagram drawn by Professor Jürgen Rohwer)

7

Grand-Admiral Karl Dönitz, who had begun the war as the Commander of the U–boats, and who in January 1943 assumed command of the whole German Navy and during the last days of the war, after Hitler's suicide, became Head of State, never believed that *Enigma* could be broken and that that was what had happened.[26] A similar view is expressed by other Germans, who during the last war also came into contact with ciphers and deciphering and used the *Enigma*. Today they accept the fact that it was broken, but continue to hold the opinion, expressed during the war, that it was only possible to achieve this with the help of betrayal.[27] This is not an unreasonable point of view if one remembers that the Polish success in 1932 was, to a great extent, based on the documents which *Asché* had sold to the French Intelligence (see Chapter 2, pp. 14–16). This speeded up the whole process, but had no real significance, since the analysts were already on the right track and would have reached the same conclusions, but a few years later.

Despite this unshakeable conviction generally shared by senior officers, precise German minds did not accept this viewpoint as absolute. What the human brain has created in order to conceal the truth, can by the very same token be deciphered and read. That is how General Fellgiebel, responsible for all secret radio communications, saw it and he shared this opinion with his subordinates. At briefing sessions they discussed technical problems very fully and sought ways further to complicate *Enigma* and its keys. It was appreciated that the more complicated the keys became, the harder it would be to break them, but that, at the same time, this would create additional problems for those operating the machine. Further complicating the keys caused mistakes in enciphering which were doubly dangerous: they endangered one's own signals and they allowed the enemy to penetrate closely guarded secrets more easily. The German experts knew that the Allies had very highly developed cryptanalysis facilities and that no technical improvement was beyond them, and they warned against doing anything which could make the enemy's task easier. According to the experts, *Enigma* equipped with plugs was unbreakable, but only when messages did not exceed twenty thousand letters with one setting. Thus they suggested that messages be limited to three hundred words. Generally speaking the rules were followed, but there had to be constant improvements, added complications and changes so that the enemy was never given a moment's rest nor allowed to slip into an easy routine.[28] As a result of this, as the theatre of war expanded, both the Army and the Air Force introduced further modifications to the daily keys and instead of changing them once every twenty-four hours around midnight, a change was made every eight hours (see Chapter

4, p. 59). All this made life hard for the enemy, but also required constant effort and instruction of one's own signallers. There were, after all, thousands of machines in use.

The German fears were well founded, in spite of their confidence since their Intelligence supplied them time and again with the most important information about the success of their enemies in deciphering their ciphers. The best example is a document dated 18 August 1943, obtained by the German Intelligence in Switzerland. This report sent by a Swiss agent in Washington to his superiors in Switzerland (see Sources) is entitled: Deciphering of the German Navycodes.

The Navy, which had first accepted *Enigma* into service, and which was the most security conscious, continued to change its daily keys only once every twenty-four hours. However, in addition to the introduction of the sixth and seventh rotors it used newer nets, with their own keys. Each of them carried its own codename and one had to be acquainted with them in order to appreciate the difficulties this caused.

The first of these nets was *Hydra*, which had come in as early as 1939, when the volume of daily signals was small and did not exceed 192. This net was used for sending signals to vessels operating in waters under German control, namely the western Baltic and parts of the North Sea. Later, when Denmark and Norway had fallen, to be followed after a few months by Holland, Belgium, Luxemburg and France, this net also embraced the sea around Norway, northern waters, the English Channel and the Bay of Biscay. Its keys were very difficult and it was only in May 1941 that Bletchley Park managed to work them out (see Chapter 6, pp. 93–4).

At the same time, towards the end of 1939, they began to use a net, codenamed *Aegir*, which handled ships operating in foreign waters, often several thousand miles from Europe. It was this net which carried traffic to the 'pocket battleship'* *Graf Spee*, which was scuttled by her captain outside Montevideo on 17 December 1939, and to her sister ship *Admiral Sheer* and others.[29]

In the second half of 1940 two new nets were set up: the first one, *Alpha*, for sending short signals to the main fleet, and *Beta* for similar ones to submarines. In that year the overall number of daily signals was small and on average numbered about 310.

At the end of 1940 and the beginning of 1941 a new net, *Neptune*, was brought into service. Its keys were especially difficult and rarely used, since it dealt solely with the main fleet and capital ships on special missions. Breaking the *Hydra* keys helped to break the secret of the *Neptune* net, but

---

*The Versailles Treaty banned the Germans from building warships of more than 10,000 tons. Therefore, they created a new class of small, but very heavily armed battleship, nonetheless exceeding the limit.

Bletchley Park had a great deal of difficulty with these keys. They solved them in the second half of May 1941, but it was an extremely slow process that took several days.

Alongside the *Neptune* net, although perhaps a little later, a special net was introduced, having no special codename, which was used for signals to individual vessels and then only in exceptional circumstances. It was restricted to armed merchantmen, such as the *Atlantis*, already referred to above, which usually operated in distant waters. Since this net was rarely used and only for individual ships, its keys were never broken. By 1941 the number of daily signals rose to 473.[30]

On 1 February 1942 the very important *Triton* net came into operation. The U-boat Commander, Admiral Dönitz, used this net to contact his vessels operating in the distant Atlantic, principally off South and North America, off Africa and also off Ireland. Later this net embraced the Indian Ocean. The cryptanalysts had a great deal of trouble with this net's keys and a year passed, marked by great losses in Allied shipping, before they succeeded in working them out. In the first week of December the Admiralty (OIC) finally received the first deciphered signals. Their numbers rose day by day and reached a total of 176; in the second week 173 were deciphered and in the third 178. The deciphered texts were not always complete and there were mistakes here and there, but this had been a breakthrough and once again it was possible to determine the position of enemy U-boats, of which there were then about one hundred at sea.[31]

It was also at the beginning of 1942 that the *Freya* net, reserved for special tasks, was introduced. It was used exclusively by the Naval High Command (*OKM*) and the Admiralty for secret communications with naval shore commands when, for one reason or another, it was inadvisable to use land communications (teleprinters and telephones). It should be added here that land communications used completely different methods of encipherment.

A little later the *Potsdam* net came into service and was used for communications with ships in the eastern Baltic operating against the Soviet fleet.

Mid-1942 saw the introduction of the *Süd* net for ships in the Mediterranean and right at the end of the year it was extended to the Black Sea. It did not embrace U-boats and since *Hydra* keys had earlier been broken, it was quite quickly deciphered. There was also a separate net only in the Mediterranean, *Schwarzmeer*, which was introduced right at the end of 1942. This was a year of great German naval activity and the number of signals sent daily by *Enigma* reached 1,200. Unfortunately, many of them were never deciphered by Bletchley Park.[32]

At the beginning of 1943 the Germans introduced the *Thetis* net, over which signals were sent to the submarine training-school in the Baltic, and the *Medusa* net for communications with all U-boats operating in the

Mediterranean. Breaking the first net allowed the British to follow the movements of many U–boats from the moment they finished trials and left the Baltic, while breaking the second one allowed them to counter the submarine threat in the Mediterranean. Just after these two nets a new one, *Sleipnir*, was introduced for vessels involved in training and torpedo-firings in the Baltic.[33]

The Far East was also not ignored and in mid-1943 the Germans started using a net called *Bertok* for communications between the Naval High Command in Berlin and the naval attaché at the Tokyo embassy. Then two support nets came into operation: *BB-Sprüche* for E–boats (as the British Navy termed the 'Schnell' or 'S–boats') and *e-e-Wetter* for transmitting weather reports.

Finally, in the second half of 1943, a new net, *Tibet*, was introduced for communications with support vessels, such as tankers and supply ships for the armed merchantmen operating in distant waters. The keys to this net were never broken. The year 1943 was the climax of operations at sea and the number of German naval signals rose to 2,563 daily.[34]

Despite these continual complications and changes, which exhausted the monitoring stations' staffs and never gave the analysts a moment's rest, the German Navy, which was unusually conscious of security, continued to work on further refinements to its cipher machine. Seven rotors were used, but only for variety, since the machine still only operated with three, but now, at the beginning of 1943, it was decided to install a fourth working rotor. This required a great deal of planning, since each surface ship and each U–boat had to receive a new *Enigma*. The British managed to intercept some information about this and later also the German Admiralty order that from midnight on 8 March all signals were to be enciphered using four rotors.[35]

At the Admiralty in London faces grew longer. It was true that the number of German U–boats sunk was increasing, but Intelligence warned that more and more of them were being constructed and that one after the other new 'wolf packs' were coming out into the open sea from the training areas in the Baltic. At a critical moment of the war when fortunes were in the balance on the Eastern front, which was receiving massive supplies from the Allies, and also in the west, where preparations were under way for the invasion of Europe, the Battle of the Atlantic played a decisive role. Bletchley Park was faced with a vitally important and urgent task.

Only those who during those years worked in radio monitoring, and above all the cryptanalysts, knew just what difficulties had been created by this fourth rotor and the constantly growing number of new nets. The monitoring staffs had to unravel messages from the thousands of Morse signals and allocate them to the correct net, and they could do this only because many months of experience had taught them to recognize the 'touch' of different German operators. By particular habits and by the way a signal was sent they could recognize who and which net was 'on the air'. When the analysts received the prepared material, they had to start the nightmare task of deciphering the new net's keys. While *Enigma* had been using three drums, this had been possible, but once the fourth one was operational, the nightmare became hell. Tasks which earlier had taken several days, now took several weeks' or even months' work. Sometimes they were unsuccessful and even when they did succeed they could not relax for a moment, for they could be told the same day that a new net had been introduced with new keys.

Day and night Admiralty Intelligence waited for information, for on it depended the safety of the convoys and on them rested the outcome of the war.

NOTES

1. Hepp, letter to the author, 8 February 1978.
2. Ibid. Also: H. Höhne, *Codeword: Director*, London, 1971, pp. 72–3. Also: I. Colvin, *Canaris*, London, 1973, pp. 45–6.
3. Bonatz, op. cit., pp. 73–4.
4. Ibid, p. 76.
5. Ibid.
6. Beesly, op. cit., p. 33.
7. Bonatz, op. cit., pp. 92–3.
8. Kahn, op. cit., pp. 453–5. Also: Hepp, letter, 8 February 1978.
9. Dr E. Hüttenhein (a former cryptanalyst from *OKW/Chi*), 'Erfolge und Misserfolge der Deutschen Chiffrierdienste im Zweiten Weltkrieg', Bonn, 1978, p. 3.
10. K. O. Hoffmann, *Die Geschichte der Luftnachrichtentruppe,* Neckergemünd, 1965/68/73, Vol. I., pp. 123–7.
11. Kahn, op. cit., pp. 461, 646.
12. Ibid. Also: Hoffmann, letter, 8 February 1978.
13. Hoffmann, letter, 8 February 1978.
14. Kahn, op. cit., pp. 436–51.
15. Hüttenhein, interview recorded in Bonn, 26 September 1977.
16. Ibid. Also: H. Bonatz, Unpublished opinion of the book *The Ultra Secret,* Mainaschaff, 5 November 1974.
17. Beesly, op. cit., p. 90.
18. Bonatz, op. cit., pp. 109 and 126–7. Also: Beesly, op. cit., p. 33.
19. Ibid, pp. 120–1. Also: Bekker, op. cit., pp. 96–7. Also: Kahn, op. cit., p. 242.
20. Beesly, op. cit., pp. 52–3.
21. Bonatz, op. cit., p. 109.
22. Kahn, p. 466.
23. Ibid, p. 560.
24. Hoffmann, op. cit., letter, 8 February 1978.
25. Kahn, op. cit., p. 464.
26. Beesly, op. cit., p. 67 (from an interview by Ludovic Kennedy with Admiral Dönitz in 1973). Also: J. W. M. Chapman, Dönitz' conferences with Hitler, 8 and 26 February 1943 (a copy in author's possession).
27. L. Hepp, E. Hüttenhein, K. Möller, K. Hoffmann, op. cit.

28. *Besprechung be Chef HNW von 15. bis 17. April 1943*. National Archives and Records Service, Washington, document No. T–312 – R–604, pp. 19–22. (HNW – *Heeresnachrichtenwesens* – Army Communications System.)
29. Jürgen Rohwer, a diagram prepared in December 1976 for a lecture at the American Historical Association (see picture p. 75.)
30. Ibid. Also: Beesly, op. cit., pp. 65 and 221.
31. Beesly, op. cit., pp. 110 and 152–3. Also: Rohwer, op. cit.
32. Ibid, pp. 65 and 72. Also: Rohwer, op. cit.
33. Ibid, pp. 65 and 112. Also: Rohwer, op. cit.
34. Rohwer, op. cit. Also: Beesly, op. cit., p. 66.
35. Ibid. Also: Beesly, op. cit., pp. 176–7.

6
By Sea and in the Air

1

On 19 July 1940 a special session of the *Reichstag* (Parliament) was held in the Kroll opera house in Berlin, during which Hitler promoted fourteen generals to the rank of field-marshal, Hermann Göring to that of *Reichsmarschall*, and gave a long speech. It had been widely expected that this speech would contain peaceful overtures towards Great Britain and so it did, but the dictator, intoxicated with victory, was unable to offer anything more than appeals to common sense.[1]

The previous British Government might have taken Hitler's Berlin speech seriously, but now that Churchill was in power there was no chance of compromise. The British were feverishly preparing their defences, arming their troops with anything they could find, building anti-tank defences and erecting mock artillery to confuse Göring's aerial reconnaissance.

After the strain of France's final days, when radio monitoring stations had been working ceaselessly, a sort of calm descended, although Bletchley Park was awaiting at any moment a fresh onslaught of intercepted signals. Hardly had the Nazi leader's shouts died away in the loudspeakers when a signal was deciphered and immediately sent to the Prime Minister on the *Ultra* net. This was Hitler's top-secret instruction, Directive No. 16, dated 17 July, on the invasion of the British Isles, which was codenamed 'Sea-Lion'. Hermann Göring passed it on to his air-fleet commanders by radio. The signal began with the words: 'Since England, in spite of her hopeless military situation, as yet shows no signs of readiness for rapprochement, I have decided to prepare a landing operation against England, and if necessary to carry it out.'[2]

The *Luftwaffe* had at its disposal teleprinters and landlines, so the fact that such a secret and important piece of information was sent over the air proved that Göring was one hundred per cent certain of *Enigma* and that no one amongst the Germans suspected that their enemies had managed to unravel its secrets.

From the directive, which appeared to be more in the nature of a propaganda tract than an order, it also transpired that, after his swift victory in France, Hitler was not prepared for the eventuality of further action and of formulating new plans in such a short space of time. He had anticipated that, after his initial victories, Great Britain would be willing to come to an agreement, which almost happened during the Norwegian campaign. After the collapse of the Western front, he was quite certain that London would find some way of withdrawing from the war; however, this had not come about and speedy attempts at improvisation had to be made. The mere fact that only one month had been allocated for these preparations testified to the great haste and superficiality of the whole undertaking.

This did not mean, however, that only after their complete success on the Western front did the Germans begin to think seriously about invading the British Isles. Although the experience of the First World War had made it appear probable that the front in France would hold out for months, nevertheless Hitler had prepared for the *Blitzkrieg* which he had used successfully in Poland, and which he wanted to repeat in the West. The idea of an invasion of the British Isles, that old, never realized, dream of Napoleon, lay deep in the subconscious of the German dictator, so he had to take some practical steps in this direction.

One proof of these early German plans were the preparations for sabotage on the terrain of the United Kingdom, to be carried out at the same time as the attack on her southern coasts. These plans went even further, for they envisaged an attempt at breaking up the country from the inside by inciting a Welsh nationalist uprising at the moment of the expected victorious landing. To this end the Germans looked for ways and agents, who would help them to convey arms and explosives into Wales and to find people there prepared for action.[2]

When the German Admiralty received these instructions, it immediately acted upon them and a preliminary plan was prepared for 28 July. It envisaged creating a bridgehead near Dover, where the English Channel was narrowest. A tight corridor would be cleared, protected by minefields, submarines and aircraft, along which in the course of three days 260,000 soldiers, 30,000 vehicles and 60,000 horses would be transported to England. Grand Admiral Erich Raeder, the Commander of the German Fleet, made, however, one firm and basic stipulation: before any naval operations could begin, the *Luftwaffe* must have complete control of the skies over the Channel and southern England.[3]

In July 1940 the air forces that Marshal Göring directed at England consisted of three fleets: the Second based in Belgium and under the command of newly promoted Field Marshal Albert Kesselring; the Third, in France, commanded by Field Marshal Hugo Speerle, also promoted in July; and the Fifth in Norway and Denmark under General Stumpff. They had between them about 3,000 aircraft, of which 1,400 were long-range bombers (*Dorniers, Junkers* and *Heinkels*), 300 dive-bombers (*Stukas*), over 800 one-seater fighters (*Messerschmitt 109*) and about 300 two-seaters (*Me 110*).

Out of this huge number of machines about 2,500 were ready for action, of these, 656 were *Me 109*s.[4]

Against these forces Great Britain could put up four fighter groups: No. 10 covering the south-west which during the battle was taken over by Sir Quintin Brand; No. 11 under Air-Vice-Marshal Keith Park covering London and the south-east; No. 12 under Air-Vice-Marshal Sir Trafford Leigh-Mallory covering the Midlands; and No. 13 under Air-Vice-Marshal Richard Saul, patrolling northern England and Scotland. The whole of Fighter Command was under Air-Chief-Marshal Sir Hugh Dowding, a quiet, calm, formal man of sixty, for whom the Air Force was his whole life and who had and sought no friends. Owing to his age and the intrigues of his rivals, he had on several occasions received official letters saying that he ought to retire. Each time the decision had been reversed, but he was kept in a state of uncertainty; during the hardest battles, when the fate of the whole war was in the balance, he was constantly being disturbed by unfounded accusations.[5]

The RAF also had some bombers and even carried out several early raids on Berlin and other German cities, but at this stage of the war they made little impact. The aerial battle, which Winston Churchill called the Battle of Britain, was beginning, and in it only the British fighters counted. In fifty-seven squadrons there were, among others, 609 single-seater fighters (*Spitfires* and *Hurricanes*), of which 531 were ready for action and whose capabilities were equal, if not superior, to those of the enemy. For a full comparison we must also take into account facilities for replacing losses, both in pilots and machines. The British aircraft industry, alongside the Navy, was one of the few areas of military preparedness which surpassed that of the enemy. German factories could produce 140 *Me 109*s monthly, while the British ones, masterfully galvanized by the press baron Lord Beaverbrook, whom Churchill had appointed Minister of Aircraft Production, could in the same period turn out 500 *Spitfires* and *Hurricanes*. The pilot situation, however, was quite the reverse. The Germans had more than enough pilots and many of them could even be considered experienced veterans, having come through the Spanish Civil War, the Polish campaign and the battles in France, while the British side had too few, even including the Polish, Czech, French, Canadian, Dutch and Norwegian airmen, and their combat experience was limited to dog-fights over Poland and France. The one advantage on the British side was the fact that the battle was taking place over England and so the German pilots had enough petrol for only thirty minutes' combat and when they were shot down and landed by parachute, they were captured, whereas the British pilots and their allies could stay in the air longer and, after parachuting down, could rejoin their units and the battle. There were cases of shot-down pilots who the same day took over new machines and went up again. This naturally caused extreme physical and mental exhaustion, while the enemy had great reserves of manpower and could send rested pilots into combat. Anti-aircraft batteries and barrage balloons lay in wait for the Germans, but the RAF pilots had to deal with bombers, which were also armed, as well as with the fighters.[6]

What was taking place before everyone's eyes was not, however, the whole story. The British Air Force was also backed up by radar, which played an extremely important part, by a network of thousands of observers reporting anything they could see, and by a superb command structure which was concentrated in underground operations rooms. Furthermore, even these essential arrangements did not represent the sum of the British defence secrets. The airmen fighting in the sky had another powerful ally about which only a few people in the whole of Great Britain knew. This was the camouflaged centre at Bletchley Park, protected like the Crown Jewels, with its team of cryptanalysts, who daily were reading the most secret German signals enciphered on *Enigma*.

2

Hermann Göring alighted from the sleeping-car of his special train, codenamed *Asia*, took out a large pair of binoculars and began to inspect the sky. The evening of 8 August 1940 was drawing in, it was the height of summer, but a strong wind was blowing, rain was falling and heavy clouds covered the whole sky. The train had stopped at a small station in the Pas de Calais, not far from the coast and through the strong glasses the chalk cliffs of the British coast could be seen. The Marshal was not in a good mood. That very morning he had issued an exceptionally important order announcing Operation *Adlertag* (Eagle Day), which was to begin on 11 August and which was to lead to an eventual German victory. 'Within a short period you will wipe the British Air Force from the sky. Heil Hitler.'[7] The order sounded conclusive, but the Marshal knew that its execution presented great difficulties. For several weeks now German bombers had been attacking English south-coast ports and coastal shipping, while the fighters had been tangling daily with British fighters, but as yet no clear advantage had been gained in these operations. Furthermore, as if on purpose, the weather had deteriorated, the forecast was bad and there were fears that the great operation might have to be postponed.

The German leader's despondent, yet energetic, expression would have changed instantly had he known that his order, sent by radio to all his three air fleets, had been intercepted and that, after its decipherment at Bletchley Park, the *Ultra* net had immediately forwarded it to the Prime Minister, Churchill, and to Air-Chief-Marshal Dowding. *Ultra* had its own specialists in the underground shelters of Fighter Command at Stanmore, near London, and hut No. 3 at Bletchley Park was linked to Stanmore by a teleprinter and all the deciphered messages on air operations were sent there immediately.[8]

The bad weather held for four days and on 12 August Göring repeated his order setting the following day as the date for the great attack. The Second air fleet was to open the offensive with a mass attack on the airfields in Kent and the Thames area. This order was intercepted and read at Bletchley Park as was its speedy cancellation and postponement until the afternoon. Chaos ensued, confusing the British more than the Germans, for Dowding, knowing the German order, had ordered an alert for the afternoon, while some German units, failing to receive the signal, had carried out their missions in the morning.[9]

Two days later, on 15 August, all three German air fleets made a great raid. Göring, suspecting nothing, gave his orders over the air and the British monitoring stations picked them up and turned them over to the cryptanalysts. It was on this key day of the great battle that it became clear just how important the breaking of *Enigma* had been. The Second and Third air fleets attacked airfields in southern England and from early morning were met by British fighters, whose commanders knew beforehand when and where the attack would go. These onslaughts were nothing new, but for the first time Göring introduced the Fifth fleet stationed in southern Norway and northern Denmark, and this attack was meant to be a complete surprise. First of all came the German bombers from Stavanger in southern Norway heading for Scotland and northern England. There were seventy of them escorted by thirty two-seater *Messerschmitts, Bf 110*s, which, laden with additional fuel tanks, were hardly in a fit state for battle. The pilots were relaxed, since no one in Britain could suspect their approach. Before they could be picked up by radar, they would be over their targets. Suddenly, still far out to sea, *Hurricanes* and *Spitfires* of No. 13 Group appeared. Half of them attacked the fighters, the other half dealt with the bombers. Within minutes fifteen German aircraft were shot down in flames with the loss of only a single British machine. Only a few *Heinkels* managed to reach their targets and drop their bombs; badly mauled, the large armada had to turn for home.

A little later on the same day fifty *Junkers, Ju 88*s, left Alborg in Denmark for the Midlands without any fighter cover at all. They were also met over the sea by fighters from No. 12 Group and, in a short engagement, seven bombers were shot down and a number seriously damaged. Once again a small number of the attackers managed to get through and cause a certain amount of damage, but this had no real significance.[10]

In the underground shelter of Fighter Command Headquarters young girls worked ceaselessly, moving aircraft symbols on a large operations table and marking the results of the fighting; up above, in the gallery, stood Air-Chief-Marshal Dowding carefully watching their swift movements. He was the only senior officer present who knew why the German surprise attack had failed and why they had had such great losses. In his most secret dreams and thoughts every commander nurses the hope that he might be able to find out his opponent's plans, and now, not in his dreams, but in reality, Dowding was able to read Hermann Göring's most secret thoughts. The information coming from Bletchley Park, linked to an analysis of German tactics, permitted the British Commander-in-Chief to develop a system which with every day seemed to become more effective. Göring's plan aimed at provoking as many British fighters as possible into combat and then destroying them. If this had happened, the road to the British Isles would have lain wide open. Dowding was aware of this plan and so sometimes sent only a dozen or so aircraft against the German formations. His subordinate commanders were angered by this and accused him of procrastination, poor tactics and even defeatism, but he knew the Germans' plans and knew he must retain as many of his aircraft as possible for the decisive moment.[11]

Adlertag was extended to a whole week, but without any evident result and the Germans once again concentrated on attacking airfields in southeast England. Göring continued to send his orders over the air and Bletchley Park daily received a great many intercepted messages. It was not possible to decipher all of them, but those which were sufficed to show that Dowding's tactics were correct. As well as running the battle, which the British had to win, the Air-Chief-Marshal continued to remember one extremely important fact: at all costs the Germans should not realize that their secret orders were being read. Therefore, from time to time, the British commander made mistakes, not serious ones, but nonetheless obvious. His enemies immediately picked on them, even though they were fighting on the same side, and attacked him mercilessly. Dowding, bound over to the greatest secrecy, did not betray his impatience by the slightest gesture. Even the group commanders were not let into the secret, although they belonged to the Air Force's élite, and some of them were Dowding's sharpest critics. On the other hand, many junior officers, who were going into action several times a day, were amazed at the accuracy of their orders.[12]

German intelligence, with its agents in the British Isles, was doing its best to provide its superiors with as much information as possible on British losses and it was from this source that Göring drew his information about the RAF's desperate situation and that it had only three hundred fighters left. Fortunately, this was incorrect and the actual figure was twice as high, but the British really were going through a serious crisis. Some of the attacks had hit aircraft factories and the flow of new machines was slackening; this was not, however, the most important factor. The number of pilots was decreasing and those still in action were at the limits of exhaustion. New men were being trained as quickly as possible, but the shorter the course, the less value the final product. But the Germans were also feeling the strain of several weeks' fighting and their morale began to suffer. Göring had reckoned that the *Luftwaffe* would sweep its opponents from the sky in a fortnight with few losses, and so German industry was not prepared for such great demands, while the confident German pilots began to feel the strain. The British command knew all this, since the Germans continued to use the radio, having full confidence in *Enigma*.[13]

There began the long, painful attacks on airfields and radar stations which dragged through the whole of August up to the first days of September. The several weeks-old battle had developed into routine, when, suddenly on 7 September, Göring sent Marshal Kesselring an order by radio to send three hundred bombers over the London docks. The attack, with a strong fighter escort, was to take place during the afternoon.

Bletchley Park received this order, immediately deciphered it and Churchill, together with Air-Chief-Marshal Dowding, had time to consider what this sudden change of tactic might mean. There were two opposite interpretations: either Göring believed that he had already won the battle in the air and was delivering the final blow, or, on the contrary, he was changing his tactics since his efforts so far had failed to produce any results.

The answer came from another signal deciphered by the analysts. The same day that the London docks and neighbouring areas were burning, the German invasion forces received the order to be at full readiness. So the attack on London was intended to distract the attention of the British commanders and draw off all the fighters. Emergency calls immediately sped around the British Isles, the Home Guard was mobilized, churches were reminded to ring their bells in the event of invasion and bombers took off to attack the ships and barges assembled in northern France.[14]

The invasion did not take place, but the air attacks on the capital continued for several days. Then a blessed rain began to fall from an overcast sky, but was followed by an improvement in the weather with a full moon. Finally Sunday, 15 September came. No one then knew that this was to be the climax of the whole great battle.

The Fifth German air fleet was out of the reckoning since the distance from Norway and Denmark was too great for fighters, so Göring could use only two fleets – the Second and the Third – but this time every aircraft which could fly took off. Kesselring and Speerle sent out 328 bombers and 769 fighters which moved on the British Isles in two huge waves.[15] Dowding, forewarned about the attack by Bletchley Park, and rightly guessing that the critical hour was at hand, for the first time changed his tactics and sent up two whole groups of fighters: No. 11 and No. 12. About three hundred *Hurricanes* and *Spitfires* met the first German wave over the coast, southern England and London and engaged it. The Germans, taken by complete surprise at the numbers of enemy fighters, hurriedly dropped their bombs and turned back. The British fighters returned to their airfields, refilled their empty fuel tanks, loaded up with ammunition and again took off to meet the second wave. For the first time Londoners could watch a battle between several hundred aircraft on the huge backcloth of a clear sky. It was a terrifying and yet wonderful sight, full of tension, the roar of engines, the chattering of machine guns and the deafening blast of exploding bombs.

The German attack ended in defeat; they lost 56 aircraft, as against merely 27 British fighters. Immediately after the battle the British information service stated that 187 German aircraft had been shot down, while the Germans asserted that the British had lost 78. Both sides exaggerated by the same amount: three hundred per cent. Some of the bombers managed to break through to London and cause a number of fires and a great deal of damage, but the British resistance was not broken and the number of aircraft which greeted the attackers showed that all earlier calculations had been wrong. The Blitz, with its awful night attacks, raged on for several weeks, but the battle's peak had passed and the initiative was moving to the British side.

Two days later Bletchley Park in great excitement read a new secret signal in which the German High Command informed all airfields in Holland that Hitler had ordered all preparations for an airborne attack on Great Britain to be abandoned. The same evening a meeting of the Chiefs of Staff, together with Churchill, took place. The Prime Minister's face was radiant and the movements of the other men showed that a great weight had also fallen from their shoulders. Hitler's undefeated, victorious forces had finally been halted for the first time, and the threat of invasion had been averted indefinitely.[16]

3

Kapitan-Leutnant Fritz Lemp, the 26-year-old commander of submarine U–30, was in excellent spirits that day. It was Sunday, 3 September 1939, the sun was shining, a light wind was blowing and the boat, which had just surfaced, was rocking gently to the peaceful rhythm of the waves. A chain of thirty German submarines surrounded the British Isles and Lemp's boat was at the very end of the chain, out in the Atlantic, about four hundred kilometres to the north-west of the Hebrides.

About half-past eleven in the morning the *Enigma* machine on board the submarine received the signal: 'To Commanders-in-Chief and Commanders afloat, Great Britain and France have declared war on Germany . . .' Lemp almost jumped for joy. So it had begun. His boat was on the regularly used sea-lane for ships plying between the British Isles and the United States, and it was clear that fate wanted him, a young commander, to strike the first blow at sea against the enemy for *Führer* and country. He gave an order and the boat began slowly to dive.

Evening was already falling and it was past 7:30 when, in the periscope, appeared the shape of a large vessel, undoubtedly a passenger ship. Lemp knew the details of the Hague conventions, and only a few hours previously had received instructions that passenger ships were to be left alone, but the desire to distinguish himself by achieving the first success at sea overrode everything. The submarine approached the ship and fired off her torpedoes. One of them hit and caused an explosion: the ship began to sink.[17]

It was the passenger liner *Athenia* of 14,000 tons and with more than 1,400 people aboard, of whom 118 were lost. Before the survivors were landed at Galway in the west of Ireland the whole world had heard the news that the terror of the First World War had returned to the sea-routes.

4

On the very same day that Great Britain entered the war and the *Athenia* was sunk an exceptional thing happened: the man who, twenty-five years earlier, at the outbreak of the First World War, had held exactly the same position, entered the Government. It was Winston Churchill, later to be Prime Minister and a great leader, who sat down behind the desk of the First Lord of the Admiralty.

Great Britain, like the other great Western democracies, was not prepared for a new world-wide conflict. The exception to this was her Navy, which stood guard over the huge far-flung Empire. The Third *Reich*, despite ignoring the decrees of Versailles and frenziedly rebuilding its fleet after Hitler's accession to power, was unable to rival the forces that Churchill had at his disposal at the beginning of the war. Every comparison favoured the British: in battleships the advantage was 7:1, in cruisers 6:1 and in destroyers 9:1. The situation with aircraft carriers was even more disparate; Great Britain had six and the Germans only two and those were being built.[18] This balance took on a somewhat different aspect if one took into account the fact that the Empire required protection of its sea-lanes and that the British Navy had to operate in the Pacific, the Indian Ocean and the Mediterranean, while the Germans were supported by the Italian fleet. The Third *Reich*, however, would have stood no chance in a naval confrontation and did not in the least seek one.

Submarines were another matter. During the First World War they had strangled the embattled British Isles to the extent that the civilian population had been on the verge of starvation and Churchill, who remembered this very well, attached great importance to the danger of submarine warfare. He was met with a pleasant surprise. In 1938 Hitler had accepted a programme of building capital ships (Z–Plan Fleet) and submarines had been low on the list of priorities. This was probably a direct consequence of the Chancellor's megalomania and his love of gigantic plans and great buildings. The result, however, was that, on the outbreak of war, Admiral Karl Dönitz, the Commander of the German submarine fleet, had only 57 vessels, of which 45 were ready for action. According to his calculations he needed at least 300 boats to carry out the tasks assigned to him.[19] These were colossal, if one realizes that on any one day in 1939 Great Britain had around 2,500 merchant vessels at sea, not counting the several hundred belonging to friendly fleets.[20]

Despite this astonishing failure on the part of the Germans to exploit experience gained in the First World War, the threat of submarine warfare was very great, particularly since the Germans concentrated above all on disrupting shipping in the Atlantic, and it was these trading routes which were the most important for Great Britain. Only continual and uninterrupted contact with the United States and a steady stream of supplies from there afforded any hope of survival and eventual victory.

The essential task confronting Admiralty Intelligence, called the Operational Intelligence Centre (OIC) under Lieutenant-Commander (later Vice-Admiral) Norman Denning, was following the movements of German submarines and capital ships, which slipped secretly out of port and lay in wait for Allied convoys. In this area the British made a bad start, for information from actual German ports was poor and aerial reconnaissance not yet adequately developed. Submarines prowled the Atlantic without serious hindrance and in addition to them there were the two German 'pocket' battleships, *Graf Spee* and *Deutschland*, which, moreover, had been at sea even before the outbreak of hostilities. In November 1939 they were joined by two battle cruisers, the *Scharnhorst* and the *Gneisenau*, which Admiralty Intelligence failed to spot.[21]

With such a state of affairs the attention of the Intelligence officers had to turn in the direction of Bletchley Park. Ships afloat could only communicate with their bases by radio; each one had *Enigma*, so the interception and deciphering of signals and reports would allow the British to pin-point the positions of German vessels. Unfortunately, here cryptanalysis was also powerless. Some years previously, in 1932, when the Polish analysts had broken the secret of *Enigma* (see Chapter 2, p. 25), they had paid least attention to naval ciphers, partly because Poland was above all afraid of an attack by land and partly because the naval ciphers were the hardest; they again turned out to be the toughest to crack. The German Navy had from the very beginning used five rotors on its *Enigma*s, with three in use at any one time, and at the start of the war they introduced another two, the sixth and seventh, which fact was discovered when a German submarine was captured at the end of 1939 (see Chapter 4, p. 59). This was an exceptional achievement, for all German commanders had strict orders to destroy their *Enigmas* and all the papers connected with it. Later, from 1943, all cipher instructions were printed on special paper which disintegrated on coming into contact with water. Yet even this wonderful booty was not enough for Bletchley Park to break the secret of *Enigma M* and during the Norwegian campaign, in which the fleets of both sides played an important role, the Admiralty had had to operate in the dark, able only to recognize that something important was going to happen by the volume of indecipherable enemy radio traffic.[22]

This state of affairs continued for several months and the situation in the North Sea and in the Atlantic in particular was becoming critical. During the first four months of the war, Great Britain, together with the Allies and the neutral countries, lost 755,392 tons of merchant shipping, of which 99.9 per cent was sunk in the Atlantic, and during the next four months the figure was 806,653 tons, all of it in the Atlantic. It was true that in the same period the Germans lost sixteen submarines and introduced only six new ones into service, while Admiralty aerial reconnaissance began to produce better results, but the overall situation continued to be very bad.[23] Added to this, the German Navy began to use some large and quite fast merchant ships with concealed armament. They lay in wait for single Allied merchantmen and achieved excellent results.

Although the cryptanalysts at Bletchley Park continued to be under great pressure and were working at full stretch and top speed they were still unable to break the naval ciphers. Fortunately, they were now reading *Luftwaffe* signals with ease, and there were a great many of them. This enabled the British to deal more effectively with dive-bomber attacks on convoys and sometimes provided information on naval plans, when the two German services worked together.[24]

The difficulty in breaking *Enigma M* lay also in the fact that the German Navy adhered to communications security rules much more strictly than the other services, and wherever possible used telephones and teleprinters, and restricted wireless traffic to a minimum. However, as the Battle of the Atlantic developed, the situation began to change. On the basis of their experiences so far and their great losses, Admiral Dönitz came to the conclusion that the tactic of using U–boats singly must be changed and that it must be replaced by flotilla operations (Grey Wolves' tactics), as a result of which the submarines' effectiveness would increase greatly and there would be fewer losses.[25] The idea was good, but it required a much greater use of radio so that submarines of the same 'wolf-pack' could maintain contact with one another. The increase in radio traffic greatly improved the chances of the Bletchley Park analysts.

For a number of weeks they had had to be content with guessing what the indecipherable signals meant. It was realized that the short ones were weather reports and the longer ones reports on completion of a mission and information about return to base. Since they knew about the sixth and seventh rotors, they were aware that their problems had increased, but this brought them no nearer a solution. When at the end of 1939 they had captured a German submarine with her *Enigma,* they had been unable to get hold of its instructions or the secrets of its keys. They had to try for another similar success. Several ships received orders to do just this. Special teams were trained to capture an *Enigma* intact together with its documentation.

The first important success came on 23 February 1941. On that date an attack was carried out on the Lofoten Islands off the northern coast of Norway and the German trawler *Krebs* was damaged. Her captain managed to throw the *Enigma* overboard and some of its papers, but then he was killed and the spare rotors, together with the rest of the documents, fell into British hands.[26] This prize enabled Bletchley Park to establish the keys of the low-grade net (*Marinenschlüsseln*) and to make some preliminary attempts at breaking the *Enigma M* ciphers. On 12 March the first deciphered naval signal was sent through the *Ultra* net, to be followed by others. They dealt not only with submarines and convoys, but also with great capital ships such as the *Scharnhorst* and *Gneisenau* and later the *Bismarck*; they were therefore enciphered on high-grade nets.[27]

This success did not satisfy the cryptanalysts, who still lacked a great many details; so they continued the hunt. On 7 May, off Iceland, the British managed to capture another trawler, the *München*, whose captain succeeded in destroying her *Enigma* but the instructions and keys fell into their hands. Unfortunately, as on the *Krebs*, they dealt only with low-grade traffic and thus had only limited use. However, fortune smiled on the British. A new opportunity arose two days later and Fate decreed that it was Kapitan-Leutnant Fritz Lemp, the same man who on 3 September 1939 had sunk the first passenger liner of the Second World War, who supplied the means. Commanding a new boat, *U–110*, he attacked a convoy out from the Hebrides, but he was unsuccessful and was himself spotted by the corvette *Aubretia*. He dived within thirty seconds and tried to escape, but was hit by depth-charges, his damaged batteries began to give off gas and he had to surface. Lemp, caught in the fire of surrounding British vessels, jumped into the sea, but when he saw that his boat was not sinking he tried to get back on board and destroy the *Enigma*, but was hit by a machine-gun bullet. The boat was captured and a specialist team found an intact *Enigma*, together with the additional rotors, the daily keys and other documents relating to the machine's setting and operation. Everything was salvaged in the greatest secrecy so that none of the rescued German crew would know what had happened.[28]

This achievement turned out to be decisive in the process of breaking

Enigma M. A submarine's patrol lasted between eight and twelve weeks and each vessel carried a list of daily keys for that period. *U–110* had only recently left port, so the captured keys were in force until the end of June and thus the naval section at Bletchley Park had no difficulty in reading signals dealing with submarines. Independently of this, the papers found aboard *U–110* afforded a deeper insight into the secrets of *Enigma M* and its ciphers. This had a decisive influence on the Battle of the Atlantic, which in its turn was of great importance to the outcome of the whole war.

5

On 5 May 1941 Adolf Hitler himself paid a visit to the Polish port of Gdynia, which the Germans had taken and renamed Gotenhafen. The two newest, recently completed 42,000-ton battleships, *Bismarck* and *Tirpitz*, lay at anchor.[29] Each vessel was a marvel of engineering. They were covered in 'Wotan' armour, built specially by Krupp; their armament consisted of four great turrets each containing a pair of 15-inch guns, and of six smaller turrets with 5.9-inch guns. Internally the ships were divided into compartments, separated one from the other by watertight bulkheads and the crew believed that they were 'unsinkable'.

There was no doubt that they were the most powerful warships of the day and it was impossible to remain indifferent on seeing them. Nevertheless, during the tour of inspection Hitler was silent and betrayed not the slightest sign of pleasure. After all every new weapon aroused his imagination and on such occasions he was always very excited and asked a great many questions.

There could have been many reasons for this silence. Hitler was a self-taught man and in many fields was a dilettante, but he did possess a certain instinct which, in addition to the other facets of his character, had helped him to the top. Perhaps his instinct told him that these marvellous mountains of steel with the very latest in equipment and the 4,700 sailors, who formed the two crews, could have been more profitably employed elsewhere. Perhaps, however, the reasons for the *Führer*'s silence and scepticism were deeper. He had indeed accepted 'Z–Plan', which envisaged the construction of capital ships, and he wanted to emulate the British enemy and beat them at sea, but in his heart he feared and admired them. When he began the war he had counted on the islanders' sense of political realism encouraging them not to become involved and to agree to his proposed division of the world. Things had turned out differently and now he was fighting the British and with every day his hatred grew, but he continued to feel a certain respect for them and in particular for their power at sea. It was for this reason that he responded coolly to Grand Admiral Erich Raeder's plan to mount a new operation in the Atlantic to be called *Rheinübung*. The *Bismarck*, whose crew had already undergone suitable training, was to take part, together with the heavy cruiser *Prinz Eugen* and other support and supply vessels. The idea was to attack merchant shipping without tangling with British warships. Raeder was very keen on this operation and Hitler, although he had a great many misgivings, did not issue the order to cancel it.[30]

The great battleship's cruise, her attempts to break out into the Atlantic, the efforts of British Intelligence to discover the Germans' plans, the battle, the final chase and the proud giant's end, have all been described in detail many times and do not need repeating. Nevertheless, it is worthwhile returning to the most important dates and facts, since, for the first time, they can be compared with the hitherto secret materials, which at the time of writing have been available at the Public Record Office for several months. These are the German naval signals deciphered at Bletchley Park between 12 March and 28 May 1941, which is the very time at which operation *Rheinübung* was being planned and was eventually executed. The file contains 236 signals, of which about 100 relate to the *Bismarck* and her fate.[31] What was the role of the British cryptanalysts in the sinking of the German battleship?

Using conventional methods, Admiralty Intelligence had been following the activities of the Germans and knew that the *Bismarck* had been completed at Hamburg docks in August 1940 and had been moved several times to Kiel and back. This information was obtained from aerial reconnaissance which took a number of pictures. This source dried up when in March the battleship was moved to the Baltic for sea trials and anchored at Gdynia. British aircraft could not fly that far and Intelligence had to be satisfied with fragmentary and second-hand information obtained by agents. One of these, in the French port of Brest, provided news that a berth was being prepared there for anchoring the German giant (probably at the end of its cruise); another one communicated directly from Gdynia.[32] But information was still scanty, time was slipping by and a source of news as to what the Germans were doing was sought. At this juncture Bletchley Park entered the picture and sent over the first deciphered signals dealing with the *Bismarck*. They were dated from 7 to 10 May and had been deciphered only after three or four days, but they were still useful, as they concerned the great ship's fitting-out and trials.[33] It was from these the Admiralty received the first sign that something was in the air. This was confirmed by observers who reported that, during the second week of May, German aerial reconnaissance activity had greatly increased from the Denmark Strait between Iceland and Greenland to Scapa Flow. It was clear that the Germans were preparing something.

On 18 May both vessels sailed out of Gdynia accompanied by several other ships, but Admiralty Intelligence knew nothing of this. Bletchley Park received a number of signals, some dated the 13th and one dated the 19th, but their decipherment took time and only one from the 13th was read relatively quickly, by the 20th. The docks at Kiel informed the *Bismarck* that she would have 2,000 tons of fuel oil to take aboard at Gdynia.[34] This meant that the ship was going to leave any day and it was possible to deduce that, at the moment of decipherment, she was already at sea. Confirmation of this conjecture came the same day. Captain Henry Denham, the British Naval Attaché at Stockholm reported that, at 3 pm, two great warships, escorted by three destroyers and five auxiliary vessels and ten or a dozen aircraft, had sailed past Marstrand (a town in southern Sweden, level with the northern tip of Denmark), heading in a north-westerly direction.[35]

Admiral Sir John Tovey, the Commander-in-Chief Home Fleet at Scapa Flow, had received definite confirmation of his fears and issued the appropriate orders. The largest cruiser in the world, the 42,000-ton *Hood*, fast, but poorly armoured and old, headed for the Denmark Strait together with the newly commissioned 35,000-ton battleship, *Prince of Wales*, still with civilian fitters aboard. They were escorted by six destroyers and the cruiser *Suffolk*. In addition to this the cruisers *Birmingham* and *Manchester* were also deployed towards the Iceland-Faroes gap, while the new aircraft-carrier *Victorious* and the battleship *Repulse* were given different tasks and ordered to remain at Scapa Flow.

Bletchley Park received a number of further signals from 19 and 20 May, but had difficulty reading them and now time was short. Fortunately, aerial reconnaissance managed to establish that the German ships, after stopping in a fjord near Bergen in Norway, had sailed from there on the evening of the 21st. They could have turned back, they could have gone to northern Norway, or they could finally have attempted to break out into the Atlantic either through the Denmark Strait or to the south of Iceland. Admiral Tovey, anticipating the last alternative, led the rest of his ships out of Scapa Flow.

For several days the weather was dreadful, the Air Force was powerless and the analysts at Bletchley Park were straining every nerve to read something, unfortunately to no avail. Operations were carried out virtually blind, for German Intelligence was also experiencing difficulties and Admiral Günter Lütjens, in command of the German squadron, had not been informed of the British preparations and was calmly steaming in the direction of Greenland. An almost chance encounter occurred; the *Hood* was sunk, the *Prince of Wales* damaged, while *Bismarck*, hit by three shells, began to lose fuel oil. The Germans had the upper hand, but they abandoned the attack and eluded their pursuers for two days.[36]

Already on 20 May the Admiralty, anticipating that the Germans would try to break out into the Atlantic, had called out three of its great ships stationed at Gibraltar: the aircraft-carrier *Ark Royal*, the battleship *Renown* and the cruiser *Sheffield*. Spanish Intelligence, which was co-operating with the Germans, immediately sent them a signal, which was sent to Admiral Lütjens on the 20th: ' . . . Spain reports, . . . that *Renown, Ark Royal* and one cruiser left Gibraltar, course unknown.' To be sure, Bletchley Park only managed to decipher this on the 26th, but it was important since it showed that the Germans knew of the squadron approaching from the south.[37] The same day the cryptanalysts began to decipher much simpler *Luftwaffe* signals. These dealt with air cover which was being prepared for the *Bismarck* as soon as she came within fighter range, and they provided the British with priceless information, since they left no doubt that the battleship was heading for France. Not only did Bletchley Park succeed in establishing the direction she was taking, but even the exact port for which the damaged vessel was making. Meanwhile German propaganda was making a great deal out of the sinking of the *Hood*, the whole world knew about it and a high-ranking *Luftwaffe* officer at Athens, who had a son serving on the *Bismarck*, inquired of Berlin the vessel's destination. He was told: Brest. The diplomatic ciphers, which were easier to break than the naval ones, had for some time been read by Bletchley Park and the signal was deciphered and found itself at the Admiralty.[38] This was a clear example of a mistake made by the Germans who departed from the rule of revealing a secret only to those who had to know. They continued to make mistakes. After the sinking of the *Hood*, Admiral Lütjens, unaware that he had effectively thrown off the pursuit, informed his superiors of his success and future plans in a long series of signals. Although the cryptanalysts had great difficulty in reading these signals quickly, the monitoring stations could easily establish the German ship's position by direction-finding.[39]

In the early hours of 26 May a British Catalina seaplane found the *Bismarck* sailing alone, since the *Prinz Eugen* had been ordered to save herself independently. Bletchley Park received a number of signals from the 24th, 25th and 26th, but before they managed to decipher them the great ship's final hours were approaching. Admiral Tovey, who inexplicably had sailed for several hours in the direction of Norway, was too far away, but the Gibraltar squadron was steaming north. By evening the distance between it and the *Bismarck* was so small that Swordfish torpedo aircraft took off from the *Ark Royal* and attacked the German vessel. One of the torpedoes damaged her steering-gear and the *Bismarck* lost the ability to manoeuvre.

During the several hours of dusk a number of signals were exchanged between the wounded giant and submarines, all of which arrived at Bletchley Park. The centre also received two signals from Admiral Lütjens, one to the Naval High Command and the other to Hitler, promising to fight to the end, together with the Chancellor's reply to the Admiral and the whole crew. It was deciphered after two days, but by then had no significance. Night brought an end to the fighting and the next morning Admiral Tovey arrived aboard the battleship *Rodney*. In an exchange of salvoes the German vessel suffered further damage and her guns fell silent. The cruiser *Dorsetshire* approached to within easy range and fired two torpedoes. At 10:36 on the morning of 27 May the *Bismarck* disappeared beneath the waves with her flag still flying at the masthead.[40]

The sinking of the German battleship, which had been achieved as a result of massive British superiority, had not only a symbolic, but also tactical significance. Henceforth the Germans ceased trying to send out great capital ships and the whole weight of the Battle of the Atlantic fell on the shoulders of Admiral Dönitz and his submarines.[41] This battle might have turned out differently, if, from the very beginning, the Germans had concentrated on undersea warfare.

The search for the German battleship was also the beginning of a very close co-operation between Admiralty Intelligence and Bletchley Park and, despite certain difficulties, it demonstrated the great value of the crypt-analysts' work. Although in May 1941 their results were not always produced sufficiently quickly, for it was just at that time the Germans were introducing a new cipher net for capital ships, codenamed *Neptune*, the breakthrough had been made and was to produce splendid results in the future.[42]

NOTES

1. Fest, op. cit., pp. 637–8.
2. Ibid, p. 638.
3. Len Deighton, *Fighter*, London, 1977, pp. 49–50.
4. Ibid, pp. 59–73. Also: Peter Calvocoressi and Guy Wint, *Total War*, London, 1974, pp. 138–9.
5. Ibid, pp. 64–5.
6. Ibid, pp. 134–43. Also: Edward, H. Sims, *The Fighting Pilots,* London, p. 41.
7. Winterbotham, op. cit., p. 67. Also: Deighton, op. cit., p. 31.
8. Ibid, p. 65.
9. Ibid, p. 68.
10. Deighton, op. cit., pp. 209–15. Also: Winterbotham, op. cit., pp. 67–9.
11. Winterbotham, op. cit., pp. 70–1.
12. Ibid, pp. 72–3.
13. Ibid, pp. 74–5.
14. Ibid, p. 78.
15. Richard Collier, *Eagle Day*, London and New York, 1966, p. 14.
16. Deighton, op. cit., pp. 265–6. Also: Winterbotham, op. cit., pp. 80–1. (The figures on aircraft taking part, shot down and involved in the Battle of Britain differ. It is impossible to be completely accurate.)
17. John Costello and Terry Hughes, *The Battle of the Atlantic,* London, 1977, pp. 1–6.
18. Ibid, p. 35.
19. Cajus Bekker, *Hitler's Naval War*, London, 1974, p. 371. Also: Costello and Hughes, op. cit., p. 35.
20. Beesly, op. cit., p. 25.

21. Ibid, p. 31.
22. Bonatz, Opinion of *The Ultra Secret*, op. cit. Also: Beesly, op. cit., pp. 37–8 and 67.
23. Costello and Hughes, op. cit. pp. 304–5.
24. Beesly, op. cit., p. 51.
25. Bekker, op. cit., p. 182.
26. Beesly, op. cit., pp. 70–1.
27. Intelligence from enemy radio communications (*Enigma*), *Public Record Office*, London, file DEFE 3/1, ZTP 1–936, 12 March 1941.
28. Beesly, op. cit., p. 71. Also: Costello and Hughes, op. cit., pp. 154–5.
29. Bekker, op. cit., p. 220.
30. Ibid, p. 220.
31. *Public Record Office,* file DEFE 3/1, op. cit.
32. Beesly, op. cit., p. 74.
33. *Public Record Office,* op. cit., documents No. 383, 384, 389, 395, 422, 589.
34. Ibid, document No. 589.
35. Beesly, op. cit., p. 76.
36. Costello and Hughes, op. cit., pp. 146–9.
37. *Public Record Office*, op. cit., document No. 770.
38. Beesly, op. cit., pp. 84–5.
39. Ibid, pp. 79–80.
40. *Public Record Office,* op. cit., documents No. 902 and 920. Also: Costello and Hughes, op. cit., p. 151.
41. Bekker, op. cit., p. 228.
42. Beesly, op. cit., p. 77. (It appears that in his excellent book the author is a bit unfair towards the work of Bletchley Park in connection with the sinking of the *Bismarck*. The book was published before *Enigma* records of the PRO were opened to the public.)

7

Secret Despatches Flow Towards Moscow

1

LEOPOLD TREPPER WAS BORN in Poland in 1904 and it was there that he went up to university, where he did not finish his course but did become a communist. In 1926 he joined a Zionist organization and left for Palestine, but he was unhappy there and both Europe and revolutionary work called him back. He went to France and there, in 1930, he joined a Soviet intelligence ring, which was organized by another Palestinian, and which was in direct contact with its headquarters in Moscow, called *Razvedupr* (short for *Glavnoe Razvedyvatelnoe Upravlenie* – Chief Intelligence Administration). He quickly learnt how to live illegally and he took easily to the techniques of intelligence work.[1]

In 1932 the whole network, with the sole exception of Trepper, was arrested. He therefore left France and reported to Berlin at the secret offices of the *Razvedupr*. He was sent to headquarters in Moscow where he underwent further training. For several years he was cut off from practical work in the field and it was only in 1936 that his great moment arrived: he was appointed to control a great spy ring planned for western Europe. Hitler had already come to power, German rearmament was well under way and Moscow had decided that preparations had to be made for a new war.

Trepper was not starting from scratch, since there were, of course, Soviet agents already operating in the West. Some of these had been trained in Russia, others were local communists, and the first task was to incorporate them into a single network. Since Soviet Russia's potential enemies in Europe were the two great Western democracies, France and Great Britain, as well as Hitler's Third *Reich*, and since the mechanics of intelligence work required that, within the bounds of possibility, the network's headquarters should be in a neutral country not far from the centre of things, Belgium was chosen. Trepper was given a contact, Johann Wenzel, a German communist from East Prussia, who had also undergone training in Moscow, was a radio specialist and who was already operating in Belgium. Trepper set up a business, which was a cover for the whole operation, made contact with a great number of communists of various nationalities, who were all in Belgium at that time, and began to build up a wide network. He quickly expanded it into France, Holland and Denmark and, within the framework of his company, he established agents in a number of German, Belgian, French, Dutch and Danish ports and was ready to begin work aimed at obtaining information on Germany, Great Britain and France.[2]

Trepper received a Canadian passport in first-class condition, which had been obtained by Soviet agents during the Spanish Civil War; he learnt all the necessary details on life in Canada, on business there and many other things which might be useful if he had to deal with the police. He finally appeared in Brussels in March 1939, using the codename *Gilbert*, but amongst his own people he was known as *Grand Chef*. Moscow headquarters, however, would not have lived up to its reputation if it had not believed that, in addition to the loyal co-operation of local communists, it had to have its own people in such an important network, if only for mutual control. During 1939 Lieutenant Mikhail Makarov, Captain Victor Sukulov-Gurevich and engineer Konstantin Yefremov arrived in Brussels and made contact with Trepper. Another officer, Lieutenant Anton Danilov, was ordered to France, but was also at the disposal of *Grand Chef*. Sukulov-Gurevich, who was usually known as *Captain Kent* became Trepper's deputy and was thus called *Petit Chef*.[3]

An analysis of the political situation of the day showed that Nazi Germany was the most dangerous country in Europe, and was the only one in a position to jolt the world into a new war. Thus it was there that espionage activities had to be the greatest. The task facing Trepper's organization, however, was made easier by the fact that Nazi Germany, despite the new Chancellor's boasting, was far from being united. Certainly opposition politicians and communists had been purged from public life and put into concentration camps, but not everyone had been caught. Furthermore the government's terror tactics and warlike policies had aroused opposition in many people. These people, outwardly loyal and often holding important positions, were secretly prepared to join opponents of the Third *Reich* in order to combat Nazism.

2

In April 1933, within the great wave of terror which swept the country after the Nazis came to power, the young editor of an opposition journal, *Der Gegner*, Harro Schulze-Boysen, was arrested. He was not such an opponent of the new order that he had to be eliminated, but rather he could be 'converted' and put to some use. He was therefore left in the hands of the *SS*. Three times he was forced to run the gauntlet of young soldiers armed with whips, who beat him unconscious shouting that one day he would be one of them. A young friend and colleague of his died under their blows.[4]

Schulze-Boysen belonged to a wealthy and influential family and his mother knew Hermann Göring personally. The young journalist was therefore released from prison and transferred to the newly created Air Force Ministry as a reserve Air Force lieutenant. Thanks to his powerful connections he was left in peace there and, after a time, since he was an excellent and intelligent administrator, his superiors acquired such complete confidence in him that in 1942 he was even once sent to Hitler's headquarters in Vinnica in the Ukraine. The hopes of the *SS* men that he would come over to their side had been vain; hatred burned within him and made him an implacable enemy of the system. He became one of those Germans who were prepared to co-operate with their country's enemies in the battle against Nazism.[5]

Another of these was Arvid Harnack, an adviser in the Economics Ministry, who almost immediately after Hitler came to power sought ways of getting in touch with Soviet Intelligence. There were also others in various key positions throughout the Nazi state. Dr Hans-Heinrich Kummerow, a communist, was a telecommunication engineer, Lieutenant Herbert Gollnow worked in the *Abwehr*'s sabotage and diversion section, Horst Heilman and Alfred Traxl worked in the secret communication department of the operations division of the Army General Staff (*OKH*), Hans Henniger was in the *Luftwaffe* equipment directorate, Colonel Erwin Gehrts was in the training division of the Air Ministry and Rudolf von Schelila in the Ministry of Foreign Affairs. Each of them had his own contacts and his own ways of obtaining information from them. Not everyone realized just how important were conversations with colleagues at work or with friends. There were also those who were not in any important position, but who nevertheless, as a result of their work, moved in well-informed circles. One of these was the writer Dr Adam Kuckoff.[6]

All these widely separated contacts relied on personal friendships and formed two groups: one led by Schulze-Boysen, the other by Arvid Harnack. They represented quite different ideologies and personalities. Schulze-Boysen was an idealist with anarchist tendencies who was fighting against Nazism because he considered it to be an enemy of freedom; the other was a Marxist with a strong sense of discipline towards the Communist Party and the Soviet Union. Despite these differences, they came to an understanding in the summer of 1939, even before the outbreak of war, and began to co-operate.[7]

3

During the German attack on Poland in September 1939 the Soviet spy ring in the West was not yet quite prepared, but this was no great drawback, since Stalin made a pact with Hitler and in this phase of the war was confident that his conditions would be met. Nothing much changed before the spring of the following year when the surprise German attack on Denmark and Norway took place. Enciphered radio messages went east producing replies from Moscow containing questions, advice and instructions, but ignoring the most important issues. For many years Soviet Russia had feared that the Western democracies would come to some agreement with Germany and create a common anti-Soviet front, so the outbreak of war between the Third *Reich* and France and Great Britain suited her greatly. The war was expanding and this could only please Stalin.

However this stage of affairs changed dramatically when Hitler attacked in the west and, contrary to all expectations, demonstrated that the *Blitzkrieg* could work. The Soviet dictator had been expecting a long war and the complete exhaustion of both sides which would have left a virtually powerless Europe at his mercy, but suddenly German might found itself unrivalled on the continent. Great Britain fought on and drew onto herself almost the whole of Hermann Göring's Air Force; Hitler ordered preparations for the invasion of the British Isles to be made, but already there was no Western Front draining away millions of soldiers and weakening the countries concerned both economically and psychologically. How long could divisions be kept idle in a state of full preparedness? Hitler had started the war in the search for living space; where could he find it?*

Trepper understood all this very well and so built up his network with great energy. The occupation of Belgium forced him to move his headquarters to Paris, where it was easier to hide, while *Captain Kent* remained in Brussels and Anton Winterinck continued to operate in Holland. New groups were formed in Marseilles, Prague, Stockholm and in Romania. At the beginning of 1941 contact was made with the Schulze-Boysen/Harnack group in Berlin.[8]

German Counter-Intelligence was aware that both in the occupied territories and within the heart of the *Reich* a Soviet spy ring was operating, because firstly it stood to reason and secondly they had picked up its radio signals. They were difficult to decipher, but their destination could be told.

---

*It is amazing to what extent Hitler's own words were ignored. In his famous book, *Mein Kampf*, published in 1924, he stated: 'We terminate the endless German drive to the South and West of Europe, and direct our gaze towards the lands in the East . . . If we talk about new soil and territory in Europe today, we can think primarily only of Russia and its vassal border states.'

The Chief Security Office (*RSHA*) was also aware of this. In Admiral Canaris's *Abwehr*, just as in all other services, a special jargon was used. Transmissions on secret enemy short-wave sets were called 'playing' while a number of enemy transmitters was given the umbrella name of 'orchestra'. The whole Soviet western network, using several stations in a number of countries, was called *Die Rote Kapelle* (The Red Orchestra).[9]

4

On 29 June 1934, just before the 'Night of the Long Knives' during which such supposed enemies as Ernst Röhm, the head of the *SA*, and General Kurt von Schleicher were murdered, Hitler had a conversation with the Chief of the General Staff, General Ludwig Beck. Their conversation turned to the Army's future and when Beck said that he was preparing it not for conquest but for the defence of the homeland, Hitler interrupted him curtly: 'General Beck, armies do not exist for the preparation of peace; they exist for the triumphant execution of war.'[10]

After this conversation and the events of the following night, the tension, which had from the very beginning existed between Hitler and the Army, increased. The German armed forces, which had not been defeated in battle during the First World War, still contained a great many officers from that time, who maintained the spirit of the old Junkers' traditions, which the new Chancellor, coming as he did from a lower social class, just could not bear. The German Republic had undergone a social revolution and people who formerly had never even dreamt of holding an important state position had come to power and they aimed to control all aspects of the life of the nation. A great change within the officer corps and the leadership of all three services seemed to be imminent.

Despite their mutual dislike and even hatred, the opposition of senior officers to Hitler was restricted at first to conversations and criticism within private circles of their friends, for the ties both of loyalty and discipline were still very strong and dominated everything, but slowly this state of affairs began to change. The universal terror, lawlessness, the barbaric treatment of the Jews, the violent and uncompromising movement towards war, all, with every day, affected ever- wider circles of disillusioned people. There was still no organization or conspiracy, but private conversations were gradually beginning to turn into a sort of loose association which could quite easily develop into a secret plot. General Beck, who continued to hold his rather exposed appointment, was a kind of spiritual leader of a group of a dozen or so people, amongst whom were Admiral Wilhelm Canaris, head of the *Abwehr*, General Karl-Heinrich Stülpnagel, the Quartermaster General,

Colonel Erich Fellgiebel, the head of Army signals, General Erwin von Witzleben, the commander of the Berlin district, and several others. The driving force behind these discreet contacts was Canaris's deputy, Lieutenant-Colonel Hans Oster, a tough, resolute and prudent man.[11]

These confidential contacts developed into something more like a secret organization, when, on 5 November 1937, Hitler, in the study in the Chancellery, outlined his expansionist plans which would assure the German nation the living space it needed. Those present were: The Minister, Field Marshal Werner von Blomberg; the Commander of the *Luftwaffe*, General Hermann Göring; the Army Commander, General Werner von Fritsch; the Commander of the Navy, Grand Admiral Erich Raeder; and the Minister of Foreign Affairs, Konstantin von Neurath. All of them were startled by these astonishing plans and all of them tried to restrain Hitler from them, only Göring supporting them without reservation.[12]

General Beck, who despite holding the highest post in the Army had not been invited to the secret meeting, was informed of it by Fritsch and Neurath and they attempted a joint intervention with Hitler, but were not even received. The conspirators began to wonder what they should do in order to prevent Germany being dragged into a war which would end only in disaster. General Beck came to the conclusion that Hitler's plans must be made known to the Western democracies.

Politicians, industrialists and high civil servants also belonged to the conspiracy. The State Secretary of the Ministry of Foreign Affairs, Ernst von Wiesäcker, was amongst its adherents, as was the conservative Ewald von Kleist-Schwenzin and the mayor of Leipzig, Carl Goerdeler. In the spring of 1938 the latter travelled twice to France to encourage the French to oppose the Czechoslovak settlement, and later he went to London on a similar mission. In France he received some rather vague and evasive answers, while in London Sir Robert Vansittart, the main diplomatic adviser at the Foreign Office, even remarked that such a mission entailed betraying one's own country.[13]

After Goerdeler, Kleist-Schwenzin also travelled to London and even met Churchill. He was followed by the industrialist Hans Böhm-Tettlebach, while others also attempted to make some contacts, but all with the same result. There was no will in the West for decisive action and an atmosphere of defeatism, concession and compromise reigned.[14]

In August, when the Sudetenland crisis, caused by Hitler's demands, arose, General Beck resigned and the new Chief of Staff was General Franz Halder. He also, however, was against expansionist plans, was in touch with the conspirators and even went further and planned a *coup d'état*. Immediately after any declaration of war, or the opening of hostilities without such formalities, General von Witzleben commanding the Berlin district was to arrest the Chancellor and his closest colleagues and try them. The Commissioner of the Berlin police, Wolf Heinrich von Helldorf, was taken into the conspirators' confidence, as were the judge, Hans von Dohnanyi, a prominent economist, Hjalmar Schact, several further generals and politicians and a number of other people.[15]

The whole plan rested on the belief that the Western powers would awaken and take Czechoslovakia's side. However events took a different turn; the Munich conference was held, only to be followed by further concessions. The conspirators retreated and everything proceeded according to Hitler's intentions. After seizing Czechoslovakia, he turned his gaze on Poland and after that country received the British guarantee it was clear that there must be war. Then came the period of Hitler's great successes: the pact with Stalin, the defeat of Poland, the conquest of Norway and eventually the completely unexpected lightning victory in the west. The Chancellor's popularity reached a new peak and any opposition was quite pointless, but the conspirators did not abandon their plans, instead they only became more discreet and even less visible. Later, however, things began to take a different turn, the reckless decision to open a new front in the east was made, Hitler himself declared war on the United States, the great bombing raids over Germany began and it was then that the conspirators again began to raise their heads and their ranks began to grow. They extended more deeply, they spread ever wider, while continuing to observe every rule of secrecy and concealment.

The Third *Reich*'s security organizations were aware that National Socialism had some passionate enemies who would not abandon their beliefs. Such people were difficult to grasp, often held high positions and it was never possible either to accuse them of anything, let alone prove it. All the authorities could do was patiently observe and wait. *Abwehr* counter-intelligence was not involved, since its chief was one of the conspirators; it was the *SD* and the *Gestapo* who were on their trail. A name had to be found for these conspirators and so, in the best traditions of professional jargon, in contrast with *Die Rote Kapelle*, they were called *Die Schwarze Kapelle* (The Black Orchestra).[16]

5

The greatest difficulty facing Switzerland during the last war was how to remain neutral. Everything else took second place during the very tense period, which had begun from the moment the Nazis had come to power. Small Switzerland, which already had enough of her own problems, began to receive an influx of political refugees who could not very well be turned away, but who were a burden from two points of view: they required care and their activities could complicate the country's difficult political situation.

From the outbreak of war these problems grew more acute, but only became serious when the Western Front collapsed. Suddenly on all sides appeared troops who at any moment might receive the order to cross the frontier. Certainly unoccupied France lay to the south-west, but even there German control was very evident. Any reckless or unnecessary move could expose Switzerland to German anger and occupation, especially since Hitler, obsessed with the idea of uniting all Germans in one state, might for no better reason order an invasion of that part of the country which spoke German.

This difficult situation resulted in Switzerland trying to maintain good relations with all the countries at war. All embassies operated normally there and not only those of free countries such as Great Britain and of course the United States, but also of defeated and occupied countries such as Poland, Belgium, Holland, Norway, France and later Yugoslavia. At the same time the embassies of both Germany and Italy were also open and the Swiss authorities did everything they could not to antagonize them. Railway lines linking Germany with Mussolini's Italy ran through Switzerland, and many Swiss factories worked for the German war industry. Soviet Russia did not take advantage of these facilities, since it had no diplomatic relations with Switzerland, but it did have a number of supporters among the local communists and political refugees and made the most of this.

In addition to political problems, overpopulated Switzerland had for many years faced pressure from people from all over the world wishing to settle there. It was impossible to refuse everyone and so the principle was introduced, which continues to be in force to this day, that a candidate, after being thoroughly vetted, had to demonstrate that he possessed sufficient means to support himself adequately. It was very much harder to obtain a work permit or permission to set up a business.

In 1936 a Hungarian, one Sándor (Hungarian equivalent of Alexander) Radó, a cartographer, settled in Geneva. He possessed all the necessary financial qualifications, fulfilled all the Swiss conditions for foreign firms and set up a business, called *Geopress*, producing maps.[17] The new arrival, about forty, shortish and fat, with glasses, was a family man with a wife, two children and a mother-in-law. He led a most respectable life and his maps, which were produced to a high professional standard, quickly acquired an excellent reputation throughout the world. Despite being a full democracy, Switzerland does have a great deal of police control, for the inhabitants themselves are conscious of security matters, and so the Hungarian cartographer was watched, but for several years he gave no one the slightest grounds for suspicion. No one guessed that he and his wife were both members of a Soviet spy ring and that for many years they had belonged to the Communist Party. In all communications with Moscow he used the codename *Dora*, while to everyone else he was known as *Albert*, while his wife was called *Maria*.[18]

Radó was preparing himself for special tasks in the event of a new war and so he worked slowly and very carefully. With the assistance of a Soviet agent, Ursula Maria Hamburger (codename *Sonia*), who was also a major in the Red Army, he built up a small net which was to be the reserve network in case Leopold Trepper's large western ring collapsed; but the swift march of events caused him to start work much earlier than anticipated. In the spring of 1940,*Captain Kent*,Trepper's deputy, arrived on Moscow's orders with a codebook and instructions dealing with secret radio communications, which were *Die Rote Kapelle*'s weak spot. Within a short time Radó already had three radio stations maintaining direct contact with the *Director* (General Ivan Peresypkin) in Moscow. The first one was located in Geneva and was operated by a Swiss married couple, Olga and Edmond-Charles Hamel, both of them communists. The second one was in Lausanne and was in the hands of an Englishman, Alexander Foote, who was a communist and who had fought in the Spanish Civil War.[19] The third station was also in Geneva and was operated by a Swiss communist, Margrit Bolli, who also worked as a courier between Radó and his people. He too, maintained contact with some long-standing members of the German Communist Party, who lived in Switzerland and ran their own intelligence network.[20]

. A few years earlier, in 1934, a German, Rudolf Roessler and his wife, Olga, had come to Switzerland and settled down in a suburb of Lucerne. Roessler was a short, slim man of about fifty, who wore glasses and who had a grey unexceptional face. He was quiet and calm and had managed to settle in Switzerland thanks to the help of some friends there, in particular Dr Xavier Schnieper, a journalist and assistant at the Canton Library. These friends also helped him set up a small publishing firm, *Vita Nova Verlag*.

Before coming to Switzerland Roessler had been a journalist and had been connected with the theatre, but now, being a passionate opponent of Hitler and professing conservative, humanist and idealist views, he began a journalistic battle with the system he hated.[21] He had some excellent contacts in Germany and frequently received letters and newspapers from them. His analytical articles on Nazi Germany were distinguished by exceptional shrewdness and were always supported by excellent facts. These articles caused him to be deprived of his German citizenship in 1937 and he became stateless. In addition to his writing, he concentrated on his business and was a model citizen of neutral Switzerland.[22]

In the summer of 1939, when the approaching war was becoming only too apparent, Dr Schnieper put Roessler in touch with Swiss Intelligence in the hope that his wide contacts in Germany and his talent for precise analysis might come in useful. Roessler agreed to co-operate, since he felt gratitude towards his new country and wanted to help it; furthermore he realized that in this way he could contribute to the struggle against Nazism and he had already earlier made his own intelligence contacts through Dr Mayer von Baldegg whom he had known before the war. In mid-1940 when the Western Front began to collapse, the Roessler secret network in Germany began to operate. No one who worked in this ring knew how information was transmitted to Switzerland, but it came very rapidly and was always accurate and important. At this stage of the war only Swiss Intelligence took advantage of this information, but this changed when Hitler's armies attacked the Soviet Union. A friend of Roessler's, Dr Christian Schneider, a German by origin, but with Swiss citizenship, who had given financial assistance to the *Vita Nova* firm, put him in touch with the Soviet spy network, connected with Sándor Radó. Thus the results of Roessler's work, which were of the highest order, began to reach Moscow in mid-1942 where they aroused great interest. Their source was not only the network inside Germany, but also various other unknown sources in the West. Moscow headquarters gave Roessler the codename *Lucy* (from Lucerne?) whence arose the name *The Lucy Ring*. Meanwhile his contacts always took good care that *Lucy* never met Radó personally.[23]

6

Otto Pünter, a Swiss Social Democrat and professional journalist, took part in the Spanish Civil War on the Republican side. There he formed an intelligence ring, which he began to develop after his return to Switzerland. In his opinion the outbreak of a new European war and even a world one was only a question of a few years. He used the codename *Pakbo*, which name was formed from the first letters of the Swiss towns to which important information from abroad was sent: *P*ontresina, *A*rth, *K*reutlingen, *B*ern, *O*rselina. He operated from Bern and extended his contacts in a number of important directions: French diplomats and journalists, Austria, the Vatican, Italy and Germany. In the network connecting his people with him, there worked about thirty persons recruited from railway men, post-office workers, customs officials, border guards and a few others.[24]

In 1940 a Russian, whom he had known in Spain and who had the codename *Carlo*, warned Pünter that a Soviet–German war was approaching and gave him an introduction to Radó, who held all the threads of Soviet Intelligence operations in Switzerland. Their intermediary was Margrit Bolli, although Pünter met Radó several times. The *Pakbo* net collected primarily political and economic intelligence from Germany, from France through Frenchmen in contact with the Maquis, from London on General de

Gaulle's activities, a great deal of interesting information from diplomatic circles in Bern and also, what was of great importance, much useful material from the Western Allies. This was organized by a French diplomat who was in touch with the British Intelligence Service and later with Allen Dulles, who from the end of 1942 headed an American Intelligence network from Switzerland. Communications with Britain went by air through neutral Portugal in the form of microfilm and packages. Communications with Moscow were arranged by Radó, for Pünter did not have his own radio station.[25]

7

After the First World War financial considerations and a sense of security caused the Swiss Intelligence Service to be almost completely closed down. This relaxed attitude changed when the Nazis came to power in neighbouring Germany, but still little was actually done and when in 1937 Colonel Roger Masson took over the Fifth Section of the General Staff (Intelligence) be found a department of five with an annual budget in excess of 30,000 francs. A year later the budget had already risen to 50,000 francs and by April 1939 it was 320,000 francs with a staff of ten; but all this continued to look rather meagre. After mobilization of the Army the Fifth Section was renamed Sub-group Ia *(Untergruppe Ia)* and at the beginning of 1941 was given the name Sub-group Ib of the General Staff. It comprised Intelligence and Security. Intelligence was divided into D Bureau (Germany), F Bureau (France) and I Bureau (Italy). In November 1939 intelligence station No. I was set up in Lucerne and was linked with other stations: St Gallen, Basel, Zürich, Schaffhausen and Lugano. The number of employees was increased and at the peak of the group's activities reached 120. There was also a much larger number of agents and informers. The budget continued to rise: by 1943 it was already 600,000 francs and in 1944 it had reached 750,000 francs. All these preparations had one aim: to safeguard Switzerland's neutrality.[26] In order to ensure this everything had to be known about the country posing the greatest threat: namely the Third *Reich*. It was essential to find out what decisions were being taken in the most important German government departments and above all in Hitler's headquarters.

The lack of substantial means and manpower forced the Swiss military authorities willingly to take advantage of the assistance of private individuals whom they knew well. Thus they eagerly accepted an offer of co-operation from a Captain Hans Hausamann, a professional photographer, who after 1933 had turned to journalism, concentrating on the political changes in Germany, had extended this to collecting secret information and, in a private villa near Lucerne, had, out of his own pocket, set up an information centre called Bureau Ha (codename *Pilatus*). Through various contacts, chief of which was a Czech, Colonel Karel Sedlacek (codename *Simpson*), the representative of the Czech émigré government, he was in touch with American, British and French diplomats and worked closely with the Swiss Intelligence station in Lucerne *(Rigi)*, but was not formally subordinated to it.[27]

In the summer of 1939, before the German attack on Poland, Dr Schnieper brought about the co-operation of Bureau Ha with Rudolf Roessler through an Austrian friend of his, Dr Franz Wallner. Throughout the war Hausamann and Roessler never actually met and followed every precept of intelligence work, but their mutual exchange of information was lively and produced excellent results.[28] In this way, by means of Roessler, Dr Wallner, Bureau Ha, Baldegg and Dr Schneiper, the director of Soviet Intelligence operations in Switzerland, Sándor Radó, made contact with Swiss Intelligence.[29] There were many intermediaries, but the link was maintained producing rapid and good results. Radó, as has been explained, was also in touch with Otto Pünter and in this way all the intelligence networks which might have information useful to the Soviet Union, were within his grasp. During the most important phase of the war, when everything was in the balance and Hitler was close to victory in the east, Radó could work peacefully and render Moscow priceless assistance. For a long time the Swiss authorities either knew nothing of this, or preferred not to know.

8

On 12 November 1940 a group of senior German officials, with the Minister of Foreign Affairs, Joachim von Ribbentrop, in front, formed up on the platform of a Berlin railway station. Ribbentrop's Soviet opposite number, Commissar Vyacheslav Molotov alighted from the train and with a slight smile began slowly to shake the proffered hands. The very same day in the afternoon the Russian guest had his first discussion with Hitler. They dealt with the German proposal to divide up the British Empire, which in the opinion of the Germans, was in its death-throes. During their discussions the air-raid sirens started up and everyone had to go down to the shelters, which caused Molotov to ask innocently whose aircraft were disturbing them if the British were already on their knees. In further talks the Germans suggested that Russia might join the Tripartite Pact which already linked Germany with Italy and Japan.[30]

Several days later the German ambassador in Moscow received Stalin's reply to Hitler's proposals. The answer was 'Yes', but the Soviet dictator insisted on so many conditions of his own that it was quite impossible for Hitler to accept them. On 18 December he issued war directive No. 21, which ordered preparations to be made for an attack on Russia with the codename *Barbarossa*.[31]

The directive was top secret, but it was not necessary either to know its contents or to be an exceptional agent to realize that the German attack could be only a question of time. Earlier preparations were now developing at such a pace and the concentration of forces was so obvious that there could be no doubt as to their eventual use.

It was for just such a moment that the Soviet spy network in Western Europe had been formed. Leopold Trepper held all its threads in his hand and he had agents in Germany and in all the Western occupied countries. In neutral Switzerland it was his subordinate, Sándor Radó, who was in control. His position was exceptionally strong since, in complete contrast to the *Rote Kapelle*, he operated in an area where there was little danger and he had three radio stations. Radio communications with Moscow, which were continually tracked by the Gestapo and *Abwehr*, were Trepper's weak spot.[32] For several months past, numerous signals had been going to Moscow and now this amount increased greatly. Their contents were alarming. From the other end of the world, from Japan, Richard Sorge, the correspondent of the *Frankfurter Zeitung*, who had been working for Soviet Intelligence since 1938, was sending similar warnings. In some strange state of blindness and mental weakness Stalin did not believe any of these reports. On one of the important messages he wrote in his own hand in red ink: 'This information is an English provocation. Find out who is doing this and have him punished.'[33]

Meanwhile, subsequent events proved that the accuracy of these reports was unparalleled. What better proof of their value than that they gave the precise day on which Hitler would launch his attack on Russia? It was only this cataclysm, about which Stalin refused to believe until he saw it with his own eyes, which radically altered Moscow's attitude. Day after day the Soviet capital sent messages pleading for information. They covered everything: the deployment of the German forces, their supplies, losses, the movement of troops in the west, plans for an attack on Switzerland and many other things. From indifference and disbelief Moscow had changed to a tone of great impatience and excitement; her messages also contained detailed instructions on how intelligence work should be carried out and how a spy net should be made secure. All messages were to be enciphered in German for additional security. But above all now there was recognition of the work done. 'Remember that your work is of the utmost importance.'[34]

In the first phase of the war on the Eastern Front intelligence information did not have a great deal of importance, since when it had warned of the impending attack, it had been ignored, and when the Red Army was in panic-stricken retreat, it was of little use. However winter arrived early,

Stalin called in the crack divisions stationed in Siberia, the front stabilized and a positional war began, and it was then that the *Rote Kapelle*'s work became invaluable, particularly the information provided by the independent, but co-operative, Sándor Radó. Moscow received details of *OKW*'s strategic plans, of the movements of the Army and the Air Force, of their losses and monthly production of replacements, of a number of other German war plans, of the political situation and many other very important matters. All this information could originate only from the very heart of German decision-making or from some other magnificently informed source.

2 July 1941. To the director.
    The Germans currently have Operational Plan No. 1 in force. The target is Moscow. The operations that have been started on the flanks are merely diversionary manoeuvres. The accent is on the central sector of the front.

Dora[35]

2 July 1943. To the director. Urgent.
    From Olga (see page 115)
    German losses from the beginning of the war to May 1943: 1,947,000 fallen, 565,000 captured, 1,080,000 severely wounded. In addition some 180,000 dead and wounded lost by the auxiliary troops. According to the 30 May figures Germany has lost a total of 3,772,000 men including 2,044,000 dead.

Dora[36]

The speed with which all this intelligence reached Switzerland was amazing. A serious and well-informed Swiss researcher of these matters, Hans Rudolf Kurz, even states that in certain cases Swiss Intelligence received advance copies of very important orders from German headquarters before even its addressees. This view has been confirmed by the *Wehrmacht*'s former Chief of Staff, General Franz Halder. 'Almost every offensive operations of ours were betrayed to the enemy before they even appeared on my desk.'[37] They might have gone straight to Swiss Intelligence, into the hands of *Pakbo*, but above all to Rudolf Roessler.
    Both witnesses and historians believe that the information was sent by telephone, mail, courier and radio. Some people hold that it was sometimes sent through Italy or via the Maquis in France.[38] All of this was possible, since in addition to secret intelligence lines of communication, many legations were working openly in Switzerland and they could take advantage of every technical means of liaison, together with radio and the diplomatic mail.
    It is at this juncture, therefore, that we must ask a most important question: who was supplying all this information to Switzerland, where was he obtaining it and how was he sending it?

9

The *Rote Kapelle* was the most useful instrument in the hands of the Soviets, since it consisted both of communists and fanatical opponents of Nazism, who had become agents of foreign power, and it is towards it that we must first direct careful attention. It had great difficulties in maintaining regular radio contact with Moscow and thus was in close touch with Switzerland where Radó had three radio stations. *Rote Kapelle* information could travel there by four different means: to Radó from his own communist contacts inside Germany; to Pünter who had similar contacts; direct to Swiss Intelligence and finally to Roessler. He knew Schulze-Boysen personally, having met him once in Berlin, and some historians believe that it was precisely the *Rote Kapelle* which was the *Lucy Ring*'s main source of information.[39] It is possible to refute this argument without much difficulty, since in the early autumn of 1942 the *Red Orchestra* was destroyed and in December of the same year eleven of its principal members were executed, and yet it was just after that time that Roessler was at his most productive.[40] Furthermore the capabilities of this net were not too good; Schulze-Boysen certainly worked in the Air Ministry, where he was trusted, but he was only a lieutenant; Harnack was an adviser at the Economics Ministry, while others were located in various areas of the German war machine, but they were all a long way from *OKW* and Hitler's headquarters. Trepper's other feelers also tended to move on the fringes of the main centres of decision-making. Their information was certainly valuable, but comprised only a part of the overall intelligence picture, which had to be supplemented by material from other more important sources.[41]

Looking for these one must turn in the direction of the other group, which German security agencies called *Die Schwarze Kapelle*. It was quite a different matter. This secret group of senior officers and politicians which was aiming to overthrow Nazism with the help of the Western Allies and reach a compromise peace with them, really did have members in all the most sensitive areas of military and political decision-making. Information might have reached Switzerland from this group but with the important proviso that it was intended for France and Great Britain and, after the collapse of the Western Front, also for the United States. The members of the conspiracy, both Junkers and democratic politicians, could not want a Soviet victory; however, as time went on and Stalin became an ally of the West, this attitude might of necessity have had to change.

Rudolf Roessler was the man of confidence of this group, but is it possible to suggest that the most senior officers of the German Army, bound by an oath of loyalty to the *Führer* and for generations accustomed to discipline and the unquestioning execution of orders, could in time of war provide their enemies with the most sensitive of state secrets?[42] If we accept that there was no other way of overthrowing Nazism, with the exception of a swift and summary defeat, this eventuality cannot be rejected, but there is no proof for it. There is also no proof that Admiral Canaris, who had contacts in Switzerland, was thus sending information to the Western Allies in this way.[43] In the search for the truth and also to divert attention from the *Wehrmacht*'s senior officers, who in the eyes of many of their fellow countrymen would never have resorted to giving away their own secrets to their enemies, the name of Martin Bormann, the *Reichsleiter* of the National Socialist Party (*NSDAP*), has been mentioned. During the last years of the war he belonged to Hitler's daily and most intimate circle, he had access to every secret and theoretically could have handed them over to others.[44] Only Roessler could have shed any light on all these puzzles, but despite incessant questions from Moscow, which wanted to know the sources of his information, and also the great postwar pressure by historians, he maintained his silence and took his secret to the grave when he died in Lucerne in 1958. Under extensive questioning he revealed only that his informer in *OKW* was *Werther*. In addition to this his informers were meant to be: *Teddy* in *OKH*, *Stefan* and *Ferdinand* (or *Fernand*) in *Luftwaffe* headquarters, *Olga* in the Reserve Army Command, *Anna* in the Ministry of Foreign Affairs and *Bill* in the munitions division of the Army. Researchers of these matters and some participants cannot agree on an assessment of these sources, some believe that these codenames were only symbolic and made up by Roessler himself, who collected fragmentary information from various sources and turned it into reports, while others go so far as to identify the christian names and first letters of the surnames of five generals and five senior officers, who were these informers.[45] Ignoring this last suggestion which turned out to be a journalistic invention, it is necessary to point out that all historians agree that Roessler's intelligence was of the greatest value.[46] Moscow reiterated this in numerous messages.

10

However, the eventual sources of the information which reached Switzerland, destined for the Soviet Union, were not restricted to the two 'orchestras', both 'red' and 'black'. The great Western democracies were keenly interested in providing such information, in particular Great Britain, which for a year had had to withstand Hitler's might almost alone and for whom the Soviet Union, attacked by Germany, was a priceless ally absorbing the greater part of the enemy's forces and suffering the greatest losses. Since Great Britain and the United States had undertaken the massive task of providing the Soviet Union with every type of military equipment and supplies, it is hard not to suppose that they also undertook to provide intelligence. Ostensibly the easiest way would have been to send it through diplomatic channels and this is just what Churchill had done at first, warning the Russians of the impending German attack. But when he realized that Stalin was not believing him, he was forced to change his tactics. The Soviet dictator had eventually come to trust the reports of his own intelligence network, chiefly from Switzerland, and so it would then have been logical to take advantage of this, supplying as discreetly as possible information for Russia, while creating the impression that it had been obtained by Soviet Intelligence.

If we accept that this reasoning is logical, the word *Enigma* must immediately come to mind! In addition to traditional methods of obtaining secret information, this was the very source which during the last war enabled the Allies to read the Germans' most secret and most well-hidden orders, and it was as a result of this that all the German military and political secrets were discovered. Furthermore, *Enigma* with its extensive centre at Bletchley Park and its widely developed radio-monitoring network, guaranteed the speedy interception and onward transmission of the most significant daily information, which played an important part in the war effort and explained a number of incomprehensible questions. Sending such intelligence from Germany, leaving aside the great risk and the moral problem for those who were collecting it and then passing it on, required either a complicated system of couriers or else using the post, which could easily be discovered. Almost every historian agrees that a direct secret radio link between Germany and Switzerland was impossible, since the monitoring service of the security agencies would have quickly intercepted signals transmitted from Berlin or Hitler's headquarters in some unknown cipher.[47] Despite the enormous number of radio messages a trained ear would have recognized a different way of sending Morse. The legations of neutral countries could possibly have maintained such a radio link, but where would they have been able to obtain daily such important information?

All these difficulties disappear if we accept the idea that the information came from *Enigma* and that it was transmitted to Switzerland by means of some very trusted British Intelligence agents, who did not have to know the source of their reports.[48]

Apart from the actual problem of obtaining the information, the most difficult task was delivering it to the right people, without the Soviet agents in Switzerland being aware that it had all been prepared by British Intelligence. The most urgent materials could have been sent by radio to the British embassy in Bern, where an immediate decision had to be made as to their destination. Firstly it would have gone to Swiss Intelligence, which would have been a logical decision, since it was in touch with Bureau Ha, and, through Dr Baldegg, with Rudolf Roessler. He could easily have sent the information to Sándor Radó at any time with a note that some of it had come from *Werther*, some from *Olga* and the rest from *Bill* and so on. Such a discreet method would ensure that Moscow would not suspect that British 'disinformation' or 'provocation' was taking place. It would also explain how Roessler came to have the most secret German orders within twenty-four hours of their issue. His identity as head of the *Lucy Ring* was sufficiently mysterious for this solution to be regarded as quite credible. This is a new explanation of this problem, but it must be borne in mind that almost every historical book and collection of memoirs on Roessler, emphasizing his great achievements and mysteriousness, was written before the secret of *Enigma* was revealed. Hans Rudolf Kurz, author of an excellent book, *Nachrichten-zentrum Schweiz*, in which he discusses at some length Roessler and his sources, now that he knows that *Enigma* was broken and is aware of the existence of Bletchley Park, completely accepts the hypothesis that Roessler could have received at least part of his information from this source. He even goes further and believes that the whole *Lucy Ring* could have been subtly prepared and set up by British Intelligence.[49] After all, the British needed to know what was happening in the most secret German circles and before the war they did not yet know that *Enigma* would prove to be such a windfall, so they might well have worked to set up a spy network in Switzerland using a man with excellent contacts inside Germany. Up to the middle of 1942 Roessler was working primarily for Swiss Intelligence and also for the British.[50] Pursuing this line of argument Kurz also believes that Alexander Foote, the Englishman working for Radó, could have been a double agent and that, independently of his communist sympathies and ties, he could have been working for British Intelligence. He also might have been receiving material gained thanks to *Enigma* and passing them on to Radó.[51] Dr Xavier Schnieper, who had in the first place contacted Roessler together with Swiss Intelligence, also believes that through various intermediaries Roessler might also have been using *Enigma* information, although at present there is no proof of this.[52]

Another way in which British Intelligence might have sent the results of the work of Bletchley Park to Switzerland was through Otto Pünter's net, and more specifically through his French diplomatic contact *Salter*. He was in touch with the Intelligence Service through Portugal. Pünter also had his own people amongst General de Gaulle's supporters, in the Maquis and in diplomatic circles in Bern. He also had important links with President Roosevelt's envoy, Allen Dulles, who in October 1942 appeared in Switzerland, officially as a member of the embassy and thus covered by diplomatic immunity, but in fact as head of the OSS (Office of Strategic Services) for Western Europe, which was more or less an intelligence post.[53] All these contacts could have been used discreetly to send information which went immediately to Radó and Moscow. The more common points of contact there were, the greater were the chances that suspicion would not be aroused. Stalin did not trust the Western Allies, used his own values to judge them and looked for tricks in everything.

It would be possible to prove this hypothesis, connected with *Enigma*, if there was a way of confirming that Bletchley Park deciphered a German signal whose text corresponded exactly to that of a message sent by Radó to Moscow and quoted in his book. Unfortunately this is impossible, at least for the time being, since the last documents quoted by Radó are dated 13 October 1943, while the materials recently made available in the Public Record Office dealing with the German Army in the East, only start at November of the same year. Earlier documents deal only with naval operations and sometimes with the Air Force where naval operations are concerned.[54] Is this accidental? Very possibly, but one may also suggest that this coincidence, apparently only superficial, demonstrates that the theory linking *Enigma* with Soviet Intelligence in Switzerland is substantially correct. Perhaps someone believes that it is still too early to discuss these matters and is holding up these documents which could throw light on a number of questions.

The theory that British Intelligence supplied Rudolf Roessler with information is not a new one. Malcolm Muggeridge suggested it in an article in the *Observer Review* in 1967.[55] Muggeridge, who worked at Bletchley Park for a time during the war, made no mention of *Enigma*, which he could not do, since its existence had not yet been revealed by anyone and he was still bound by the Official Secrets Act.

However, another former Bletchley Park employee, Constantine Fitzgibbon, made the point quite openly in his book, *Secret Intelligence in the 20th Century*, which came out in 1976, and so after Winterbotham's revelations, in which he wrote:

> Since the Russians would not accept military intelligence from any but their own sources, Ultra and much else was 'fed' to the Russians via the 'Lucy Ring' and undoubtedly with the help of Swiss intelligence. It was supposed to come to Roessler through his Berlin General Staff and *Herenklub* contacts. . . . How aware Roessler was that he was a tool of British intelligence to the Russians is of minor importance. They believed him, they moved more Siberian divisions to the Volga, and they won the Battle of Stalingrad – just.[56]

This is a most convincing statement since it has been made by an historian who during the war was in personal contact with the problem of *Enigma* and who worked in Intelligence. Nevertheless, we shall have to wait for the eventual clarification of this secret. Only when all the Bletchley Park documents are made public will the whole truth about *Enigma* and the extent of its influence be open to examination.

NOTES

1. Höhne, pp. 43–5.
2. Ibid, pp. 40–8.
3. Ibid. Also: Schellenberg, p. 324.
4. Wilhelm von Schramm, *Verrat in Zweiten Weltkrieg*, pp. 41–2.
5. Ibid.
6. Höhne, pp. XIV–XXVIII, 47, 138, 163–4 and 298. Also: Schellenberg, pp. 325–6.
7. Ibid, pp. 119–20.
8. Ibid, p. 55.
9. Ibid, p. XV.
10. Anthony Cave Brown, *Bodyguard of Lies*, p. 149.
11. Royce, Zimmermann and Jacobsen, *20 Juli 1944*, pp. 13–23. Also: Fest, p. 559.
12. Fest, pp. 539–40. Also: Karl Heinz Wildhagen and others, *Erich Fellgiebel*, p. 273.
13. Ibid, p. 559.
14. Ibid, pp. 559–60.
15. André Brissaut, *Canaris*, pp. 112–17.
16. Brown, p. 148.
17. Sándor Radó, *Codename Dora*, pp. 8–12.
18. Ibid, p. 13. Also: Hans Rudolf Kurz, *Nachrichtenzentrum Schweiz*, p. 49.
19. Alexander Foote, *Handbook for Spies*, II-nd edition, p. 51. Also: Radó, pp. 34–5.
20. Kurz, pp. 49–54. Also: Radó, pp. 44–7. Also: Foote, pp. 24, 43–51 and 66.
21. Dr Xavier Schnieper, an interview recorded in Lucerne, 18 August 1977. There is wide dispute as to Roessler's political views. Kurz, op. cit., p. 31, believes that he was a communist. Dr Schnieper knew him very well and his opinion appears to be correct.
22. Otto Pünter, *Der Anschluss fand nicht statt*, Bern and Stuttgart, 1976, pp. 102–3. Also: Kurz, op. cit., pp. 29–31.
23. Kurz, op. cit., pp. 29–54. Also: Schramm, op. cit., pp. 19–28. Also: Schnieper, op. cit.
24. Pünter, op. cit., pp. 104–9. Also: Werner Rings, *Schweiz im Krieg, 1933–1945*, Zürich, 1974, pp. 351–2.
25. Pünter, letter to the author of 10 January 1978 and his book, op. cit., pp. 104–24. Also: Kurz, op. cit., pp. 54–8.
26. Kurz, an interview recorded in Bern, 22 September 1977.
27. Edgar Bonjour, *Geschichte der Schweizerischen Neutralität*, Basel and Stuttgart, 1970, p. 95. Also: Rings, op. cit., pp. 349–50. Also: Kurz, op. cit., pp. 213 and 42–4.
28. Alphons Matt, *Zwischen allen Fronten* (Der Zweite Weltkrieg aus der Sicht des Büros Ha), Frauenfeld and Stuttgart, 1969, pp. 9–19 and 191.
29. Rings, op. cit., p. 372.
30. Aleksander Bregman, *Najlepszy sojusznik Hitlera* (Hitler's Best Ally), 4th edition, London, 1974, pp. 117–21.
31. Barton Whaley, *Codeword Barbarossa*, Cambridge, Massachusetts and London, 1973, pp. 18–19.
32. Höhne, op. cit., p. 58.
33. Ibld, pp. 39 and 57.
34. Ibid, p. 59.
35. Radó, op. cit., p. 69.
36. Ibid, p. 199.
37. *Der Spiegel*, 16 January 1967. Also: Kurz, op. cit., pp. 19–20 (he states that a German courier officer made the secret mail available and that another officer in Hitler's HQ transmitted the information).
38. Kurz, p. 45.
39. Schramm, pp. 73 and 85.
40. Ibid, pp. 22, 102, 115 and 141. Also: Höhne, pp. 157–61 and 202–3.
41. Höhne, pp. 234–47.

42. Schramm, p. 18. Also: Bonjour, p. 97. Also: Foote, p. 79.
43. Brissant, pp. 318–19 and 324.
44. Schramm, p. 178.
45. Ibid, pp. 150–63. Also: Foote, pp. 77–8.
46. Pierre Accoce et Pierre Quet, *La Guerre a été en Suisse, 1939—1945*, p. 80. Also: Kurz, p. 113, footnote 28 (he states that the authors admitted that the names and initials were all fabricated).
47. Schramm, p. 73. Also: Schnieper, interview.
48. Winterbotham, Transcript, *The Secret War*, p. 12 (in his opinion the information from Bletchley Park helped the Russians considerably during the latter stages, just before Stalingrad).
49. Kurz, interview.
50. Bonjour, p. 98. Also: Kurz, pp. 82–3.
51. Kurz, interview.
52. Schnieper, interview.
53. Allen Dulles, *The Craft of Intelligence*, p. 4.
54. Public Record Office. For example some dispatches were selected: XL 4251–4500, dated 31 July 1944 and 2 August 1944.
55. *The Observer*, 1967.
56. Fitzgibbon, pp. 277–8. Also: Alfred Friendly, 'Confessions of a Code Breaker'.

8

Uncle Sam and the Mikado

1

EARLY ON THE MORNING OF 7 December 1941, the Japanese fleet launched a surprise attack on the American naval base at Pearl Harbor in Hawaii. Torpedo-carrying aircraft took off from their carriers and within a few minutes eight battleships: *Arizona, California, Maryland, Nevada, Oklahoma, Pennsylvania, Tennessee* and *West Virginia* were just a ball of fire. At the same time dive-bombers, escorted by fighters, attacked the airfields and almost all the American planes were destroyed on the ground.[1] Despite great damage, only two battleships, the *Arizona* and *Oklahoma*, were completely destroyed. The *Maryland, Pennsylvania* and *Tennessee* were fairly quickly repaired, while the *California, Nevada* and *West Virginia* also returned to active duty after extensive refits.

American society, which had until then been rather indifferent towards the more than two-year-old war and which had unwillingly supported President Roosevelt's attempts to help Britain, and later the Soviet Union, when they were attacked by Hitler, was shaken by this brutal and treacherous attack. Now the anger of a nation whose pride had been wounded within a few hours changed the whole situation, and the very next day the United States entered the war.

Anger towards the perfidious Japanese unleashed great forces within the United States, producing the will to mobilize rapidly, and urgently put the economy on a war footing. At the same time this anger turned against those authorities, both political and military, which had allowed such a catastrophe to happen. Where was American Intelligence while the Japanese fleet had been crossing the huge expanse of the Pacific and creeping up on the American base? How had the base command allowed itself to be surprised in this way? What form would this anger have taken if the American people had known the most closely guarded secret and realized that American experts had been reading the most confidential Japanese ciphers even before the attack, and that Japanese war plans were no secret to American Intelligence?[2]

121

2

During the First World War Japan had fought on the same side, but now the United States saw in her a rival in the Pacific, and a rival who was yearly growing in strength. Thus the Americans were interested in Japanese secret plans. American cryptology began to develop in 1917, after the United States' entry into the war, and in June of that year the Army Intelligence Cipher Office was formed with Herbert Yardley, a good cryptologist and an ambitious man, in charge. This office began to intercept signals and to struggle over deciphering them; an American 'black chamber' was set up and its first serious success was the breaking of the Japanese diplomatic code in 1920. This allowed the Americans to read Japanese messages between Tokyo and Washington the following year during the disarmament confer- ence, which was establishing amongst other things the parity of British, American and Japanese fleets in the Pacific.[3] The Japanese were then using relatively straightforward methods of encipherment and, despite constant progress in the field of cryptology, this state of affairs might have continued until the Second World War, were it not for the Americans themselves, who committed a serious indiscretion.

New ideas and new offices always bring with them misunderstandings, duplication of effort and friction among ambitious people. This occasion was no exception. In addition to the Cipher Office the Army started building its own Signal Intelligence Service run by the outstandingly talented cryptologist, William Friedman, who had been born in Kishinev in Romania (now in territory annexed by the Soviet Union). He was three years old when his family emigrated to the United States. In 1929 the Army Chief of Staff decided that the 'black chamber' should be incorporated into Radio Intelli- gence and the 'chamber's' head, Yardley, defending his independence, turned to the State Department. There he painted a colourful picture of his achievements over the previous years and demanded an increase in his budget, but he was met by a surprising rebuff. The new Secretary of State, Henry Stimson, who was poorly informed, knew nothing of the existence of the Cipher Office and was a naïvely idealistic man, declared that 'gentlemen do not read each other's mail'. This attitude caused the immediate with- drawal of the yearly subsidy of $40,000 which was synonymous with the abolition of the 'black chamber'. Yardley did receive an offer to lead the Signal Intelligence Service, but on a much lower salary; he refused and, finding himself in difficult material circumstances and very bitter, decided on a step which brought very considerable consequences. In 1931 he pub- lished in the *Saturday Evening Post* three extracts from his forthcoming book, the *American Black Chamber*.[4]

The publication of the most carefully guarded intelligence secret caused

Friedman to protest, and Congress passed a special act to withold publication of a further work, *Secrets of Japanese Diplomacy*, but the damage had already been done. The Japanese abandoned their technical achievements to date, withdrew nearly all their codes and started from the beginning again. The small American cryptological team was also forced to do almost the same thing.[5]

The Japanese language, using syllabic script and as many as five thousand symbols, was completely unsuited to modern ciphering, so the Japanese used the Latin alphabet. Pursuing this line and using foreign models, they became interested in German cryptological achievements and in 1934 bought a commercial version of *Enigma*.* Just as in Germany, it was the Navy which first accepted the machine into service, followed by the Foreign Ministry, the Army and a great many other important departments and ministries. By 1937 it had definitely been adopted.[6]

The Japanese were not satisfied with what they had, for although Nazi Germany had common interests with them, it was impossible for the two great powers to have the same cipher machine. After their experience with the Americans, the Japanese were determined to build a system which would be as different as possible from those used by their potential enemies. Japanese Intelligence succeeded in getting hold of some construction details of the American *Sigaba* (M–134–C), which had been built by Friedman and, like *Enigma*, was based on a system of rotors, the British *Typex* and Boris Hagelin's Swedish invention, which was already in use with the French and in which several other countries might have been interested. This machine which had five rotors and which, unlike *Enigma*, was able to print out deciphered signals, had a number of models. The B–21 model was bought by the Swedish Army in 1926, the French bought the C–36 in 1936 and the M–209 aroused great interest in the American Army. The Japanese knew about all this and introduced a large number of changes and new ideas into their machine. These concerned above all the plugs of which there were a great many and which were in a separate box. From this box an electrical connection led to another box containing the rotors. In addition to this, the machine used two electric typewriters: on the first one the signal was typed out in clear, while the second typed it out already enciphered, after it had gone through the boxes with the plugs and the rotors.[7] The Japanese called it *97-shiki-O-bun In-ji-ki*, which meant Alphabetical Typewriter 97. The figure '97' came from the Japanese calendar. The year in which this machine

---

*Masanori Tabata from Japan (see Bibliography) states that in 1942 Japan imported 50 *Enigma*s from Germany. Some minor changes were introduced to them, but the alphabet letters were left intact. Masanori is quoting a former officer of the Imperial Japanese Navy, Masaharu Yamamoto, who believes that these *Enigma*s were used by Japanese submarines to coordinate their operations with German U–boats. He rejects the idea that the Japanese ciphering machine was based on *Enigma*.

was developed, 1937, was 2597 in the Japanese calendar. The Americans for simplicity used the name *Purple*. The Japanese, like the Germans, who, in order to complicate the system, used nets with different keys, employed at least a hundred different codes to make their machine harder to break. *Otsu* was the Army's tactical code, *IC* was for intelligence agents, *Hato* the Foreign Ministry, *J* was for Europe-based diplomats and so on.[8]

The Japanese paid special attention to the Hagelin M–209 which had been bought by the American Army. Hagelin went to the United States in 1937 and 1939, but no agreement was signed then, since Friedman suggested a series of improvements. Only when war broke out in Europe did American interest revive and when the Germans attacked France, Hagelin managed at the last minute to get through to Italy by train via Berlin and catch the last ship sailing for New York. He was extremely fortunate, for in his suitcase he was carrying diagrams and two machines in parts. The deal was eventually signed and between 1942 and 1943 the Americans produced 140,000 M–209s, which were used from divisional to battalion level, that is to say for matters of secondary priority. The most secret signals were enciphered on the *Sigaba*.[9]

Japanese Intelligence* did what it could to discover details of the Hagelin machine, but without success; it was impossible to capture one in battle, since American and Japanese land forces only met face to face in the later stages of the war. The Japanese, therefore, went straight to the source and, through their embassy in Stockholm, bought up a few prototypes. This transaction was cloaked in the greatest secrecy, while the actual movement of the machines from Sweden to Japan was even more discreet and unexpected. With German connivance Japanese submarines sailed into the Baltic several times and secretly carried away the valuable cargoes.[10] Now it was not a case of looking for ways to further complicate their own machine, but of breaking American secrets so as to read their deadly enemy's signals.

3

The Americans, who were struggling with the complexities of *Purple*, were faced with the same difficulties which several years previously had beset the Polish, French and British cryptanalysts. Despite Japanese inventiveness

---

*In 1978 the United States National Archives in Washington received thirty thousand pages of documents from the National Security Agency. The documents show that during the last war Spanish diplomats spied for Japan in the United States. American code-breakers knew about the spy ring, but the Government allowed these operations to continue rather than disclose their own knowledge of secret enemy codes (Reuter, 11.9.78). *The Times*, London, 12.9.1978.

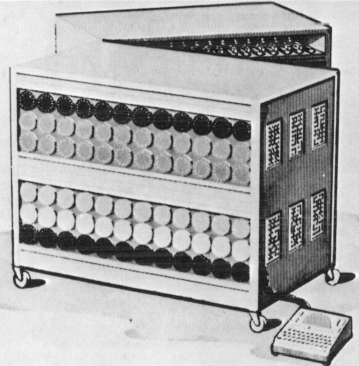

21 Two surviving huts at Bletchley Park
22 British *Bombe* (about six feet high)

23 German *Enigma* in its box

REF: CX/MSS/T266/67   XL 4708

ZZ

((XL 4708 £ 4708 SH 88 £ 88 SHA 34 £ 34 TA 22 £ 22
FU 26 £ 26 ON YK ZE EF 32 £ 32 ST 16 £ 16 DL 23 £
23 NX 21 £ 21 %

FLIVO TWO ONE PANZER DIVISION EARLY FOURTH.   ALLIED
PRESSURE STRONG)) IN MORNING CHECKED BY GERMAN
COUNTER MEASURES.   HEIGHTS THREE NOUGHT ONE, THREE
TWO ONE AND TWO NOUGHT FIVE (COMMENT TARE SEVEN
FOUR SIX FOUR NINE NOUGHT, SEVEN THREE EIGHT FOUR
EIGHT NINE, SEVEN T O ONE FOUR FIVE FOUR) ONCE
MORE IN GERMAN HANDS.   IN EVENING FRESH ALLIED
ATTACK WITH TANKS AND INFANTRY ON HEIGHT TWO HUNDRED,
TARE SEVEN ONE FOUR THREE.   HEIGHT IN ALLIED HANDS

CAZ/RFB/

EVB   0419542/8/44

24 A typical signal deciphered and sent from Bletchley Park, concerning the fighting in France after
the landings. *Top left:* the general reference number for Ultra material. *Top right:* reference number
for a hut where the decript was processed. *ZZ top centre:* the priority marking (from Z to *ZZZZZ*).
Below ZZ: the signs for the headquarters to which this signal was transmitted. Nine lines of signal.
Bottom left: the initials of the individuals concerned with the issuing of this signal. *Bottom right:* the
time of origin from Bletchley Park. The date of this particular signal is: 4 August 1944, at 19.54 hours.
£ is a shorthand symbol for 'repeat'

The Purple Machine

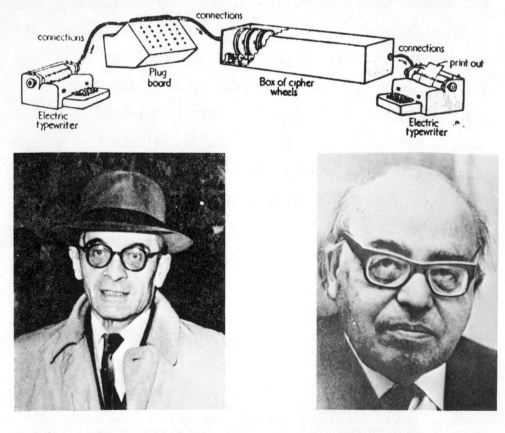

25 William F. Friedman   26 Boris Hagelin
27 The reconstruction of the *Purple* machine
28 Rudolf Roessler   29 Sándor Radó

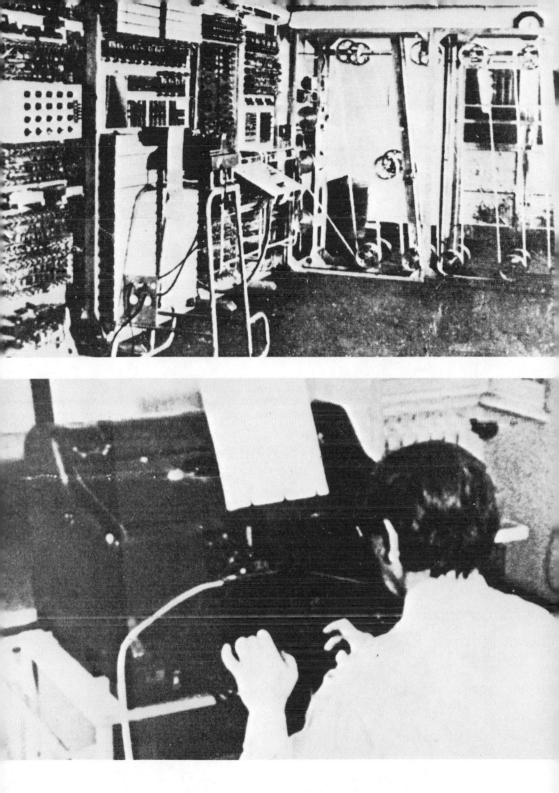

30 The Colossus at Bletchley Park in 1943
31 The *Geheimschreiber*

32 General Erich Fellgiebel
34 Colonel Claus Schenk von
   Stauffenberg
36 Captain Hans Hausamann

33 Admiral Wilhelm Canaris
35 Lieutenant Harro
   Schulze-Boysen
37 Otto Pünter

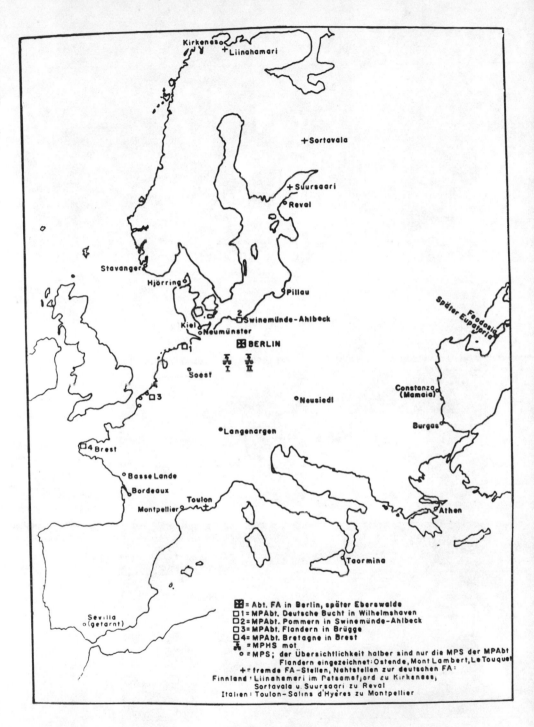

Kirkenes
Liinahamari

Sortavala

Suursaari
Reval

Stavanger
Hjörring
Pillau

Kiel
Neumünster
2 Swinemünde–Ahlbeck

BERLIN
I II

Später Eupatoria
Feodosia

1
Soest

3
Neusiedl

Constanza
(Mamaia)

Langenargen
Burgas

4 Brest

Basse Lande
Bordeaux
Toulon
Montpellier
Athen

Taormina

Sevilla
o(getarnt)

= Abt. FA in Berlin, später Eberswalde
1 = MPAbt. Deutsche Bucht in Wilhelmshaven
2 = MPAbt. Pommern in Swinemünde–Ahlbeck
3 = MPAbt. Flandern in Brügge
4 = MPAbt. Bretagne in Brest
= MPHS mot.
o = MPS; der Übersichtlichkeit halber sind nur die MPS der MPAbt
   Flandern eingezeichnet: Ostende, Mont Lambert, Le Touquet
+ = fremde FA–Stellen, Nahtstellen zur deutschen FA:
Finnland: Liinahamari im Petsamofjord zu Kirkenes,
   Sortavala u. Suursaari zu Reval
   Italien: Toulon–Salins d'Hyères zu Montpellier

38 German B-Stellen

39 Stalin, Churchill
and Roosevelt (Teheran,
30 November 1943,
Churchill's 69th
birthday)

40 Cipher Office in a
tent on Yalta airfield
during the conference

41 MC-570, modern
ciphering machine

and cunning, their cipher machine was based on the same essential principles as the German ones and, in order to break its secret, a similar method had to be used. What was needed above all was to intercept as many signals as possible enciphered with the same key. An examination of them produced similarities which formed a basis of common rules. At this juncture it is worth emphasizing that the Americans' difficulties were greater, since the Japanese were quite impenetrable when it came to the ability of foreign intelligence agencies to infiltrate them and the Americans were not fortunate enough to receive the sort of assistance that *Asché* had afforded the Poles by courtesy of the French (see Chapter 2, pp. 14–16). The commercial *Enigma* which Friedman had bought in Germany in 1929 was of some help, as was fragmentary intelligence out of Germany, but the lack of any further information forced them to rely almost entirely on mathematics, permutations and intuition.[11]

Fortunately American cryptology had in William Friedman a man at the height of his powers and a specialist endowed with an outstanding mind, exceptional stamina and fine intuition. It was mainly thanks to him that, after many months of uninterrupted work, many failures and disappointments and many false starts, the desired success eventually came. On 25 September 1940 the first Japanese signals enciphered on *Purple* were partially read.[12]

This was a great American achievement and there is no need to diminish it; however it is difficult not to raise the question whether those who earlier broke *Enigma* did not play some part here. This would have been perfectly logical.

Certainly no details of the Polish successes reached the United States, since it was not until July 1939 (see Chapter 3, pp. 41–5) that they were revealed even to Poland's natural and traditional allies, the French, and to the British who had become allies. Later, during the 'phoney war', there was no reason why the two great powers, Great Britain and France, preparing Hitler's downfall, should have shared such a great cryptological secret with the then neutral United States. The situation however changed when France fell and Great Britain found herself almost alone facing the savage might of the Germans. A great aerial battle began over the British Isles; every day the Battle of the Atlantic grew more intense; Hitler threatened an invasion and British eyes turned daily in the direction of the great Western democracy. Help could come only from that quarter and that was where it had to be sought. The United States could find itself in a war with Japan, which was allied to the Third *Reich*, and it was also interested in overthrowing Hitler and altering the European balance. Churchill saw this when dealing with Roosevelt for the sale of a good number of destroyers and saw the chance of obtaining war supplies and starting patrols in the north and west Atlantic. This help he did receive, but he had to have something to offer in exchange, in addition to bases in the West Indies, so as to bring the United States closer to the war. It would have been logical if in that difficult situation the British had made some of the secrets of Bletchley Park available to the Americans. No one there knew for certain just how far the American specialists had got in their efforts to break the Japanese ciphers, but Intelligence must have been aware that Tokyo had bought a number of *Enigmas* in Germany and that they probably formed the basis of the Japanese cipher machine. The British Empire extended to the Far East, its fleet operated in those waters, the defence of Singapore, Burma and Australia were of vital concern and Bletchley Park had a section working on Japanese ciphers.[13] Is it conceivable that in those circumstances there was no Anglo-American co-operation in the field of cryptanalysis? After all such co-operation had existed between Poland, France and Great Britain before the war even began, and had continued as long as the Western Front had held.

At the beginning of July 1940 Lord Lothian, the British Ambassador in Washington, met President Roosevelt and, on Churchill's instructions, informed him that Great Britain was prepared to make available some of her most closely guarded technological secrets to the United States. They dealt with radar, submarine detection and radio interception. Several days later the Ambassador wrote to the President asking whether he accepted such an exchange of information. This was the first step, followed by the departure for the United States of Sir Henry Tizard, who was a radar expert, but was also very well informed about other British secrets. This visit brought nearer the day when technological co-operation between the two countries would become reality. Both sides needed this badly and so, towards the end of November, an understanding was signed on the exchange of cryptological secrets.[14] This did not mean that earlier exchanges had not taken place. The Americans received everything on *Enigma* and the newest German nets and keys, while the British were promised one of the first *Purple* machines reconstructed in Washington. In mid-January 1941 two Navy and two Army officers arrived from the United States at Bletchley Park together with two *Purple*s and other equipment. This marked the start of some real and valuable work. Every day radio messages from Washington brought the keys of *Purple* to Bletchley Park. In the later months the British received other Japanese cipher machines (*Red* and *J–19*), and the Americans further details of *Enigma*. Thanks to this they were able to build their first primitive computer called *Madame X* based on the principle of the Polish *Bombes*.

The immediate future showed how important these contacts were. Co-operation between Bletchley Park and Washington increased greatly and began to produce valuable results. The enemy ceaselessly complicated his machines and changed the keys and the ciphers and there was a constant race between the two sides. The analysts could not relax for a moment, for new problems continually arose, but the exchange of information, materials and solutions[15] between the British and the Americans grew daily and enabled the establishment of a world-wide system.[16]

The British-American co-operation in circulating the results obtained by Bletchley Park was also very important. This was the work of *Ultra* directed by Squadron-Leader Winterbotham. From the moment the United States came into the war, it was necessary to train quickly a number of American officers to enable them to take over functions in the Special Liaison Units (SLU) (see Chapter 4, p. 55). They were usually recruited from among reserve officers, mainly lawyers, but also teachers, engineers, journalists and civil servants. Ernest L. Bell says that of twenty-eight American officers who worked for *Ultra* at one time in the European theatre of war, only two came from the regular army and had received full military training.[17] They were accepted subject to a very extensive investigation and were sent to Bletchley Park for special training. There not only was the secret of *Enigma* revealed to them, but they were taught to use the British cipher machine, *Typex* (used on the lower level), the basic principles of codes and ciphers, intelligence technique, type-writing and other practical matters. They also had a period of training with operational commands. They were all bound by the strictest security rules and sworn to complete secrecy, even in relation to their own superior officers. They were utilized to the full when the landing in North Africa took place, during the campaign in Italy and, naturally, at the time of the great operation of landing on the northern coast of France (see Chapter 8, pp. 130–1; Chapter 9, pp. 140–2; and Chapter 10, pp. 155–65).

4

Many months had passed since Bletchley Park had succeeded in deciphering its first German signal (see Chapter 4, p. 53). By 1942, in addition to the main building, there was a complex of several dozen small wooden huts, housing the cryptanalysts and other specialists who needed peace and quiet, and of several large barracks, each holding about a hundred people, such as translators, typists and other clerical staff. There were also canteens amongst the barracks and a number of low brick buildings.

Such a large number of people concentrated in a small area and working in rather primitive conditions could have produced a number of difficulties. Amongst the specialists there were quite a few outstanding minds with idiosyncratic tendencies who were used to praise and distinction, and now these men were supposed to blend into the background. Furthermore, the strictly enforced security rules imposed special discipline which forbade any conversation whatsoever on the work being carried out. The specialists from the various huts who already knew each other could meet in their spare time, but their conversation could cover everything with the exception of their absorbing daily problems. They needed some favourite pastime since the unusually intense concentration which their work demanded required breaks and periods of complete relaxation. The same applied to everyone working there, although their problem was different: they needed entertainment to kill the monotony and boredom of their work, which was often organized on a three-shift system. Short holidays were hardly adequate.[18]

The small town had little to offer and so they had to organize their own entertainments. Some of the analysts played chess and bridge, arranged dances and went skating in winter on the frozen pond, and in summer they played cricket matches, while others organized concerts, lectures and discussions; sometimes a cinema came round. But the atmosphere was not very congenial and led to quarrels which in different circumstances would never have occurred. However, the overall standard of the people working at Bletchley Park was high. Amidst the great mass of different naval, air force, American and British uniforms, sprinkled with civilians, amidst the great differences in intellect, temperament and habits and amidst the different nationalities (for as well as the Americans there were also Belgian and French wives of some of the Englishmen), amidst all these there was a general recognition of the fact that there was a war on and that, although housing and food were not of the best, life at the front would have been very much worse. They all also took the security rules seriously, not because they had signed the Secrets Act with its threat of serious consequences, but because of their personal sense of discipline which was stronger, since not enforced.[19]

The centre's expansion was caused by the increase in work facing the British cryptanalysts. For the first two years the war was fought only in Europe and North Africa, which did not mean that the only problems were caused by the German *Enigma* and its complexities. Its commercial predecessor had not only been available for a long time on the open market, but had even been offered to the armed forces of a number of countries (see Chapter 1, p. 9), and so some of them must have become interested in its capabilities. As well as the German forces, the Belgians, Bulgarians, Romanians, Spaniards, Swiss and Italians had bought it.[20] Belgium had been invaded by the Germans and her ciphers had ceased to have any significance, she was on the Allied side anyway, but the remaining countries either belonged to the allies of the Third *Reich* or were co-operating with it. This applied also to Switzerland, although her sympathies certainly lay with the Allies (see Chapter 7, pp. 106–7). The radio signals of these countries had to be intercepted and their ciphers broken in case they contained any interesting and important information. This particularly applied to Italian signals, since the Mediterranean Basin played an extremely important role in British strategic thinking.

Of all the thousands of people who worked at Bletchley Park the most important were the cryptanalysts. There were about fifty of them divided into small teams of ten to twelve people, located in specific huts and concentrating on a single or a few types of message. Some worked on German naval signals, others on *Luftwaffe*, Army, *Abwehr*, Japanese, Italian and others. For instance, hut No. 3 worked on *Luftwaffe* signals and dealt with *Ultra*; No. 6 worked on Army signals and others and housed the *Bombes* and later *Colossus*, when cryptanalysts had to deal with the problem of *Geheimschreiber* (see Chapter 9, pp. 146–7); No. 8 concentrated on naval signals, No. 12 dealt with *Abwehr*.[21]

Towards the end of 1942 there was a change of command at the centre. Commander Denniston, already exhausted and no longer young, was transferred to London and his place taken by Commander Edward Travis, a small, energetic man in his mid-forties. He was not a cryptologist, but he had worked in Signals in the Navy[22] and was well acquainted with some of the problems connected with his new appointment. His essential task was the organization and efficiency of the work as well as its speed. The vast area of operations, from Europe through Africa and Asia to the Pacific, all required Bletchley Park's assistance and everyone counted on it.

5

General Montgomery did not have much faith in the *Ultra* intelligence he received, although he knew its secret, since he belonged to the small group of people who had been informed about *Enigma*. Yet in the Mediterranean Basin a number of successes had been achieved as a result of deciphering German and Italian signals. Amongst these had been the naval battle of Cape Matapan in which Admiral Sir Andrew Cunningham had scattered the Italian fleet in March 1941, sinking three cruisers, *Fiume, Pola* and *Zara*, and damaging the battleship *Vittorio Veneto*, chasing it into ports out of which, with small exceptions, it did not venture until the end of the war. The same source had also provided information on General Erwin Rommel's Africa Korps, about its movements and its sea supply-routes which gave the British the chance to cut him off from his supplies and halt his offensive aimed at capturing Cairo.[23]

Montgomery knew all this and yet he continued to treat casually all the information which arrived secretly and urgently from London, rather as if he believed that the traditional methods of obtaining information on the enemy were more effective. It is possible that his ambition as a front-line commander was also involved, since in his opinion he should have been the only person to receive such information on his own theatre, whereas both Churchill and the General Staff in London received it, which was the cause of a quarrel later between Montgomery and Menzies.[24]

The other side was also not without information from a similar source, for Rommel's cryptanalysts were reading British Army technical despatches. Moreover, Berlin for a long time had been able to decrypt the reports sent to Washington by the American Military Attaché in Cairo, concerning the war in North Africa.[25]

It was possible to pretend to treat *Ultra* intelligence lightly, but in the situation which at the end of August 1942 was developing in the desert, it would have been madness to reject it. This Montgomery did not do, and used as much of *Ultra* as he could, but at briefings he pretended that it was his intuition which told him that Rommel would try to outflank the Eighth Army to the south, driving deep into the desert. Bletchley Park's priceless information allowed him to prepare a riposte to this German manoeuvre and to halt this dangerous attack whose aim had been to break through to the Suez Canal. At the end of October and the beginning of November and after careful preparation and achieving great superiority, Montgomery finally defeated Rommel, continuing to use information provided by the breaking of *Enigma*. This victory coincided with the Allied operation on a large scale, for on 8 November American and British divisions, under the command of General Dwight Eisenhower landed in Morocco and Algeria, which were still in French hands.

This complex operation, bearing the codename *Torch*, was given much assistance by Bletchley Park which read messages circulating between *Luftwaffe* Field Marshal Kesselring, the German Commander in Italy, and Hitler's General Headquarters. The landing required large-scale naval activities, since the divisions with their equipment had to be brought direct from Great Britain and the United States, and so it was extremely important to find out what the Germans knew about the attack. Admiral Dönitz, who was largely preoccupied with the battle in the Atlantic, could divert his submarines towards Gibraltar and within a dozen or so days could concentrate about fifty of them there. Fortunately, despite the fact that as early as October Kesselring had been uneasy and had cabled Hitler asking for reinforcements, it was really only the landing which produced any reaction. Bletchley Park also read a series of messages dealing with the movement of German divisions and Air Force units to Tunis.[26]

The very next day after the Allied landing in North Africa, Hitler gave the order for his divisions to move south and occupy the whole of France. There was nothing unusual in this, for the occupation of the African coast provided a springboard for an invasion of Europe from the south. This order was intercepted and read, which allowed London to react quickly in the matter of the French fleet in Toulon. The British contacted General de Gaulle with the view to convincing the French to join forces with the British fleet in the

Mediterranean, but the influence of Vichy was still so strong that they managed only to achieve a compromise: the French scuttled their own ships.[27]

In mid-January of the following year and taking advantage of the successful landing in Morocco, a conference between Churchill and Roosevelt took place in Casablanca, with the participation of many senior commanders and staff officers, which was to establish strategic military objectives for the whole year. During the ten days of discussions Churchill was kept constantly informed by *Ultra* about German plans; he used this information in his difficult discussions with the Americans, who were amazed by British efficiency, particularly in the field of intelligence.[28]

Unfortunately on the last day, during the press conference, Roosevelt, without Churchill's approval, stated that both leaders were prepared to continue the war until Germany, Italy and Japan surrendered unconditionally. It was difficult to repudiate the leader of the world's most powerful country, but it was not long before the fatal results of his statement made themselves evident. Hitler was in an unusually difficult situation after the defeats of Stalingrad and Alamein, *Die Schwarze Kapelle* had not for a long time been in such a favourable situation and just at the moment when the *Führer*'s authority might have been undermined and he might have been deprived of the support of the German nation, the concept of 'unconditional surrender' saved the situation for him. The Minister of Propaganda, Goebbels, launched the slogan 'total war' to the last soldier, for in any case the Germans would be at the mercy of their ruthless opponents, and the slogan caught on. The deft handling of the propaganda on secret weapons which might any day be introduced, was an excellent bonus.

An interesting intelligence detail is connected with this conference. The Germans found out that there was to be a meeting between the two leaders of the Western world and they desperately wanted to discover where it was to take place. There was always the chance of picking up some scraps of information and decisions, or even of a sudden attack and an attempt to kill their two most dangerous enemies. Intercepting radio signals, tapping Churchill's telephone conversation with Roosevelt[29] and using every other means of intelligence-collecting, they succeeded in establishing that the meeting would take place in Casablanca. This information was quite correct, but sophisticated intelligence minds could not believe that it could be so simple and decided that Casablanca must mean the White House in Washington.

6

The occupation of southern France also influenced the fate of the French,

Polish and Spanish cryptologists who were working there. After the collapse of the Western Front, Bertrand took them in two aircraft to Oran and later to Algiers where they stayed for several months. When the situation in unoccupied France, governed by Pétain, clarified itself and there arose opportunities for the partial rebuilding of the cryptology centre they were all brought by ship to Marseilles and quartered in the castle of les Fouzes near Uzès, not far from Nîmes. There were fifteen Poles, ten Frenchmen and seven Spaniards. Bertrand had French documents made for the foreigners and set up a Country Building Firm which provided adequate cover from the eyes of inquisitive German agents. Monitoring equipment was secretly brought in, as well as radio-transmitters and cipher machines, and everything was carefully hidden and work begun. The whole unit was given the codename *Cadix*, while the Polish team, which was still commanded by Lieutenant-Colonel Langer, received the name *Group 300*. They began to intercept and read German signals and they set up a secret radio link with Great Britain.[30]

Right at the very start of the secret centre's work it was apparent just how vital it was. Some of the deciphered German signals were being sent by locally based agents observing movements in French and North African ports and using portable transmitters to send information to Stuttgart. Since the terms of the armistice forbade this type of activity, the alerted French police carried out a raid in Marseilles and arrested a dozen or so agents, which was made easier by the fact that they all had suitcases of the same shape and colour. The centre was also able to provide assistance for various underground organizations which were operating in that area. A great many secret radio stations were there, maintaining contact with Britain and tracked by the Germans. Their monitoring centres were at Marseilles, Montpellier and Pau and they received information from the field by telegraph and not radio. The French Post Office workers, who were partly collaborating with the resistance, intercepted these calls and diverted them to their leaders, who were in secret contact with *Cadix*. The ciphers were simple and were read daily and so many German surprises were avoided. The Poles also broke the secret of the Swiss *Enigma*, based on the German commercial version, and read messages dealing with economic and military matters. The latter ones caused a great deal of difficulty, since they were enciphered in German, French and Italian, but on the other hand they had the convenient feature that on a given day all the signals were enciphered with the same key.[31]

The secret cryptanalytical centre operated for two years and only in October 1942 did it have to leave the castle in a hurry when the Germans were getting close. It had already earlier deciphered a number of signals which suggested that German detector units were on the trail of the *Cadix* radio station. Bertrand hoped to find a new site, but before he could do this the German divisions moved south. The cryptologists scattered to look for shelter, even in the Italian occupation zone. The Poles decided to go to Great Britain via Spain and Portugal, but Colonel Langer, together with three other members of his group, fell into German hands at the frontier and, unrecognized, spent the rest of the war in a prisoner-of-war camp. The two analysts Rejewski and Zygalski managed to cross the frontier and in January 1943 they found themselves on the Spanish side. The third one, Jerzy Różycki, was no longer alive, for he had gone down with his ship while crossing the Mediterranean from Algeria to France. Their freedom in Spain was short-lived, since within a few hours they were arrested by the police and spent several months in gaol. After this they were at liberty for a few months under the protection of the Polish Red Cross and by the summer were in Portugal. From there they travelled on a British destroyer to Gibraltar where, on 30 July, they boarded a plane to England.[32]

Cryptanalysts, and particularly good ones, continued to be badly needed, but there was no question of bringing Rejewski and Zygalski to Bletchley Park, which was the most secret place in Britain. For two years they had certainly been in unoccupied France, but nevertheless under German control, and when it was occupied they had gone into hiding, and later had spent several months in a Spanish gaol. The strict rules of security would have required the two specialists to be screened for many months and meanwhile they would have been quite inactive. After a short stay in the 'Patriotic School' (an institution under the auspices of Counter-Intelligence which screened everyone who during the war landed in the British Isles in suspicious circumstances), they were turned over to Polish military authorities.

Within a few days they were posted to Boxmoor near London, where a small cryptanalysis unit had been set up, which was attached to the signal battalion of the Polish General Staff, stationed in Stanmore, under the command of Staff Major Tadeusz Lisicki. The unit was in constant touch with the Intelligence Department of the Polish Staff and also Bletchley Park, which allocated the Polish experts a task. This was to read the German *Doppelwürfelverfahren* cipher, which was used by *SS* formations. Rejewski and Zygalski had already worked on it in France and had been breaking it, so the task was not too difficult. During the last years of the war this cipher assumed a certain importance, since *SS* units, which were responsible for security in Germany and the occupied countries, used it to report the results of Allied bombing and other details on the running of the war.[33]

The fate of the French and Spanish cryptanalysts is unclear, and Colonel Bertrand remained in France, where he was arrested in 1943 by the *Abwehr*, but managed to escape in very peculiar circumstances and in 1944 arrived in England. Having been in German hands he was a security risk and therefore not allowed to visit Bletchley Park.[34]

NOTES

1. Basil Collier, *The War in the Far East, 1941–1945*, London, 1969, pp. 120–3.
2. Clark, op. cit., pp. 128–31.
3. Ibid, pp. 25 and 90. Also: Kahn, op. cit., p. 5.
4. Ibid, pp. 82–9.
5. Ibid, p. 89 (he states that this took place in 1933).
6. Ibid, pp. 88 and 104. Also: Kahn, p. 6.
7. Norman, op. cit., p. 114 (there is a diagram of the Japanese machine).
8. Clark, op. cit., pp. 88 and 105.
9. Ibid, pp. 110–11. Also: Kahn, op. cit., pp. 426–7.
10. Stürzinger, an interview recorded on 22 September 1977 in Zug, Switzerland, where there is a cipher-machine factory and museum, Crypto AG, which was set up by Hagelin in 1952 (he was unable to establish it in Sweden because of excessive taxation).
11. Major P. W. Evans, aide to the American Military Attaché in Berlin, report on *Enigma* of 2 July 1931. Archives and Record Service, Washington, document No. 4131–B–2.
12. Clark, op. cit., pp. 105–8.
13. Mrs Ruth Thompson (she worked in Bletchley Park), an interview recorded in Oxford on 9 December 1977.
14. Clark, op. cit., pp. 115–21. Also: Kahn, op. cit., p. 486.
15. Ernest L. Bell, III, a letter to the author of 18 April 1978.
16. Clark, op. cit., p. 121.
17. Ernest L. Bell, *An Initial View of Ultra as an American Weapon*, New Hampshire, USA, 1977, pp. 22–3.
18. Mrs Thompson, op. cit.
19. Golombek, op. cit. (he states that the penalty for indiscretion was seven years' hard labour). Also: Mrs Thompson, op. cit.
20. J. Vanwelkenhuyzen, director *Centre de recherches et d'Etudes historiques de la seconde guerre mondiale*, Brussels, a letter to the author of 9 November 1977. Also: Brown, op. cit., p. 21. Also: Kurz, an interview, op. cit.
21. Golombek, op. cit. Also: Gordon Welchman, Transcript *The Secret War – Enigma,* Project No. 06246/2–36, 1976, p. 9. Also: Peter Calvocoressi, letter to the author, 17 February 1979.
22. Ibid. Also: Jones, op. cit., p. 62.
23. Winterbotham, op. cit., p. 98.
24. Ibid.
25. Beesly, op. cit., p. 66.
26. Ibid, pp. 149–50. Also: Winterbotham, op. cit., pp. 119–30.
27. Winterbotham, op. cit., p. 121.
28. Ibid, p. 126. Also: Brown, op. cit., p. 246.
29. Kahn, op. cit., pp. 555–6. Also: Deighton, op. cit., p. 122.
30. Rejewski, *Memoirs*, op. cit., pp. 73–81.
31. Ibid, pp. 75–92.
32. Ibid, pp. 92–5.
33. Ibid.
34. Bertrand, pp. 158–9 and 204–5. Also Renauld, p. 47.

The Slide Towards Victory

1

HENRY KAISER HAD MADE a fortune building bridges and dams and was well known to those who appreciated his great organizational abilities, but he had never yet turned his hand to shipbuilding. Although America had not yet come into the war, and the isolationists were arguing with the advocates of intervention, the slogan 'Ships for Britain' had already been coined.[1] President Roosevelt loved people who did things on a grand scale and so he received Kaiser when the latter approached him with an offer. It was clear what was in the industrialist's mind and so the President assembled a number of senior naval officers, led by the caustic and energetic Admiral Emory S. Land, who headed a committee to speed up the rapid shipbuilding programme. The sailors' faces mirrored their amazement as the President carefully listened to the explanations of this multi-millionaire, who was quite incomprehensible to the assembled experts. Instead of bows he said front, instead of stern, back, he mixed up his words and sometimes he just did not know the right terminology and supplemented his monologue with sweeping gestures. Nevertheless a clear picture of Kaiser's proposition emerged from this jumble of words, apparently unrelated figures and shrugs of the shoulder. He was offering to build ten thousand-ton merchant ships in record time on a production-line basis.

The specialists incredulously shook their heads, but the President accepted the suggestion and an amazing race against time began. Such high-speed methods could be used only for the simplest and slowest type of vessel and so British designs for a steamer, dating from 1879, were adopted and work was begun using a car production-line technique. Pre-fabricated parts were transported to the shipyard where they were joined together. Each ship had its own name, but they were all called 'Liberty Ships', EC2 (Emergency Cargo 2/large capacity). Construction of the first ship took six months, but later efficiency was improved to such an extent that by November 1942 it took barely four days and fifteen hours. The first of Kaiser's 'Liberty Ships' was launched in September 1941 and 2,700 of them were built before the end of the war at one and a half million dollars each. American shipyards expanded and the number of workers employed rose from one hundred thousand to seven hundred thousand, of which thirty per cent were women.[2]

This great effort to build merchant vessels played a very important role in the Battle of the Atlantic, which began on 3 September 1939 and ended on 8 May 1945. At the beginning of the war British tonnage involved was larger than that of the Americans, 8.3 million tons as compared with 6 million, but British needs and the distances involved were much greater and the losses very much more painful. Furthermore, the British had to import foodstuffs and raw materials about which the Americans did not have to worry at all. During 1942, despite the shipyards' great efforts, Great Britain's merchant fleet decreased by 1.4 million tons, while the size of the American fleet rose by 2.7 million and was still growing. Yet this increase was too small in comparison with the needs of the moment when the United States entered the war and had to supply Europe, sending massive supplies of goods and later armies and equipment across the Atlantic. In addition, the Americans had also to contend with the Pacific theatre where they were at war with the Japanese.[3]

The Germans were aware of the British and American efforts in the shipyards through their own intelligence, but failed fully to appreciate them and got their sums wrong. In May 1942 Admiral Dönitz claimed that during 1942 the Western Allies would build 8.2 million new tons and 10.4 the following year, but that these figures were almost certainly incorrect, since they came from Allied propaganda. In practice, he stated, the figure would be nearer 5 million in 1942 and so the level of Allied tonnage sunk monthly should be kept at 700,000 tons in order to gain the upper hand and win. The reality however was different: thanks to Henry Kaiser, monthly American production alone was greater than Allied losses. In 1942 the monthly excess was 700,000 tons and reached 1.5 million tons in 1943 and 2 million in 1944.[4]

2

Anglo-American supply lines across the Atlantic were under constant attack by German aircraft and surface vessels, whose success, however, was small, not exceeding 20 per cent of losses inflicted and so, as in the First World War, submarines bore the main brunt of the battle. In the first phase of the war the Germans had too few of them, but they very quickly increased production, stepped up the training of crews and in 1942 the number of vessels in the North Atlantic exceeded eighty.[5] Of these only half were always actually on station, while the rest were on the way to or from their bases. Although they could receive fuel and other supplies at sea from

1,700-ton submarine tankers called *Milch Cows*, no voyage lasted more than eight, or at most ten weeks. A return to base was essential for repairs and a general overhaul.

Admiralty Intelligence (OIC), supported by Bletchley Park, played a great part in Allied operations against enemy submarines. All the secret threads of this work were concentrated in the hands of Rodger Winn, a barrister by profession, who showed exceptional aptitude for his new work. He was in charge of a special section of the OIC, alled the Tracking Room, whose task was to collect every piece of information connected with the operations of enemy submarines.[6] The watchful eyes of agents observed them in their home ports, airmen photographed them from the air and Direction Finding Stations (D/F), located in Iceland, Newfoundland, along the American seaboard, Bermuda, Freetown, on Ascension Island and at Cape Town, intercepted as many signals as possible.[7] These were immediately sent off to Bletchley Park where work was started on deciphering them. Conventional intelligence could establish the exact number of operational vessels and even their location, but only a reading of their signals to and from their bases could provide information on their plans and knowledge of allied convoy activity.

The year 1942 began well for the Allies. Bletchley Park was reading German naval signals and there appeared to be signs of a decrease in the amount of merchant tonnage lost when, suddenly, on 1 February, they were given an unpleasant surprise. Intercepted signals began to arrive which just could not be broken and it turned out that the German Admiralty had introduced a new net, codenamed *Triton*, with new keys, for traffic with submarines on long-range operations off the coast of the United States, in the North Atlantic, off Africa and later off the west of Ireland (see Chapter 5, p. 78). This was not all. In 1941 the German Admiralty introduced a fourth rotor into all its submarines and after six months of preparation, at exactly the same time, February 1942, this rotor, called *Alpha*, started to be operational.[8]

Bletchley Park did everything it could to break the new German secret; they tried, at least partly, to establish U–boat operations by reading signals enciphered on different nets *(Hydra, Freya)* and Air Force messages. Meanwhile, losses in the Atlantic began to rise alarmingly. While in January 1942 the Germans sank less than 300,000 tons, the following month this figure leaped to 440,000, in March it was 562,000 and in May 652,000 tons. The German underwater pirates operated mainly off the American coast, for there it was much easier to plunder. The United States had only entered the war the previous December, was still unprepared and had no tactics for protecting its merchant vessels, nor methods of combating the underwater threat.[9]

The months passed, the end of 1942 was drawing near and the situation began to look serious. Although the United States and Canada had allocated their fleets to the protection of Atlantic convoys, and although the efficiency of conventional intelligence and air reconnaissance had improved, losses remained at the level of 500,000 tons monthly. Suddenly, in December, there was a breakthrough: the Bletchley Park analysts finally broke the secret of the *Triton* net and, what was much more important, the secret of the rotor *Alpha*. This had an immediate effect on the level of Allied losses. In December they fell to 300,000 tons and in January 1943 they were little more than 200,000. It appeared that the threat had been finally averted, when, quite unexpectedly, the figure again leapt up to 500,000 tons in March. The reason for this was the German Admiralty's introduction that month of another fourth rotor, called *Beta*, into all submarines which provided the cryptanalysts with a new headache. By an unfortunate coincidence Bletchley Park suffered a great loss about the same time: on 27 February Dillwyn Knox, who had been one of the most outstanding analysts and who had been working on German naval ciphers, particularly connected with U–boats, died. He had been ill with cancer for several years, had undergone two operations and for the last few months had been so weak that he had been unable to come into the centre and had worked lying in bed at home at Courn Wood.[10]

The analysts had just started to penetrate the new German secret when in July all submarines got another fourth rotor, called *Gamma*. All these 'Greek' rotors were used separately and always on the left side of the three operational rotors, the positions of which were constantly changed.[11]

The German Admiralty had high hopes of this new refinement and anticipated that its ciphers would now definitely be beyond the capabilities of the enemy, although it continued to hold the opinion that the secret of its machine could not be broken. After the sinking of the *Bismarck*, Grand Admiral Raeder's Chief of Staff, Admiral Kurt Fricke, set up a special commission, under the chairmanship of Captain Stummel, which was to decide whether or not the British had broken *Enigma*, and the enquiry came to the firm conclusion that this had not been the case. Nevertheless the Germans did introduce the fourth rotor, for they had to take into account the possibility of betrayal or the seizure by the enemy of a ship with the details of its *Enigma* keys intact. At that time the Germans also had a great deal of faith in their own *B. Dienst*, which was having its greatest successes. It had managed to break one of the British ciphers and had read transmissions dealing with convoys; it was also helped by being able to read signals of Allied air cover.[12] U–boat Command immediately exploited this exceptionally favourable achievement and deployed three 'Wolf Packs', *Raubgraf, Stürmer* and *Dränger*, numbering 38 submarines in the North Atlantic. Two great Allied convoys, SC.122 and HX.229, consisting of almost one hundred merchantmen, sailed calmly for Britain unaware of what awaited them and that while the Germans were reading their signals, Bletchley Park was unable to provide warning, since it was feverishly trying to solve the problem of the fourth rotor. Thus, in the second half of March, the North Atlantic was the scene of a tragedy in which 32 vessels, with a combined tonnage of 186,000 tons, were sunk. One destroyer was also lost from the escort, which, operating in the dark, was unable to sink a single U-boat and managed only to damage two. It was only after the engagement that a bomb from an aircraft struck one of the German raiders sending it to the bottom.[13]

Once again the situation appeared to be grave and yet it proved to be the Germans' last great success in the Northern Atlantic, rather like the return of an illness which, decisively beaten by the doctors and the body, strikes once more, but without any fatal consequences. The cryptanalysts' magnificent efforts led to a speedy solution of the problem of the new *Enigma M* and once again they began to read the U-boats' signals, although sometimes it took a week to decipher the more complicated ones. In addition to breaking the *Triton* net and the fourth rotor, Bletchley Park also unravelled the keys of the new *Thetis* net, which was introduced at the beginning of 1943 and which was used for sending signals to the U-boat training-school in the Baltic (see Chapter 5, p. 78). This allowed the British to follow every U-boat from the moment it left the shipyard, through its trials and training evolutions to its leaving the Baltic and setting off on its first voyage from a French or Norwegian port.[14]

Victory was still in the balance for a few more months, but May 1943 was a watershed. The Germans managed to sink more than 200,000 tons, but they lost 42 submarines in the process and never recovered. Although they continued to commission new vessels monthly, thus making good their losses, their crews were hastily trained and lacked combat experience, while the frequent sinkings sapped morale. These losses were in fact very high. While the first quarter of 1942 had seen the sinking of only 11 U-boats and the second, 10, the first quarter of 1943 saw the figure of 40, the second, 73, the third, 71 and the last, 53.[15] The results of Bletchley Park's work, in conjunction with increased convoy protection provided by the introduction of auxiliary aircraft carriers, which supplied air cover to the previously 'blind' spots, added to the equipping of the convoy escorts with new HF/DF and new 9-cm radar, finally decided the battle in the Allies' favour. On 24 May Admiral Dönitz, who now commanded the whole German fleet, issued the order to withdraw the U-boats from the North Atlantic convoy-routes. This difficult decision coincided with a personal tragedy for him: his two sons were among the dead submariners. Engagements at sea continued until the end of the war, but the vital battle for the sea-lanes had been won.[16]

3

In June 1943 Bletchley Park deciphered a signal from which it transpired that *Luftwaffe* Field Marshal Albert Kesselring, who had commanded the Second Air Fleet during the Battle of Britain and who was now German Commander-in-Chief in Italy, had his forward headquarters on Sicily. The British managed to establish that it was located in the San Dominico Hotel in Taormina at the top of a cliff which descended straight into the sea, and the RAF duly bombed it. One of the bombs hit the officers' mess killing many of those present; Kesselring survived because he was in Rome that day.[17]

This accurate bomb was a warning that soon the Allied attack on Italy would begin. This was to be the first operation of its kind and would involve landing on a coast which was also defended by the Germans, and so the Anglo-American High Command was taking it very seriously. After the landing on the tiny island of Pantelleria, everything pointed to an attack on Sicily, but an elaborate disinformation campaign had already been prepared to deceive the Germans and divert their attention. One operation of this campaign was called *Mincemeat*, but has gone down in history as *The Man Who Never Was*. A submarine sailed stealthily into the Spanish coast near Huelva and at high tide threw overboard the body of an officer holding tightly a briefcase of secret documents. These papers suggested that the Allies were apparently preparing an attack on Sicily, but that in reality they would strike at Greece and Sardinia. The *Abwehr* had an agent in Huelva and so the briefcase with the documents was rapidly despatched to Berlin.[18]

Meanwhile Bletchley Park was reading the exchange of signals between Kesselring and Hitler's headquarters, which provided information on the deployment of German and Italian forces on Sicily. The fact that these forces were reinforced by only one panzer division, the Hermann Göring, was perhaps proof that the attempt at disinformation had succeeded. However, on the other hand, it appeared also from the intercepted signals that the German Air Field Marshal was expecting an attack and that he believed it would be directed at Palermo in the northern part of the island. Nevertheless, he was not certain of this and so he grouped his forces mainly in the centre of Sicily so as to be able to commit them wherever the landing should take place. Allied cryptanalysts revealed this strategy, and so airborne landings were planned for the narrow mountain roads to cut off the panzer units from their objectives.[19]

The battle for the island which became a clear race between the British General Montgomery and the American General Patton, lasted barely more than a month starting on 10 July and finishing midway through August. The defenders were formally commanded by the Italian General Guzzoni, but in fact the brunt of the fighting was borne by the Germans who retreated in good order to the Italian mainland. Kesselring had obtained Hitler's permission for this by radio, which did not escape the attention of the British cryptanalysts.

The Western Allies believed that after the first successful landing on Italian soil, Mussolini's fascist régime would totter and fall, and that the Italians would withdraw from the war. This is in fact what happened: on 25 July the Fascist Grand Council passed a vote of no-confidence in the dictator, he was arrested the same day and the premiership was taken over by Marshal Pietro Badoglio, who immediately started secret negotiations with the Allies. On 3 September the Italians signed an act of capitulation, on the 8th it was made public and the following day the Allies landed on the Italian peninsula, near Salerno, to the south of Naples.[20]

The removal of the dictator, however, could not of itself mean the immediate end of fascism, which had ruled the country for over twenty years and which still retained some of its influence. The fall of fascism was also unacceptable to Hitler for whom the Italian capitulation frustrated his strategic plans, exposing his southern flank at a time when a critical situation was developing on the Eastern Front. Although he despised his Italian ally, he needed him for political propaganda purposes, and so he decided on a rescue. On the *Führer*'s orders, *SS* Colonel Otto Skorzeny carried out a daring raid on 12 September and rescued Mussolini from his heavily guarded place of exile on the Gran Sasso mountain and brought him to Germany and then to northern Italy. A provisional fascist republic was set up there and thanks only to the Germans survived until the spring of 1945.[21]

The Italians had capitulated, but the war continued, since Kesselring's divisions still faced the Allies, while the northern part of the country remained under the occupation of German troops commanded by Field Marshal Rommel, Kesselring received a clear order from Hitler to defend vigorously and retreat as slowly as possible, a task which he carried out magnificently. The advance through Italy went very slowly and the situation hardly changed when, on 13 October, Marshal Badoglio's government declared war on Germany. The fighting dragged on, the wet and windy Italian winter set in and tanks and guns drowned in the mud. It was impossible to open the road to Rome, which was blocked by the Monte Cassino outcrop, which was finally captured, after numerous attempts by other units, by the Polish Second Corps, under the command of General Władysaw Anders, on 18 May 1944. So the Allies launched a new offensive and in January 1944 landed their forces near Anzio, fifty kilometres to the south of Rome. This operation almost ended in disaster.

4

The capitulation by the Italians meant that there was no further need to intercept their signals and break their ciphers. The Germans, however, continued to be a most dangerous adversary despite the great burden of the Eastern Front and the continual Allied air offensive. In the second half of 1943 Bletchley Park was easily reading their signals, of which there were a great many since Kesselring was in constant communication with *OKW* by radio. Just as in the Sicily campaign, the Allies continued to know the German commander's every thought and plan and could adjust their strategy accordingly. The attack was launched at Salerno for the very reason that Kesselring was expecting it to the north of Naples from where the road to Rome was short and relatively easy. This brought certain tactical advantages, since the Germans were on the point of withdrawing, but these advantages did not last long. The local German commander, General Heinrich Vietinghoff, launched a counter-attack and the assaulting divisions found themselves in a difficult situation. The German Air Force also posed a serious threat and caused considerable losses to the Allied fleet which was supporting the landing. The new German guided bombs damaged the British battleship *Warspite*, the cruiser *Uganda*, as well as two American cruisers, the *Philadelphia* and *Savannah*, and they sank five supply ships, eight landing craft and one hospital ship[22].

All this was made possible by the Germans' own cryptanalytical successes in reading Allied signals. Their efficiency in this department was remarkable. Behind the front lines ran special trains in which cryptanalysts worked day and night on Allied ciphers and immediately sent the results through to their headquarters (see Chapter 5, pp. 69–70). The exceptionally difficult conditions at the front in no way hindered the scope of this work, nor weakened the resolve or the nerve of those doing it. It was this very efficiency which made the Allied landing at Salerno anything but a walkover. The American general, Mark Clark, was confident that he would achieve complete surprise, but things turned out quite differently. The Germans had intercepted and deciphered radio orders, had confirmed them by aerial reconnaissance, and then had prepared themselves and met the attackers with such a concentration of fire that the situation was only brought under control with the very greatest difficulty. The same thing happened again at Anzio, with an even worse result for the Allies in that progress only became possible after a number of weeks.

The winter battles were marked by serious losses on both sides without any clear territorial gains and only a few select people knew that, during these painful positional struggles, the greatest successes belonged to the cryptanalysts of both sides.

5

The war in the west was developing very favourably for the Allies: the important and even perhaps decisive Battle of the Atlantic had been won, North Africa had been cleared, Mussolini had been set aside and Italy been brought to its knees, while the air offensive was reducing German cities to rubble. In the east the Soviet ally, helped by massive deliveries of supplies, was pushing the Germans back and was obviously in a very strong position, so it was for that very reason that Anglo-American co-operation required immediate rationalization. Churchill and Roosevelt had already met several times, but so far these encounters had had a purely propaganda character (such as the occasion when the Atlantic Charter, which outlined in general terms their war aims and recognized the right of the occupied countries to independence, was signed by the two leaders on 11 August 1941 on board a British battleship), or had dealt with specific pressing military matters. Now, when the war was entering its decisive phase, all the most important political problems had to be resolved, dealing first of all with Europe, since President Roosevelt had agreed that this theatre of war should take priority.

In August 1943 two great delegations met in Quebec. Churchill sailed to the port of Halifax in Nova Scotia aboard the luxury liner *Queen Mary*, accompanied by a staff of 250 specialists. The British were surprised that the Americans, contrary to their usual practice, were also there in large numbers. It had been intended to hold a conference between two good friends fighting a common enemy, but the obstinate and serious faces on both sides showed that it would in fact be a difficult confrontation between two different views of Europe's and the world's future.[23]

And so it was. The United States, which for the second time had been obliged, because it felt its own security to be imperilled, to intervene in a war started by the European powers, now had much more far-reaching plans in mind. President Roosevelt made no secret of his view that the British Empire, acquired in the spirit of conquest, should now be dismantled, which meant the end of Britain's leading place in the world, but at the same time he envisaged a similar role for the United States.* His country's great economic strength and size gave him real ground for believing this to be possible. This assumption became the basis for strategic military plans and political solutions affecting the countries involved in the war. The British, although

---

*Knowing this, it would be, however, a mistake to go as far as the former Spanish diplomat and spy, Señor Angel Alcazar, who recently claimed in Madrid that the Americans closed their eyes to the Spanish spy ring in the States informing the Japanese about the positions of British ships in the Far East. Alcazar said that an American agent gave this information and that as a result of it the British battleship, *Prince of Wales*, was sunk in 1941 off the Malayan coast (Reuter). *The Daily Telegraph*, London, 23.9.1978.

islanders, had been historically tied to Europe, knew its problems and had always worked for the maintenance of a balance of power there; now they were worriedly looking at the might of the Soviet Union, which was also achieving great propaganda successes. The British wanted the Russians to defeat the Germans in the common cause, but wanted their influence and territorial gains to be limited. Roosevelt saw the matter quite differently: he wanted to finish the war in Europe as soon as possible and the balance of power there did not really interest him. He made the Poles, amongst others, various promises, but only so as to secure the millions of Polish votes in the coming US elections. Since the atom bomb continued to be in the experimental stage, he expected therefore a difficult campaign against the Japanese and laid much store on the co-operation of the Russians, for which he was prepared to pay out of other people's pockets. The European countries bordering the Soviet Union were to be sacrificed to this vision, and amongst them Poland, the West's earliest ally.

Churchill, realizing full well what would happen, envisaged an invasion of the Continent from the south in order to reach the heart of Europe before the Red Army; therefore, together with his staff of advisers, he fought for an expansion of southern operations, for a landing on the Italian peninsula, for landings in Greece and Yugoslavia, followed by a swift drive northwards. The Americans, however, came with a firm idea that the main invasion of the Continent must come from the British Isles towards France, and they had no intention of changing their minds. They wanted no conflict with Soviet Russia, while the ambition of a country moving towards first place in the world led them also to believe that only an American could command such an undertaking.[24]

This point of view, to which the British had to accede, produced the most extensive political consequences. Despite his deepest convictions, Churchill was forced to agree to decisions which divided Europe into spheres of influence. The Continent was split in two along a line which followed more or less the route of the 'iron curtain', and Soviet Russia was given the whole of Central and Eastern Europe and was allowed to enter Berlin first. These were astonishing decisions, which gave Stalin what he had only dreamt of in his most daring dreams. Yet he had not even been present at Quebec! Had he been there, he would have been unable to secure better conditions for Russia. In reality the conference had been a confrontation between two visions and two worlds; one slowly declining and the other elbowing its way into first place in the world arena. Churchill, the experienced politician, who had spent all his life fighting at conference tables, in parliament and at international meetings and who was a master of such gatherings, had never yet encountered such difficult negotiating conditions. Unfortunately, he achieved only secondary victories at Quebec and had to admit defeat on the most important matters.

Both leaders naturally had on their staff a number of discreetly disguised cryptologists, who were in constant touch with their headquarters and who were receiving all the most important information. Churchill was also accompanied by several officers of the *Ultra* Special Liaison Unit (SLU) to help him when things began to get difficult. This is what happened during the planning stages of the Italian campaign, which the Americans opposed, not wishing to commit large forces in the Mediterranean area so as to be able to launch the bulk of their divisions against France. Churchill was able to show them a signal containing information that the Germans were massing heavy forces with the intention of occupying northern Italy and Italian positions in the Balkans. This caused the Americans to reconsider and General Marshall recognized the wisdom of the British suggestions and the need for an attack on the Italian peninsula.[25]

At the time of this conference cryptological co-operation between Great Britain and the United States was in full swing; American specialists worked at Bletchley Park, Britons were in Washington and both sides had revealed a great many of their secrets to each other. However the discussions at Quebec were so difficult and important for the future divergent fortunes of both countries, that it is difficult to imagine that each country did not have its own secrets, which were carefully guarded solely for its own use. This must have included British monitoring of American signals and similar American activities. It would be extremely naïve to believe that one should not read the secret signals of one's ally, in the way that a husband and wife should not open mail addressed to one other. This sort of morality does not exist in politics; all means are acceptable when they achieve the desired result and so we must assume that both Churchill and Roosevelt were secretly aware of their fellow negotiator's secret communications.[26]

Reading these secret signals depended on having already broken each other's cipher machines: the American M–134–C, known as the *Sigaba* (see Chapter 8, p. 123) used by Roosevelt, and the British *Typex*. Both machines belonged to the most closely guarded state and military secrets, which were not even revealed to one's closest allies. Consequently British experts had not been allowed to examine the American machine and had responded in similar fashion, denying access to their own *Typex*, but only of the most complicated type, used on the highest level (see Chapter 8 p. 127). Nevertheless co-operation required the exchange of enciphered information and both machines were adapted accordingly. The *Sigaba* could encipher a signal which could then be read by the *Typex* and the same took place in reverse.[27] This certainly eased the task of breaking each other's ciphers, and the rest was accomplished by conventional intelligence-gathering and the efforts of analysts on both sides of the Atlantic.

Since the two Western Allies were reading each other's signals, it would be logical to assume that they were likewise reading the communications of their third partner: the Soviet Union. We must accept that efforts were made to do so, but there is no hard evidence that they were successful. It was certainly easier to break front-line communications, which by the very nature of things were enciphered in haste and so were less accurate and used simpler ciphers, but these would have been of interest to the Germans and not the Western Allies. The British and Americans were interested in political communications between Moscow and its embassies, but these were all enciphered using the one-time pad system, which was impossible to break.[28] It appears that the leaders of the Western powers had to be content with the results of conventional intelligence alone in the area of secret information on the Soviet Union.

On the other hand what of the problem of keeping the secret of Bletchley Park and the breaking of *Enigma* in relation to the Soviet Union? Did Moscow know of the British achievements? David Kahn in his well-known book, *The Codebreakers*, says categorically that in 1942 the Russians were already reading German despatches enciphered on *Enigma*, but he does not say how that came about.[29] Perhaps by way of *Die Rote Kapelle* to which belonged men who had access to German cryptological secrets; perhaps they were helped by Rudolf Roessler, thanks to his contacts. Another possibility must be considered: they could have been informed of this by their prominent agent, Kim Philby. His position in the Secret Intelligence Service (SIS) was so strong that he could have learnt the secret of *Enigma*. It is known that he tried his hardest to get into Bletchley Park, and he may have succeeded.[30]

This matter still requires much fuller and precise research.

6

Despite their deep conviction that *Enigma* was unbreakable, the methodical and well-organized Germans had another cipher machine, called the *Geheimschreiber* (secret-writing machine), which in the language of British analysts was known as *Fish*. It was in use only on the very highest level: Hitler directed that it be used for his overall strategic plans and orders to distant commands; the Ministry of Foreign Affairs employed it for maintaining contact with its embassies in neutral countries; the Navy used it for teleprinter messages. It was considered to be completely safe.[31]

Like the *Enigma* it resembled a typewriter, but was very much larger; it also had rotors, ten of them, but all rotating simultaneously. It had the great advantage that it automatically enciphered a signal typed on it in clear and sent it to the telegraph or radio stations, at the rate of sixty-two words a minute, without the need for a cipher clerk, which was one of *Enigma*'s great weaknesses. In order to receive the message a similar machine was needed, which automatically typed out the text at the end. It was in essence a teleprinter, based on the telegraph code of Baudot and Murray (see Appendix). This code contained thirty-two separate elements embracing twenty-six letters, ten numbers, punctuation, teleprinter functions, line feed, carriage return, letter spacing and letter and number shift. In order to fit all this into thirty-two elements, the code had to be used twice over: in a lower case for letters and in an upper one for numbers and puctuation. The keys were changed daily.[32]

The *Geheimschreiber* was in use from the beginning of the war and Bletchley Park worked on its ciphers, but it is difficult to establish when the British broke it. The first task was to reconstruct an identical machine and the easiest way to achieve that was to capture one from the enemy. This happened during the North African campaign when two such machines fell into the hands of the Eighth Army. At the same time, in the second half of 1942, the analysts managed to read some of the ciphers and thus succeeded in constructing a fair imitation of the German *Fish*, which was reasonably close to the original.[33] It is not impossible that a German mistake might have helped the experts, such as sending the same signal twice, enciphered once on *Enigma* and also on the *Geheimschreiber*.

However, knowing how the machine worked and reconstructing it was not enough. Every day it was essential to know what key setting was being used for the rotors, whose combinations reached into billions. There arose the need for an additional machine, similar to the Polish *Bombes* and its newer, more refined relation, the *Oriental Goddess*, used for the solution of *Enigma* keys.

7

The earliest ideas of building an artificial brain, which would work faster than the human brain, were born in the nineteenth century, but it was only in 1936 that Alan Turing presented a paper in which he suggested practical means for realizing this dream.[34] There was no great hurry at first to put his thoughts into action, but war, which always speeds up such things, came and now, while the British experts were agonizing over the *Geheimschreiber* and looking for some way of reading its ciphers and keys very much faster, they turned to Turing's ideas. This work was taken up by Professor Max Newman, a Cambridge mathematician, who was recruited to Bletchley Park in September 1942 and who built up around himself in hut F a team of experts. These included: Alan Turing himself, Gordon Welchman, Dr Jack Good, Donald Michie, Dr Wynn-Williams, T. H. Flowers and others. Several of these men had come from the British Post Office Research Station at Dollis

Hill, and so they set about constructing a working model which had already been extensively analysed in the cryptology centre. They developed a machine which looked like an eight-foot high cupboard, used electronic principles for the first time and was based on a statistical system of breaking codes and was capable of scanning two thousand telegraphic symbols a second. It was assembled at Bletchley Park in April 1943 and the girls working on it dubbed it 'Heath Robinson' (after the famous satirical cartoonist who drew weird machines).[35]

The machine began to operate and even achieved some results, but these were very far from what had been expected. It heated up very quickly and smoke would pour from it; the tapes with numbers and letters kept breaking and had to be stuck together again and, anyway, it was too slow to be of much use. The model was unsuccessful, but in one respect it did carry out its task: it showed that the statistical method was the right one and that on the basis of it future attempts should be made to create something new and really worthwhile.[36]

In January 1943 Professor Newman, who was still leading the discussions and analysis in the group he had himself set up, selected from it T. H. Flowers and his colleague from the Post Office Research Station, S. W. Broadhurst, and together they set about improving the 'Heath Robinson'. This produced no results, so Flowers proposed that they design something quite different. Newman took to the idea enthusiastically and began to design the new machine, while Flowers was to develop it in his workshop.

The 'Heath Robinson' already used electronics and electric valves, which worked like mechanical switches but were very much faster. The trouble was that they kept breaking down, but by experimenting Flowers came to the conclusion that they were reliable if left on all the time and not continually switched on and off.

Since they were planning to construct a machine which would speed up greatly the reading of the *Geheimschreiber*'s keys and ciphers, they had to keep to its specifications and thus the new model also had ten rotors. In the British version these had to rotate very much faster so as to go through the limitless number of combinations and provide an answer in time. Each of these rotors had its own tape with a key, and each one had to be read in conjunction with the tape which contained the enciphered message. This model contained the huge number of 1,500 valves (the 'Heath Robinson' had only 80) and was capable of reading five thousand symbols per second. They started building it in February 1943 at the Post Office workshop at Dollis Hill and in December the completed machine was installed at Bletchley Park.[37]

This was the first electric computer, the first electric statistical brain containing a memory and which did not make mistakes. It was named *Colossus Mark I* and forthwith it was put into service and began producing results. The Germans' most complex cipher machine was now no longer a secret.

Similarly to *Enigma* the *Geheimschreiber* was constantly being improved and during the war there appeared five versions (models 52AB, 52C and others). One of the modifications consisted of some of the rotors rotating irregularly, retaining their 'eccentricity'. This required changes in the Mark I *Colossus* and so in the first half of 1944 the Mark II model appeared, which made allowances for all the changes in the German *Fish*. It had 2,500 valves and, thanks to five parallel means of reading texts, it could pick up 25,000 symbols per second. This was an astonishing speed, which for many years was not bettered even by the vastly more precise post-war computers. The new model was hastily installed in Bletchley Park, for the invasion of the Continent was approaching. On 1 June 1944 it was already in use.[38]

8

However, it was not enough for the Germans to have just *Enigma* and the *Geheimschreiber*. The experts, who were continually trying to develop better machines and add further refinements to existing ones, now turned their attention to a new invention, called the *C–41*. The story behind this cipher machine is interesting and sufficiently typical to be worth describing.

During the thirties the French had approached Boris Hagelin in Sweden with a proposition to design for them a small mechanical cipher machine, which would fit into the pocket of a uniform. Within a short time the machine was ready, was given the name *C–35* and the French Government accepted and started producing it. Production began just before the outbreak of the war and the finished design was called the *C 36*. The Swedes had earlier offered it to the Germans, who had turned it down, since their experts believed that in practice it would be worthless.[39]

Later Hagelin interested the Americans in his invention, convinced them, carried out a number of modifications at their request and sold them the machine, which became known as the *M–209* (see Chapter 8, pp. 123–4). Mass production began, 140,000 were made and used at lower-command levels.

In 1941 the Germans managed to obtain a few of these machines and began to redesign them to be something quite different and impossible to break. This was a slow process and it was only in 1944 that they succeeded in producing a prototype and built six hundred machines. They called it the *C–41*, since it was in 1941 that they had captured a model for the first time and started work on it. The *C–41* was an excellent machine, also based on the principle of rotating drums, printing out the text in clear by itself after deciphering it and very difficult to break. Who knows how the cryptology battle would have turned out if the Germans had accepted the Swedes' proposition before the war and had had the *C–41* from the first war years. It is also worth mentioning that Hägelin himself received one of the German-developed models from Norwegian resistance, which had somehow managed to capture one from the occupying force.[40]

9

Joseph Stalin never left the Soviet Union for fear of an attempt on his life, but now the time had come when he had to decide on such an undertaking. It was true that the Quebec conference had granted him everything that he demanded and desired, but the conference's results were still secret: the world did not yet know of them, and furthermore these decisions had been taken by the two Western leaders and they could still change their minds. The Soviet dictator, himself a shrewd and cunning politician, trusted no one and preferred to have these questions officially settled, and so he aimed at joint decisions which would give him everything in his expansionist plans. The need for an international conference with Churchill and Roosevelt was becoming essential and it had to be organized somewhere. The recent Russian victories, in particular the great tank battle at Kursk, had strengthened his position, but not so much that he could suggest a meeting on Russian soil, and his whole nature rebelled at the thought of staying in a country which was not under his control. After sounding out and discovering the views of the Western leaders, it was suggested that the meeting might be held in the Persian capital, Teheran. The city lay near the Soviet frontier and Moscow's influence there was strong and visible, for Soviet soldiers could move around without hindrance. Naturally the conference was to take place in the Soviet embassy, which was surrounded by barbed wire and mines and guarded by numerous uniformed and plain-clothes NKVD men. It later turned out that they had been everywhere, even in the British delegation's living-quarters.[41]

From the very beginning of the talks, on 28 November, it became clear that the tactic of both Roosevelt and Stalin was to force their own point of view, leaving Churchill on one side. On the pretext that German agents under the command of *SS-Brigadeführer* Otto Skorzeny were preparing an attempt on the President's life, Stalin persuaded Roosevelt to move to a villa in the grounds of the Soviet embassy. As a result the Soviet leader was immediately able to have his first conversation with Roosevelt alone and prepare the ground for subsequent decisions.[42] Roosevelt, although the youngest of the three leaders (Churchill was just turning 69, Stalin was 64, while Roosevelt was 61), was exhausted by illness and the long tenure of his demanding position as President of the United States and it was perhaps for that reason that he behaved so naïvely and settled some of the world's problems in such a hurry. In Churchill he had a loyal ally and a man with a Western way of thinking, but he preferred to charm the Soviet dictator with the dying embers of his personality and easily swallow the pills of his discreet flattery, for which many countries had to pay with their independence and millions of people had to suffer humiliation and misery.

The conference lasted four days, but one was enough in which to settle Stalin's demands. In Europe he was given Poland, Romania, Bulgaria, Hungary, Austria, the Baltic states and part of Yugoslavia, he was promised the Japanese Kurile Islands, and he was to be permitted to incorporate half of East Prussia into his empire. In exchange for all this he promised that Soviet Russia would enter the war against Japan after helping to defeat Hitler.[43]

The remaining three days were devoted to military matters and further war plans. Churchill, solitary and powerless, tried to fight for an Italian front and for landing in the Balkans, but Stalin, supported by Roosevelt, was firmly opposed to these ideas. It was decided that the Italian offensive would not advance beyond the Gothic Line (from Pisa to Rimini) and that all available forces should be concentrated for an attack on north-west France (*Overlord*), which was to take place not later than May of the following year and that it was to be supported by a landing in the south of France (*Anvil*).[44]

During the conference, which for Churchill and the war aims of the British Empire came too late, the British Prime Minister continually used *Ultra* information, but the situation at the conference table cancelled out the value and effect of even the most secret and important information.[45] There was no strength left to use it. Roosevelt was likewise well supplied with information on the progress of the war, particularly in the Far East, thanks to the breaking of *Purple*, but it did not affect the direction of his thinking nor did it slow down his erroneous decisions.

German Intelligence found out about the conference and tried hard to obtain information about its course and decisions. Monitoring stations picked up every signal in the hope that they might be read and reveal the necessary information, but this met with no success. Instead it was, surprisingly, conventional intelligence which supplied the details.

In October 1943 the German embassy in Ankara, where the ambassador was Franz von Papen, was approached by a man claiming to be the butler of the British ambassador, Sir Hugh Knatchbull-Hughessen. This man offered to provide photographs of top-secret British documents for £20,000. For those days that was a great deal of money, but after some enquiries on the unknown man (who was of Albanian origin, was named Elyesa Bazna and who really was the Ambassador's butler), and after receiving permission from the minister and the highest security agencies, the Germans decided to accept the offer. The results surpassed all their hopes. The photographed documents contained embassy correspondence with London, the Ambassador's hand-written notes on British relations with Russia and Turkey, details of Lend-Lease aid for Russia, a reference to Operation *Overlord*, a Foreign Office report on a Foreign Ministers' conference in Moscow in October 1943 and a report of the Teheran Conference containing the Allies' political and military decisions.[46]

Von Papen immediately sent a message to Ribbentrop followed by a courier with the film, Hitler was kept informed of everything, since the documents could be the basis of important decisions, and Walter Schellenberg of the security office took control of the other aspects of the whole operation. He made contact with General Fritz Thiele, who amongst other things was head of the Cipher Office (see Chapter 5, pp. 68–9), and showed him a copy of the photographed documents. They contained a number of important details, first among which were the Ambassador's own comments written on the margin of various documents, which could help in breaking the British diplomatic code. The most important matters were enciphered using the one-time pad system, but longer texts were enciphered by more orthodox methods and these had to be tackled immediately. The German experts got down to the task and within a few weeks had achieved a partial success.[47]

The documents provided by the Albanian, who was given the codename *Cicero*, were so vital and had been so easily obtained that the Germans suspected a British trick. In fact the butler had obtained the Ambassador's own set of safe keys and during the night had opened the fire-proof safe and photographed the documents with an ordinary Leica camera. Eventually, despite the intelligence's great value, it was not used nor were German war plans altered. Hitler, when he was told about the information and discovered his enemies' political and military plans, saw fit only to continue the total war and destroy his adversaries completely, although he no longer had the forces to achieve this. The rest of the intelligence was lost in intrigues between the security office and the Ministry of Foreign Affairs.[48] *Cicero*, whose motives were never established, also came out badly from the affair, since the Germans paid him in counterfeit five-pound notes, which had been produced in the concentration camp at Sachsenhausen.[49]

NOTES

1. Costello and Hughes, op. cit., p. 171.
2. Ibid, pp. 217–18.
3. Calvocoressi and Wint, op. cit., pp. 441–2.
4. Costello and Hughes, op. cit., p. 218.

5. Ibid, p. 201.
6. Beesly, op. cit., pp. 20–1.
7. Ibid, p. 111.
8. Rohwer, diagram, op. cit. Also: his letter to the author, 22 February 1979.
9. Costello and Hughes, op. cit., pp. 194 and 305.
10. Fitzgerald, op. cit., pp. 254–6. Also: Rohwer, letter to the author, 22 February 1979. Also: Meckel, letter to the author, 22 July 1978.
11. Rohwer, letter to the author, 22 February 1979.
12. Jürgen Rohwer, *The Critical Convoy: Battles of March 1943*, London, 1977, p. 195. Also: Beesly, op. cit., pp. 160 and 177. He states that during twenty days in March 1943 the German *B. Dienst* succeeded in reading 175 signals sent by the Allies to the Atlantic convoys. Fortunately, the Germans used only 10 of these operationally. Also: J. W. M. Chapman, a letter to T. Lisicki, 28 April 1978. He states that U–boat commanders and their radio officers received new codes each week which they had to remember and which thus could not fall into enemy hands in document form.
13. Rohwer, *The Critical Convoy . . .*, op. cit., pp. 186 and 228. Also: Beesly, op. cit., p. 177.
14. Beesly, op. cit., p. 112.
15. Costello and Hughes, op. cit., p. 305.
16. Rohwer, *The Critical Convoy . . .*, op. cit., p. 188. Also: Beesly, op. cit., p. 173. Also: Brown, op. cit., p. 259.
17. Winterbotham, op. cit., str. 133.
18. Calvocoressi and Wint, op. cit., p. 375. Also: Brown, op. cit., pp. 282–4.
19. Winterbotham, op. cit., pp. 133–4.
20. Calvocoressi and Wint, op. cit., pp. 378–9.
21. Ibid, p. 382.
22. Brown, op. cit., p. 298.
23. Ibid, p. 292.
24. R. W. Thompson, *Generalissimo Churchill*, London, 1973, pp. 232–3. Also: Brown, op. cit., p. 294.
25. Brown, op. cit., pp. 295–6.
26. Brian Johnson, author of *The Secret War,* an interview in London, 2 June 1978.
27. Clark, op. cit., pp. 152–3.
28. Kahn, op. cit., pp. 650 and 662.
29. Ibid, p. 649.
30. Patrick Seale and Maureen McConville, *Philby: the Long Road to Moscow*, London, 1973, pp. 143 and 145.
31. Hans Meckel, a letter to the author, 22 July 1978. Also: Johnson, op. cit., pp. 338–9.
32. Johnson, op. cit., p. 339. Also: Rohwer, an interview in London, 7 July 1978.
33. Ibid, pp. 342–3.
34. Randell, op. cit., p. 1.
35. Ibid, pp. 14–18.
36. Dr Jack Good, Post-production script of *The Secret War* (producer Brian Johnson), Proj. No. 06246/2036, 1977, pp. 18–20.
37. Randell, op. cit., pp. 19–22. Also: Johnson, op. cit., pp. 343–5.
38. Ibid, pp. 23–7. Also: Johnson, op. cit., pp. 346–7.
39. Stürzinger, an interview in London, 23 July 1977 and 28 July 1977.
40. Ibid.
41. Joan Bright Astley, *The Inner Circle*, London, 1973, p. 123.
42. Brown, op. cit., p. 384. Also: Astley, op. cit., p. 121.
43. Calvocoressi and Wint, op. cit., p. 345.
44. Calvocoressi and Wint, op. cit., p. 347. Also: Brown, op. cit., pp. 385–7.
45. Winterbotham, op. cit., p. 141.
46. Schellenberg, op. cit., pp. 388–90. Also: R. A. Haldane, *The Hidden World*, London, 1976, p. 116.

47. Ibid, p. 390.
48. Ibid, pp. 394–7. Also: Haldane, op. cit., pp. 116–17.
49. Recounted to the author on 16 June 1978 in London by Józef Pawlica, a former inmate of the camp and a printer by profession.

10

The Finest Hours

1

FIELD MARSHAL ERWIN ROMMEL stood on a headland jutting out from the French coast and examined the horizon through a pair of high-powered binoculars. Four years earlier, on almost the same spot, another German marshal, Hermann Göring, had stood surrounded by his staff and had also looked at the British coastline through powerful glasses, and yet how much had changed since then. In 1940 the watching German's heart had filled with boundless joy and in his mind he could see the magnificent vision of thousands of German aircraft circling over the conquered British countryside and thousands of tanks breaking down every obstacle. And now? The wonderful moments of victory had long passed; in the east the front had been pushed back onto Polish soil; in the south the Allies had established themselves on the Italian peninsula, while Germany's recent ally there had declared war on her; in the Far East the Americans were capturing island after island from the Japanese; and here, at the western end of Europe, Allied superiority in the air and the concentration of troops on the other side of the Channel were so great that a decisive move could be expected any day. Erwin Rommel was a fine, brave soldier with many victories to his credit, and yet he was fearful and his thoughts revolved stubbornly around a single endlessly repeated question: when and where would they attack?

This was a problem which absorbed the mind of the Field Marshal as a soldier, but Rommel, in addition to the sense of discipline and duty appropriate to his high rank, also felt himself to be a citizen responsible for the fortunes of his country. His great popularity, which had been gained during the North African campaign, had given him a position which could also be useful politically if the right situation were to arise. Rommel, like many other reasonable Germans, realized that the war was already lost and he believed that some agreement must be reached with the Western Allies, even at the expense of great concessions, and that together with them some stand might have to be made against the menace approaching from the east. He was a soldier with a strong sense of duty and he would have preferred to have received Hitler's blessing for such a move, but when he realized that that was quite impossible and when, moreover, an inspection of the 'Atlantic

Wall' further disillusioned him, he decided that action must be taken, even contrary to the *Führer*'s will. Thus at the beginning of 1944, through his military friendships, he made very cautious contact with *Die Schwarze Kapelle*. General Karl-Heinrich Stülpnagel, the military governor of France, acted as intermediary.[1]

Contact with the conspirators placed Rommel in an exceptionally difficult position. On the one hand as a soldier and commander he was prepared to do everything to push back the invaders into the sea, on the other hand deep within himself he did not believe in the possibility of victory and, in secret contact with *Die Schwarze Kapelle*, he preferred to see attempts made to secure a ceasefire in the west.

While these problems, which were certainly a reflection of the mood of many other highly placed German military and political leaders, were tormenting the Marshal, on the other side of the Channel Allied minds were working on the plans for an attack on western Europe. Fortunately, no one was experiencing Erwin Rommel's agony, but there was far from full harmony over the strategic plans. Despite the American-imposed decisions of the Quebec conference and their confirmation, with Stalin's support, at Teheran, Churchill had not abandoned his views and continued to try to change the course of events. His vision of post-war Europe urged him to fight for a decision to attack in the Balkans and when this plan was definitely abandoned at Stalin's insistence, he returned to operation *Jupiter,* prepared as early as 1942, which envisaged an attack on Norway.[2] He was motivated by a fear that Soviet Russia, as well as sweeping up central Europe, would also want to take over the Scandinavian countries. He also failed to force through this idea, since it was countered by the argument that the operation would be even more costly and difficult than a landing in France, that it would entail a violation of Sweden's neutrality and would not bring the Allies any closer to the heart of Germany. There remained, therefore, the northern coast of western Europe, stretching from Brest through Brittany and Normandy to Belgium and Holland.

The Germans deduced that all the other options had been rejected and that the attack would be directed at western Europe, for although they put little trust in *Cicero*'s information (see Chapter 9, pp. 151–2), many easily-perceived signs pointed towards such a decision. Vast convoys were crossing from the United States to Britain and a huge concentration of forces was being gathered in the south of England; it was easy to observe the massing of ships and a continual air offensive was being waged in northern France, principally against ports, roads, bridges and airfields. Nevertheless the threatened coastline stretched for over five hundred kilometres and presented a number of different possibilities. The narrowest stretch of water, between Dover and Calais, was barely thirty-five kilometres wide and appeared to be the easiest place for an assault, but at the same time the

German defences were strongest there, while the British ports in the area had too small a capacity. To the east stretched the coast of Belgium and Holland, which was very much farther from Britain, which also had no suitable ports opposite. If one looked westwards, it could be seen that the distance between the two coastlines increased and that from Portsmouth to Le Havre was already more than one hundred kilometres, but there were on the British side excellent large ports and Intelligence had established that the German defences were very much weaker in that area.[3]

For the Allies it was extremely important to discover the German commanders' line of thought and Hitler's own views. Bletchley Park came to their rescue by deciphering a number of important signals in the spring of 1944. From these it appeared that von Rundstedt, the German Commander-in-Chief in the West, expected an attack on the Pas de Calais and therefore had concentrated most of his divisions there; Rommel disagreed. The latter, who had great experience in fighting the Allied commanders, expected the attack to come in Normandy. He took advantage of his direct personal telephone link with Hitler's field headquarters, which was a great distinction, to try by every means to bring the *Führer* round to his way of thinking. Hitler hesitated; his intuition, which once again was prompting the right decision, pointed to Normandy, but his ears were filled with the arguments of specialists, amongst whom was General Heinz Guderian, the panzer expert, who supported von Rundstedt. They maintained that four reserve panzer divisions which, if quickly and suitably deployed, could tip the balance against the invaders, should remain near Paris to be used wherever the main attack might develop. Hitler considered this, vacillated and finally accepted that the reserve should remain near the French capital and that it would come under his personal command.[4]

All these details were known to the Allied Command thanks to the work of the cryptanalysts, and the Allies were able to use every means to stimulate the differences of opinion in the German camp, keep them alive and create even greater doubt. They debated and discussed various types of decoy and deception and also a most devious campaign of disinformation to confuse the Germans totally and prevent them from accurately forecasting the time and place of the landing.

2

Just as at Bletchley Park, quite unknown people, having no military or political rank, were carrying out exceptionally important work and thus having a significant influence on the course of the war, so too in the field of subtle deception of the enemy, which could affect the success of difficult operations, did unknown people come to the fore. One of these was Colonel John Henry Bevan of the London Controlling Section (LCS), who belonged to a group of people working on operation *Bodyguard*. LCS was the organization within the Joint Planning Staff which was responsible for devising the co-ordinating strategic cover and deception schemes in all theatres of the war, including the Far East. LCS had the right to require services of M.I.6., OSS, SOE, the British Foreign Office and the American State Department. His task was to prepare and execute various ideas, running into the hundreds, which were to cover Allied strategic plans for north-west Europe in 1944 with a fog of deception and conceal them from the eyes of the Germans. In this area the Colonel was given enormous powers: he could impose a veto on top people revealing in public something which could betray one of the carefully prepared cover stories and he had the right to advise the Prime Minister on what he could say in Parliament.[5] A lie, as everyone knows, requires the person concerned to keep to his story consistently; how much harder the task is when the lie concerns a million-strong army and is meant to deceive equally shrewd opponents.

Disinformation was, of course, nothing new, it had been in use in time of war for hundreds of years, but only during the last war was it turned into a really dangerous weapon. The *Reich*'s Minister of Propaganda, Joseph Goebbels, developed it enormously, interweaving it with war reports, whispered propaganda, psychological warfare and terror. His was the idea that the 'Fifth Column', first set up during the civil war in Spain, was to be composed of Germans and German sympathizers and was to operate in each country which the Nazis intended to occupy. It was used to create panic and foster the impression that nothing could stop the Germans, thus making it easier for the panzer columns. That is how it had been in the first phases of the war and it must be admitted that Goebbels's propaganda achieved great results, but now the situation had changed and the Germans were to experience for themselves what psychological warfare and first-class disinformation really meant.

In two areas the Germans had at all costs to be deceived and made to believe something quite different: namely the time and place of the landing. At Teheran the Western leaders had promised Stalin that the attack in the west would begin not later than 1 May 1944, now they had to reveal to the Russians that the invasion could not take place before June and get them to agree to co-operate with *Bodyguard*. The Germans, even without specific intelligence, had to expect that the invasion in the west would be synchronised with a new Soviet offensive, thus making it impossible for them to transfer forces from one front to the other. The problem was, within the framework of *Bodyguard*, to get the Russians to create the impression that they would not advance before 1 July. To arrange this Colonel Bevan flew to Moscow and there, assisted by the American and British military missions, he obtained Soviet agreement.[6] This was extremely difficult, since the eastern ally was very suspicious and looked for a trick in everything; on the other hand the Colonel had to be careful not to reveal to the Russians more than was really necessary. It was already the spring of 1944, the most important battles on the Eastern Front had been won and Stalin had all the trump cards in his hand, so his continual insistence on the need for a second front might no longer be sincere. On the contrary, he might even secretly feel that it would be better if the landing was launched and then failed. German forces would be tied down there, not a single division could be transferred to the east and the western Allies would be left licking their wounds on the beaches of England just as after Dunkirk four years earlier. Who then would halt the Soviet divisions in their advance westwards not only beyond Berlin but even to Paris?

Nevertheless it was even more important to conceal the site of the landing than its timing. Here the Russians had a much smaller role to play, pretending to co-operate with the western Allies in a landing in Norway and another on the shores of the Black Sea in Bulgaria and Romania. The attack on Norway was to be justified by the need to capture the nickel mines near Petsamo and the Balkans invasion by the seizure of the Romanian oil field near Ploesti.[7] There was, however, little hope of these deceptions succeeding, since German Intelligence must from very many sources have already drawn the conclusion that the attack was to be expected in north-west Europe. The whole weight of the disinformation campaign to mislead the Germans fell thus on the British and the Americans.

3

General George Patton, a tall, well-built man, became the leading American field commander as a result of his excellent and exceptionally dynamic leadership in the North African and Sicilian campaigns, but these great achievements were obscured by his violent character and his brutal treatment of subordinates. He had twice struck shell-shocked soldiers in the face; this had been picked up by the American press, public opinion had been aroused and the General found himself in difficulties. Eisenhower valued him highly as a front-line commander and managed to save him from a court-martial, but during the Italian campaign he had been unable to give him any command.[8]

Patton was left on the sidelines, but German Intelligence which had to know the names and appointments of all the senior American commanders, did not lose sight of him. This was not difficult, for the General attracted wide attention refusing for one minute to be parted from his white bullterrier, his huge revolver and a pizzle hanging from his right wrist. The Germans had experienced his fighting qualities at first hand and they were unable to believe that he had been removed from command as a result of quite a minor matter, and they suspected a trick. Allied propaganda and disinformation continually referred to the Mediterranean countries suggesting that any day there would be a new attack either on Greece or Bulgaria, or on southern France, and German Intelligence assumed that General Patton must be associated with these plans. Suddenly his colourful personality vanished from the scene.[9]

The General's disappearance was closely related to a new assignment. Under the umbrella of *Bodyguard* a huge fantasy was concocted, based on the 'creation' of an entire 'First United States Army Group' composed of more than fifty divisions, which was assembled in south-east England. Some of these divisions really did exist, but were already under the command of General Omar Bradley of the USA or of General Montgomery. The aim of the fictitious army was to convince the Germans that the first assault of the invasion would definitely be launched in the Pas de Calais. General Patton was 'appointed' to command this army for the very reason that his colourful personality was easily recognizable and thus it could be assumed that German Intelligence would discover him quickly. He was an ideal appointment for a commander of the first decisive assault and there was a very high chance that the Germans would find this convincing. However, a commander was not enough to create the illusion of a great army group. It was necessary to appoint commanders of specific large units, some of them real, some fictitious; it was necessary to build hundreds of dummy huts, put up hundreds of road signs, set up a field postal service and operate several radio stations which would transmit regularly over the area. Naturally they could not afford to overlook the convoys which were to bring the non-existent divisions over from the United States, nor the hospitals, nor the supplies of petrol, the military police, the fights with the local population, the subtly planned 'leaks', in a word nothing which makes up an army of a million-strong could be forgotten. Many people, including the Home Guard, unknowingly took part in the deception. The whole of this complex operation, which was to convince the Germans that the imaginary army really did exist and would certainly launch an attack on Boulogne and Calais, was given the codename *Quicksilver*.[10]

4

The strongest British weapon for feeding the Germans false information in the almost certain knowledge that they would believe in it was the Germans' own intelligence network in Great Britain. The insular character of the country and its highly disciplined society meant that it was extremely difficult for a German agent to gain a foothold. The Third *Reich* had begun building its network several years before the war and had expanded it systematically, but the rapid collapse of the Western Front and the resultant opportunity for an invasion of Britain caused this process to be speeded up in 1940. The Germans used parachute drops, brought in people aboard small boats and landed them in the south of Ireland from whence it was much easier to get into Britain. Haste, however, brought bad results; the agents were inadequately trained, their radio equipment broke down and they did not have enough firm contacts on the ground. Few of them succeeded in surviving for any length of time; they were usually found out after a few days and fell into the experienced and thorough hands of British Counter-Intelligence.[11]

All of these people could have been brought to court, condemned to death and shot, but security services rarely operate in that way. A dead agent is of no use, while a live one can turn out to be extremely useful. Sometimes there were executions, if only to prevent the Germans from believing that things were going too well or if the agent was a particularly tough man, but in the vast majority of cases the officers of British Counter-Intelligence (M.I.5) were able to convince the unfortunate agents that they ought to come over to their side, if only to save their own lives. As far as Germans were concerned this argument was not usually enough and political persuasion was used, that is the British tried to convince them that the good of their country required the overthrow of Nazism.

The task of preparing a double agent was very difficult and had to be carried out with extreme care so that the German Intelligence in no way found out that it was being deceived. The recruited agent continued to maintain radio contact with his superiors, continued to behave as if he were free and operating independently and continued to send reports with all the hallmarks of hard-won intelligence. The sole, but significant, difference was that now these reports were prepared by the British and were a classic example of disinformation.

In January 1941 the XX–Committee (the name of which derived from the two crosses representing the Double-Cross System) was set up directly responsible to W.Board, a joint inter-service board dealing with the most secret matters, and was composed of outstanding experts from different fields. The Committee's task was the closest control possible of the German double agents (The Double-Cross System) so as not to make a mistake and betray the nature of their work. The Committee had also to decide what information to release to the agents and to adjudicate between the requirements of different departments and services, such as the Navy, the Air Force, the Army, the Foreign Office and so on. The Committee was responsible for the success of the whole subtly contrived plan, the more so since it had been possible to catch all, or almost all the German agents;* it was conceivable, therefore, that the *Abwehr* was not receiving any other reports from Great Britain.[12]

The XX–Committee dealt with a number of German agents (Masterman lists thirty-nine) of different abilities and usefulness to the Allied cause. One of them, however, had been recruited by the Germans in such unusual circumstances that his case is worth recounting. He was a Polish Air Force officer, Captain Roman Garby-Czerniawski, who, after the collapse of the Western Front, set up in France an intelligence network, made contact with British Intelligence and up to November 1941, that is up to his arrest, sent radio reports on the dislocation of German units and airfields and on the movements of vessels in French ports. Fortunately he was arrested by *Abwehr* Counter-Intelligence and not the *Gestapo*, which gave rise to a situation which usually only takes place in thrillers or films. Colonel Oskar Reile, knowing the sort of pressures there are on a prisoner, for more than sixty of his subordinates had been arrested, and valuing the Pole's work highly as a result of discovered documents, offered him the chance of collaboration. Czerniawski was to be released under the guise of an escape, he was to get over to Great Britain and start undercover work among young Polish officers who were disillusioned with the Western Allies due to their placatory attitude towards the Soviet Union. He was also to set up a radio station and transmit intelligence information in a prearranged cipher. The Captain accepted, on condition that his agents would be treated as prisoners of war and that he would not be followed after his 'escape'. His third condition, that after the war Poland would reap some benefit from all this, surprised the German, but he accepted it. After reaching Great Britain in October 1942 by means of Spain and Gibraltar, Czerniawski revealed his exceptional situation to the head of Polish Intelligence and with General Sikorski's agreement was handed over to the British.

The W.Board at first rejected the XX–Committee's suggestion to use him, concluding that the risk was too great and that it was difficult to imagine that the Germans trusted Czerniawski. A further complication was created by the fact that the Captain was not a German, totally confident in the rightness of what he was doing, but a Pole whose nation had two enemies: Germany and Russia. Towards the end of 1942, although the official decisions were yet to be taken, it was already known that Stalin would take over eastern and some of central Europe and that the Western democracies were not going to

---

*The assertion that all German agents in the British Isles were caught is based on Counter-Intelligence files and there is no reason to doubt it; on the other hand one must assume that the Germans could nevertheless have had agents, in particular 'residents', who were inhabitants of the British Isles and who were not caught and continued to communicate with Germany.

prevent him. Was it possible to be quite certain that the young officer had not succumbed to German propaganda warning the Poles of Western and Soviet scheming at Poland's expense? It was, however, finally decided to use Czerniawski, he was given the codename *Brutus*, was helped to set up a radio station and was supplied with introductory information, which had been particularly carefully prepared and which at first was completely true. The Captain was ostensibly an officer on the Polish Staff and any agent could easily spot him there.[13]

Long months of secret preparations went by, the XX–Committee worked on the materials which were passed on to the double agents, the cover story of the First United States Army Group grew, the Germans intercepted and deciphered fake signals from it and, thanks to Bletchley Park, it was clear that they had swallowed the bait of perhaps the biggest trick in military history since the Trojan Horse. *Brutus*, who had at first been treated with great caution, came to be the outstanding double agent and from the questions which he received from his German contact it was clear that he had his German masters' full confidence. The information prepared for him turned out to be excellent and resisted all scepticism, double-checking and examination from German Intelligence. Its value depended on being very largely true, especially during 1943, and subsequent events proved its authenticity. This extended even to the invasion's landing-site, for *Brutus* gave Normandy, but for a date six weeks later and with the proviso that, after the initial landing, the main assault was to be on the Pas de Calais. D–Day approached and *Brutus'* information sent by radio to Germany turned out to be the most effective in operation *Quicksilver*.[14]

5

About 2 am on 6 June the German Naval Command in France picked up on its radar the approaching massive fleet and immediately informed Hitler that the Allied attack had begun. The signal was sent to Berchtesgaden, where he had gone for a few days and where he was receiving people and making decisions; but before this important news reached him, he had gone to bed with strict instructions not to be woken. The Head of OKW, Field Marshal Keitel, did not believe the accuracy of the report and did not dare to waken the dictator, whose next military conference was to take place only in the afternoon.[15] Von Rundstedt received the same report and also did not believe it, but just in case he put the XV Army, opposite the Pas de Calais, on full alert. His order was intercepted and the Bletchley Park analysts deciphered it immediately. It was an invaluable piece of information, since it confirmed that the trick had succeeded and that the Germans were expecting an attack at the Channel's narrowest point. The VIIth Army in Normandy continued to sleep peacefully, although the first paratroopers had already landed in its area. Only one division, which by chance happened to be training to repel an invasion, put up immediate resistance. The four panzer divisions, which were under Hitler's personal command, were also asleep and unaware of the developing drama. Erwin Rommel, quite deceived by the Allies' masterly disinformation campaign, was at home near Ulm on the occasion of his wife's birthday.[16]

These initial hours of German indecisiveness decided the success of the whole landing and proved that the long months spent in preparing the gigantic bluff had been repaid a hundred times over. Rommel had been right when he said that the only chance for the Germans was to push the attackers back into the sea immediately, for later on their huge superiority, especially in the air, would make this impossible. It was only at about 5 pm that Hitler issued the order that 'the enemy is to be annihilated at the bridgehead by evening of 6 June' and released the XII reserve *SS* panzer division for von Rundstedt's use.[17]

Despite these decisive German mistakes and the Allies' establishment on the French shore and their total superiority in the air, the situation of the British and American divisions was by no means easy, for the Germans, although exhausted by a long war, fought splendidly. Furthermore, Hitler, contrary to the hopes of Rommel and other German generals, attached great and even decisive importance to the Western Front. 'If the invasion is not repulsed, the war is lost for us.'[18] Therefore, to the dismay of his advisers, he ordered two panzer divisions, the IX and X, to be withdrawn from the Eastern Front and committed in the Caen area. Two further divisions, I and II *SS*, were withdrawn from Belgium and Toulouse. At the same time the XV Army remained inactive in the Pas de Calais, for Hitler continued to believe that the main assault would be launched there by Patton's fictitious Army Group. The importance which the dictator attached to the Western Front expressed itself in his personal visit to France to his field headquarters at Margival in the area of Soissons, which had been prepared in 1940 for the planned invasion of the British Isles. There on 17 June he met von Rundstedt and Rommel, coldly heard their reports and then ordered them to fight for every square metre. With great animation he drew before them a picture of the destruction of Britain when the retaliation V-weapons and jet aircraft came into use. When Rommel tried carefully to raise the question of ending the war, Hitler disposed of him with the single sentence that he was to think of an invasion and not of politics.[19]

Many of these details were known at the time to the Western Allies, for radio communications between Hitler and his commanders in the West became very lively and were monitored and regularly deciphered by Bletchley Park. In this way they found out that German panzer divisions, although reaching their forward areas after forced night advances, were then faced with various difficulties, not least that of delays in the fuel supply. They also found out that von Rundstedt had ordered Rommel to counter-attack, that Hitler had ordered Bayeux to be retaken and that he had left the garrison in Cherbourg no other option but to fight to the last man. The cryptanalysts also provided the commanders with information on the transfer of panzer divisions from the Eastern Front, from Belgium and southern France.[20] This permitted swift changes of plan in further stages of the fighting, speeded up the capture of territory, decreased their own losses and also gave the Western leaders a clear idea of the German dictator's thinking. It was a revelation for them, since they had imagined that the protection of the *Reich* from the approaching Red Army was more important for Hitler.

By the beginning of July the Allies already had in France about a million men and five hundred thousand tons of supplies and they were advancing. Hitler, who had already for some time been living in a world of his own, responded by removing von Rundstedt and appointing in his place Field Marshal Günter von Kluge.[21] His first signal as Commander-in-Chief in France was read by Bletchley Park. It contained the order that, in accordance with Hitler's wishes, all positions were to be held. A few days later Rommel also left the field of battle, seriously wounded after his car had been shot up by an Allied aircraft.

The departure of Rommel made the cryptanalysts' task harder, since he had been in frequent radio contact with Hitler and his signals had been deciphered, revealing much important information. Von Rundstedt's replacement was also awkward, since Intelligence had known his habits, behaviour and reactions, making it possible to guess his decisions. Von Kluge was new to this theatre and the Allies had to collect a great deal of information in order to build up a picture of him. Fortunately he was a frequent user of the radio and deciphering his signals produced a great deal of interesting information. It was possible to establish from them the quality of the forces he had at his disposal, as well as the extent of his losses, particularly in armour. These turned out to be higher than the figures of the Allied commanders.[22]

The second half of August saw the decisive phase of the Normandy battles. Near Falaise the Germans found themselves in a pocket, they lost more than sixty thousand men either killed or taken prisoner, the whole line fell back and the Allied divisions advanced against minimal resistance. That was the reality. Hitler, however, did not wish to recognize it and in his imagination saw everything quite differently; while German resistance was crumbling, he ordered von Kluge to counter-attack, break through the American sector and then push the Americans into the sea. Bletchley Park deciphered this signal which revealed more than the most precise intelligence analysis.[23]

6

When, during his visit to France, Hitler had painted an optimistic picture of the destruction that the new weapons would wreak in Britain, von Rundstedt and Rommel had listened to him respectfully, but inwardly they had been unable to control their scepticism. Goebbels's propaganda machine had already so many times promised a dramatic reversal of the tide of war due to most astonishing new inventions, and it had so many times proved to be illusory, that it was becoming difficult to believe, and yet this time Hitler was not far from the truth. Four days previously the first flying bomb (V–1) had landed on London, its numbers were growing and they were only the forerunners of the real threat, the V–2 rocket, which was to come into use any day and against which there was no defence.

Experiments with secret weapons had been well under way when the Nazis came to power, the *Reichswehr* had quite soon shown some interest in them and had paid particular attention to two prototypes: the pilotless aircraft, also called a flying bomb (V–1), and the rocket (V–2). Each of these weapons had its supporters and when Hitler came to power and the armed forces expanded dramatically, the *Luftwaffe* took over the V–1 experiments and the Army the rockets.[24]

Each system provided the means to land one ton of explosives on enemy territory, but the V–1 was merely a small, pilotless jet aircraft within the range of a fighter aircraft and anti-aircraft artillery, while the V–2 flew through the stratosphere attaining a speed of 1,700 metres per second, which made any defence out of the question. It had a great future and at that time represented an impressive technical achievement. A young scientist who worked on the V–2, one Wernher von Braun, was to become famous after the war when, working now for the Americans, he was instrumental in achieving the first space flights.[25]

From the very beginning Hitler disregarded the rockets and he did not agree to the project being given top priority. Despite his scepticism, the experiments progressed and in 1936 they were moved to Peenemünde at the mouth of the Oder on the Baltic. The western part of the northern promontory was occupied by the Air Force with the V–1, while the Army took over the eastern part with the V–2. The whole area was surrounded by a security cordon.[26]

In addition to British Intelligence, which already before the war had been on the trail of German experiments and had tried to discover what new weapons were being prepared for the moment of revenge, the underground resistance movements of the occupied countries were also interested in this secret work. Their intelligence in Belgium, Denmark, France, Holland, Luxemburg and Poland watched everything which might provide a clue and sent off reports to London, where these countries' governments or national committees were to be found. Contrary to their own security regulations, the Germans, faced with the constant problem of an inadequate labour force, set up near Peenemünde a camp for foreign workers who were brought by force. Near this was a concentration camp and a little farther away a prisoner-of-war camp. Although foreigners, even specialists, were not allowed into the actual experimental workshops, their close proximity allowed them to observe tests of both secret weapons and to make under-cover intelligence contacts. In this way the Intelligence department of the Polish Home Army, which was the underground army in occupied Poland controlled by the Polish Government in London, as well as the French and Luxemburg resistance movements, managed to obtain information on the secret work being carried out at Peenemünde and transmit it to London. A comparison of the results achieved by the Intelligence Service with aerial photographs enabled the British to pinpoint precise targets. On the night of 17 and 18 August 1943 over four hundred bombers carried out an attack on the V–2 installations at Peenemünde. Several hundred specialists in the residential area were killed and the damage to the buildings was so great that the work had to be stopped for several months.[27]

The Head of the *SS*, Heinrich Himmler, had for a long time been trying to gain control over the secret experiments, arguing that only his units could provide complete security, and, when the British raid showed that the enemy had precise information about Peenemünde, he finally managed to convince Hitler and work on the rockets passed into his hands. He cast around for a new site out of range of the Allied bombers and his choice fell on Blizna, a small forest village in southern Poland, where the *SS* had a range called *Heidelager*. Home Army Intelligence quickly found out about this move and in December 1943 the first reports on this went to London via Warsaw.[28]

Over the next few months the Poles provided more information, but it was not only reports from that source which formed the basis of British Intelligence thinking. Peenemünde continued to function, for in addition to further work on the V–1, the V–2 installations were rebuilt and work restarted. There was regular radio contact between Peenemünde and Berlin and it was intercepted, sent to Bletchley Park and deciphered. The first fragmentary information from this source was compared with the despatches from Poland and confirmed that tests had been moved to Blizna. The night photographs from the air confirmed this as well: the Germans were carrying out the final test flights of the V–2 in Poland, and within a short time the rockets would probably start falling on London.[29]

Among the British scientists working for Intelligence there was no agreement as to the seriousness of the threat from the rockets. From the fragmentary reports efforts were made to establish the rocket's dimensions, but only a specimen in as near-perfect condition as possible could provide a full answer.

The first success to be recorded was in June 1944, when one of the rockets launched from Peenemünde went out of control, changed course and crashed in southern Sweden. London was able quite quickly to send out its experts and in mid-July bring back about two tons of surviving equipment and fragments. The scientists got to work on them at Farnborough near London and quickly established that the rocket had remote-control equipment, which pointed towards great technical sophistication and large destructive capability. At the same time information came in from Poland that the Home Army had managed to obtain another rocket which was also only slightly damaged. A report, together with the rocket's important parts, among them the radio, was picked up from Poland on a secret flight and arrived in London on 28 July. After a swift examination of the materials, those involved in the affair could breathe again. The radio brought from Poland was simply an apparatus for receiving and transmitting signals, without any means of remote control. In fact it turned out that the rocket which crashed in Sweden was exceptionally equipped with a radio-guidance system designed for another smaller rocket, called 'Wasserfall', which had been developed for anti-aircraft purposes. Other details of the rocket, together with the information gleaned from the Swedish specimen, established that this dangerous weapon could carry to London only one ton of explosives, the same as a flying-bomb.[30] The result of this co-operation between the Intelligence Service, the intelligence branches of the various resistance movements and Bletchley Park was that when, on 8 September, the first rocket exploded in the British capital, there was no panic, for its destructive power was already known.

7

The first attempt on Hitler's life took place when he was still the little-known leader of the German National Socialist Party (*NSDAP*), but a real threat appeared in 1938 during the Sudetenland crisis. General Beck left the post of Chief of Staff, to be replaced by General Halder, and it was then that the conspirators of *Die Schwarze Kapelle* decided that as soon as the Chancellor declared war or began it without this formality, he would be arrested and, together with his closest associates, would be put on trial (see Chapter 7, pp. 105–6).

Nothing came of these plans, since the conspirators had counted on the help of the Western democracies, but these had submitted to Hitler's demands, and so the German attack on Poland had taken place without any internal opposition. After this, with the great successes of the *Blitzkrieg* and the Chancellor's great public popularity, there was no chance of any attempt on his life. His internal enemies lay low, but continued to maintain contact among themselves, carefully going about recruiting new adherents and waiting for the moment when the tides of war would begin to turn. This was brought on by Hitler himself, who voluntarily opened the huge Eastern Front and embroiled the *Reich* in a war on two fronts and, towards the end of 1941, committed a further blunder by declaring war on the United States.

In 1943, as the war with Russia was turning into the tragedy of the German Army, attempts on the life of the man responsible for this state of affairs increased. In the middle of March two senior officers, Henning von Trescow and Fabian von Schlabrendorff, placed some explosives in the dictator's aircraft; later Colonel Rudolf-Christoph von Gersdorff resolved to blow himself up, together with Hitler and his retinue, during an inspection of the Berlin Arsenal. The bomb did not explode, for at altitude the detonator connections froze, while the Arsenal plan failed due to a sudden change in the planned visit. Again another colonel, Helmuth Stieff, planned to plant a bomb during a military conference in Hitler's headquarters and a young captain, Axel von dem Bussche, wanted to sacrifice his own life by hurling himself at Hitler with a bomb while the latter was looking at some new uniforms. Once again nothing came of these plans: the first bomb exploded too soon, while the second one was not used, for the dictator changed his plans at the very last moment. He was doing this now more frequently since he knew that he had deadly enemies around him, and so there were sudden changes in his programme which affected even people like Göring and Himmler, in whom he should have had confidence. Fate also smiled on him, quite indispensable in his position and amidst such a tangle of dramatic events. Towards the end of December 1943 a new figure appeared on the scene: Colonel Claus Schenk von Stauffenberg was thirty-seven and in the desert war had lost an eye, his right arm and two fingers from his left hand. He had now become Chief of Staff of the reserve army, which gave him the right to take part in military conferences at Hitler's headquarters. He belonged to the group of young officers who had recently joined *Die Schwarze Kapelle* and who had introduced an element of decisiveness and dynamism.[31]

The situation of a professional soldier, who furthermore came from an old aristocratic family with a great tradition, was exceptionally difficult, but von Stauffenberg managed to overcome any inward scruples and became one of the leading military conspirators. He had also to accept the fact that the Western Allies had adopted a policy of 'unconditional surrender' and that any attempt to make contact with them had met with failure. The aim which stood clearly before him was the removal of Hitler by an attempt on his life, and it overcame all his scruples, doubts and hesitations.

During this phase when the group was growing and its members were filling important appointments in the armed forces all over Europe, a very serious problem was that of communication between them. This task was carried out by General Fellgiebel who had all the technical resources under his command. He formed around him a small group of highly trusted officers, who knew what was happening and on whom he could rely. This would be extremely important in the event of a successful assassination attempt, since there would be an immediate need to inform all the conspirators of the result so as to gain control of the armed forces within three or four hours. He was already in touch with von Stauffenberg and he knew that the next attempt on Hitler's life was to be carried out by the young colonel.[32]

The Allies' successful landing in France intensified all the problems facing the conspirators. The rapid American and British advance into France and the threat to the *Reich* itself could yet present some chance of negotiating with the Western democracies, as long as Adolf Hitler was not still representing Germany. Meanwhile the *Gestapo* and the *SD* were tightening their grip on the group of people who had taken the risk of trying to carry out a *coup*. On 4 July Julius Leber and Adolf Reichwein were arrested; they had been trying to expand *Die Schwarze Kapelle* to include various left-wingers; information was coming in of more danger from the police. Von Stauffenberg was twice summoned to Hitler's headquarters at Berghof on 6 and 11 July and both times he took explosives with him, but he abandoned each attempt for neither Göring nor Himmler appeared and he wanted to kill them as well. On 15 July he had another opportunity, but once again nothing happened, since the Colonel did not have enough time to connect up the detonator before the start of the conference. On 17 July the conspirators received information that an order had been issued for the arrest of Carl Goerdeler, who had been chosen as chancellor in the event of a successful *coup*.[33] The decisive time had come and the very next opportunity had to be used.

What happened on 20 July in Hitler's 'Wolf's Lair' in East Prussia is well known. Once again by chance the dictator came through alive, although this time von Stauffenberg's bomb did explode. The switching of the conference from the concrete bunker to a wooden hut, and the accidental shifting, by one of the participants, of the briefcase containing the bomb to behind a thick oak table-leg prolonged the life of a man who was leading his country to total disaster, while the conspirators' mistakes and lack of decision during the most decisive hours did the rest. It transpired that the long traditions of the officer corps, its habits and its concepts of honour and loyalty were stronger than cold reason and a rational appraisal of the country's plight. If Hitler had been killed, their hands would have been untied; since he was still alive, their personal oath to him was still binding. It was possible to raise one's hand against him, but impossible to break the oath. This decided everything and the conspirators fired not a single shot. Their National Socialist opponents saw reality differently and had no trouble reconciling immediate action with their views.

The same night von Stauffenberg and several high-ranking officers in Berlin were shot, General Beck committed suicide and the security office carried out a large programme of arrests on the adherents of *Die Schwarze Kapelle*. This was in accordance with Hitler's orders, since he had said that for some time he had suspected treachery around him and that now he would be able to strike with the utmost ruthlessness. General Fellgiebel was arrested on the following day, when he was summoned back to the 'Wolf's Lair'; his deputy, General Fritz Thiele, a little later; Carl Goerdeler, Field Marshal Erwin von Witzleben, Generals Heinrich von Stülpnagel, Paul von Hase, Helmuth Stieff and a great many other senior officers and politicians shared their fate. A few months later Admiral Canaris was in gaol, having already been relieved of his duties. They were all tried and sentenced to death by hanging. Erwin Rommel, spared a public trial, was forced to commit suicide. Hitler's revenge extended also to their families, and young children and old people were also rounded up. The wave of arrests lasted until April 1945 and embraced several thousand people.[34]

8

During the cross-examination before the 'People's Court' between the President, Roland Freisler, and Schwerin von Schwanenfeld, one of the members of *Die Schwarze Kapelle*, the following exchange took place:

Freisler: What do you really have against National Socialism?
Schwerin: I had in mind the numerous murders.
Freisler: Murders?
Schwerin: Yes, both here and abroad.
Freisler: You are a miserable wretch. You have behaved disgustingly. Answer yes
   or no. Have you?
Schwerin: Mr president!
Freisler: Yes or no, answer clearly.
Schwerin: No.
Freisler: You will not be able to do anything more. You are a small, despicable
   animal, without any self-respect.[35]

All the cross-examinations were carried out in this fashion on people who had just undergone brutal interrogation with torture, for both the *Gestapo* and the *SD* wanted to extract as many names from them as possible. Their methods were harsh, but in that political system nothing else was to be expected. Furthermore, the court's fury was to some extent justified: a *coup d'état*, particularly in wartime, is the greatest crime that can be committed against the legal government of a country. Hitler stood at the head of the Third *Reich*, a position which he had attained by way of parliamentary elections, and those who had made an attempt on his life had taken a special oath of loyalty to him.

There can be no doubt that the members of *Die Schwarze Kapelle* were, in strict legal terms, committing a great crime for which they had been preparing for a number of years, but the whole problem must be first seen from a moral point of view. Today, when all National Socialism's crimes are known, as are the destruction and misery which the war started by them brought, the conspirators' actions must be seen as completely justified. They had been in contact with the Western Allies, who were the Third *Reich*'s enemies, but they did this to avoid a new war. They had received no encouragement from them, they had no luck on 20 July and they lacked the resolution so essential to such a cause, and so they suffered the consequences of an unsuccessful *coup*, but history, written by others and by the Germans themselves, has recognized their moral stance as correct and has endorsed it.

There is, however, another problem connected with the story of *Die Schwarze Kapelle*, which requires examination. Owing to the presence in their ranks of General Fellgiebel, who controlled everything to do with *OKW*'s communications, the conspirators had access to top-secret national and military information sent by radio and enciphered on *Enigma* and the *Geheimschreiber*. Since the plotters were striving to overthrow National Socialism even before the war and were thus trying to come to an agreement with Great Britain and France, and during the war also with the United States, the hypothesis arises that, once hostilities had begun, they might have revealed to the Allies some of these secrets in order to end the war as speedily as possible.[36]

This problem is quite different from a prepared *coup d'état*. A struggle for power, even supported by exterior forces, is recognized by international law and a successful overthrow is quickly accepted by foreign governments, which initiate diplomatic relations with the new authorities. In a word, a *coup d'état*, if successful, not only is not considered a crime and does not shame those involved, but on the contrary, gives them political power, international recognition and the support of most of the country, which victors usually receive. On the other hand, secret contacts with an active enemy and the passing over to him of classified information is universally regarded as treachery and is shameful. The argument that an attempt on the life of the head of state is also treason and shameful is not widely accepted. Let us use an example: murder for material gain is a crime, while the same act committed out of political motives can be recognized as an act of heroism. The dividing line between the two actions is narrow and sometimes invisible; it is often moved and exploited, but modern ethics accept it.

In the light of these deliberations we must ask the following question: is it possible that General Fellgiebel, a high-ranking professional officer, whose membership in the conspiracy for moral reasons is not in doubt, could, in his fight against Nazism, have taken the great step of maintaining secret contact with the intelligence services of the *Reich*'s enemies? Can one suppose that he, or one of his subordinates with his consent, could have passed over top-secret political and military information, for instance to Switzerland, to Rudolf Roessler (see Chapter 7, pp. 114–15)?

Such Germans as Leo Hepp, Johannes Möller, Karl Otto Hoffmann and Erich Hüttenhein, to whom this has been put and who at the time were directly involved, have decisively rejected such an idea, using the arguments outlined above. In their opinion a German officer was incapable of such an action, particularly General Fellgiebel, a man of transparent honour. In the light of the events of 20 July and afterwards, this point of view appears to be justified. None of the officers implicated in the affair undertook any action when he heard that Hitler was still alive, none tried to escape, none tried to save himself during the interrogations by false confessions, all of them tried to protect their subordinates. Their behaviour, bordering sometimes on the naïve, was in accordance with their oath and pride in their uniform.[37] That is how Fellgiebel saw it and that is how he behaved during his trial.[38] He was fighting National Socialism and not his own country. An additional argument against the General being in touch with Roessler is the fact that the latter had been working for the Soviet Union from 1942. Russia was certainly an ally of the West and Russian victories were hastening the end of the war, but *Die Schwarze Kapelle* represented conservative views whose greatest fear was that the Red Army might reach Berlin before the British and American divisions.

German historians, however, see this problem in a different light. Wilhelm von Schramm is of the opinion that Roessler's principal contact was Schulze-Boysen from *Die Rote Kapelle*, but at the same time he puts a question mark by the names of General Fellgiebel, Colonel Oster and Dr Wilhelm Scheidt when he discusses them as possible informants of the Allies.[39] Jürgen Rohwer prefers the view that Fellgiebel did not maintain links with foreign intelligence, but does not exclude the possibility.[40] At its critical moments the war attained such a level of brutality and the German nation was facing such total destruction that people capable and willing to salvage something, might have taken the ultimate step. The Swiss historian, Hans Rudolf Kurz, has expressed a similar view,[41] while the English writer, Constantine Fitzgibbon, has written bluntly that 'Colonel Oster was a confirmed anti-Nazi, who would have preferred to see Germany lose the war than that Hitler should win it. He, and several like him, deliberately betrayed German operational secrets to the Soviets, both before and during the war. They were engaged upon what in any country and at any time would be called high treason.'[42]

Despite the confident tone of this opinion and others like it on this question, it belongs to the category of hypothesis, supposition and guesswork. There is no proof that *Die Schwarze Kapelle* was passing over secret information to the enemies and that the secret of *Enigma* was somehow involved. We shall probably never find such proof, since it is unlikely that the documents still exist and witnesses are long since dead.

Passing over classified materials to the enemy was technically feasible, even by radio, although historians dispute this. It was also feasible, despite the principles held by the German officer corps, because Nazism had aroused extreme moral and political passions, but it is far more likely that the German conspirators restricted themselves to a struggle for power and that the Third *Reich*'s greatest secrets were discovered by the Allies as a result of breaking *Enigma* and the *Geheimschreiber* and of Bletchley Park's work. Thus did London receive its intelligence, which it then probably passed on in moderation to beleaguered Moscow via Switzerland, using all caution and without betraying its sources (see Chapter 7, pp. 115–18).

NOTES

1. Fest, op. cit., p. 703. Also: Brown, op. cit., pp. 429–30.
2. Olav Riste, 'The Norwegian Government in Exile and the Allies, 1940–1945,' a lecture given during a Conference on Governments Exiled in London during the Second World War, 24–7 October 1977, pp. 14–18.
3. Calvocoressi and Wint, op. cit., pp. 513–14.
4. Winterbotham, op. cit., pp. 154–7.
5. Brown, op. cit., pp. 432–5.
6. Ibid, pp. 439–45.
7. Ibid, p. 443.
8. Ibid, pp. 473–4.
9. Ibid, p. 474.
10. Ibid, pp. 474–5. Also: Roman Garby-Czerniawski, an interview recorded on 13 July 1978, in London.
11. John C. Masterman, *The Double-Cross System in the War of 1939 to 1945*, Sphere edition, London, 1973, pp. 41–9.
12. Ibid, pp. 10–11.
13. Garby-Czerniawski, op. cit. Also: Masterman, op. cit., pp. 140–1.
14. Ibid. Also: Masterman, op. cit., pp. 141–2.
15. Fest, op. cit., p. 705.
16. Cornelius Ryan, *The Longest Day*, New York, 1960 (paperback edition p. 35). Also: Winterbotham, op. cit., pp. 162–3.
17. Fest, op. cit., p. 705. Also: Winterbotham, op. cit., p. 165.
18. Ibid.
19. Ibid, p. 706.
20. Winterbotham, op. cit., pp. 164–6.

21. Fest, op. cit., pp. 206–7.
22. Winterbotham, op. cit., p. 175.
23. Ibid, p. 180.
24. Garliński, op. cit., pp. 2–12.
25. Ibid, pp. 8–14.
26. Ibid, pp. 14–20.
27. Ibid, pp. 51–63 and 78–99.
28. Ibid, pp. 114–16.
29. Jones, op. cit., pp. 430–1.
30. Ibid, pp. 431–45.
31. Fest, op. cit., pp. 697–703.
32. Karl Heinz Wildhagen and others, *Erich Fellgiebel* ('Rolle General Fellgiebel in militär-ischen Wiederstand'), Hannover, 1970, pp. 283–94.
33. Fest, op. cit., pp. 704–8.
34. Royce, Zimmermann and Jacobsen, op. cit., pp. 118–20 and 202–12. Also: Fest, op. cit., pp. 708–14.
35. Royce, Zimmermann and Jacobsen, op. cit., p. 206.
36. Brown, op. cit., p. 310 (he states that Hans Bernd Gisevius, using diplomatic immunity, contacted Allen Dulles, the United States representative in Bern, as an emissary of *Die Schwarze Kapelle*).
37. Fest, op. cit., pp. 713–14.
38. Wildhagen, op. cit., pp. 321–2.
39. Schramm, op. cit., pp. 85 and 171.
40. Rohwer, an interview in London, 7 July 1978.
41. Kurz, an interview in Bern, 22 September 1977.
42. Fitzgibbon, op. cit., str. 242–3.

11

In the Bunker

1

THE PACIFIC OCEAN WITNESSED above all the great effort and victories of the United States, whose economic strength decided the outcome of the war. The British Empire, however, was also deeply involved there. Australia, New Zealand and Hong Kong were possessions which required protection, as did India, Burma and the Malaysian peninsula. The Royal Navy operated in those distant waters and the British Army fought in the jungle against the fanatical Japanese.

The main burden of breaking Japanese ciphers fell on the Americans, who thanks to their success with *Purple* (see Chapter 8, p. 125), found themselves in an extremely fortunate situation. Bletchley Park, however, also kept an eye on Japanese cryptological development and had a special section which handled Japanese ciphers, preparing material for intelligence use.[1] This was received by the *Ultra* net, which passed it on to the relevant people in the Far East. Squadron-Leader Winterbotham set up units in Delhi, at the Head-quarters of the Commander-in-Chief of the British forces in India, General Sir William Slim; in Kandy on Ceylon at Admiral Lord Mountbatten's South-East Asia command and at Brisbane in Australia. He carried out a personal inspection of all these areas and checked that everything was operating swiftly and efficiently. *Ultra* was also working for the American Army supporting Chiang Kai-shek in China through the agency of an American officer, Captain Inzer Wyatt, who had undergone training at Bletchley Park.[2]

It was precisely there, in the Far East, that Anglo-American co-operation in the field of cryptanalysis was the most effective. Thanks to it the Japanese were eventually defeated in a number of sea battles, which affected the outcome of the war. The most important of these took place between 4 and 6 June 1942 near the island of Midway and was significant for the fact that the Japanese fleet, possessing great superiority over the Americans (eleven battleships against none), never brought its capital ships into action. The reason for this was fear of the American dive-bombers, a fear which turned out to be justified, since the bombers decided the battle's outcome and brought Admiral Chester Nimitz a great victory. The Japanese lost all their 4 aircraft-carriers, *Akagi, Hiryu, Kaga* and *Soryu*; 1 heavy cruiser; 322 aircraft and 3,500 sailors; while the Americans lost 1 aircraft-carrier, *Yorktown*; 1 destroyer; 150 aircraft and 307 sailors.[3] This victory had been made possible as a result of the exemplary co-operation of both British and American analysts, who in May had broken Japanese naval signals dealing with the attack on the island of Midway and the diversionary attack on the Aleutian Islands with weaker forces which were, however, to have drawn the American commander's main attention. As a result of this information, Admiral Nimitz did not divide his fleet and turned it towards Midway, knowing, furthermore, the exact position and strength of the Japanese dispositions.[4]

This victory was almost bought at the price of a great defeat in the field of secrecy, for an American journalist somehow discovered the cryptanalysts' achievement and disclosed it in the press. There was an immediate reaction from Churchill and no such thing occurred again. A second such mistake was made when the American Air Force, in possession of Japanese secret signals, shot down the aircraft carrying the Commander-in-Chief of the Japanese fleet, Admiral Isoroku Yamamoto. Fortunately the Japanese, like the Germans, believed that their ciphers, and in particular the naval ones, were unbreakable and drew no conclusions from these two incidents.[5]

2

The Germans finally lost the battle for France, von Kluge committed suicide, Paris was liberated, the Allies landed on the French Riviera and British and American divisions marched on Belgium and approached the German frontier. In a daring attempt to throw the Germans out of Holland in order to protect London from the threat of a rocket attack, the Allies carried out an airborne descent at Arnhem. This attempt met with failure and halted the Western Allies' impetus; they had to reorganize their rear and it appeared that the fast-approaching winter would see a slow positional campaign.

A similar situation existed in the east, on the central sector of the front, but for quite different reasons. The Teheran Conference (see Chapter 9, pp. 150–2) had decided that the Soviet Union would absorb Poland, among others, in its sphere of influence, entailing complete domination and a communist government dependent on Moscow. The Poles did not accept this, the government-in-exile in London tried to influence Western leaders to change their minds, and the underground army in Poland mobilized its secretly prepared forces and attacked the retreating Germans. This was carried out in tactical co-operation with the Red Army, but with the attendant intention of greeting its units on Polish soil in the role of hosts. The

Poles' help was accepted, but after the fighting their units were disarmed. By the end of July 1944 the divisions of the First Byelorussian Front were in the suburbs of Warsaw on the east bank of the Vistula. Since the Poles were taking to open battle throughout the whole country as soon as the Red division appeared, how could they not do the same in Warsaw, the capital? On 1 August the Home Army attacked the Germans. Polish political and military leaders believed that this time the Russians would co-operate tactically and that the capital would be liberated within a few days.

Things turned out differently. Stalin, putting his political plans into operation with Western acquiescence, had no intention of helping the insurgents and restrained his forces, which entered Warsaw only in January of the following year. Soviet propaganda tried to explain the sudden halt in the offensive by a German counter-attack, which did in fact take place, but only in the first two weeks of August. After sixty-three days of some of the most bitter fighting seen in the war, the uprising was suppressed at the cost of about 200,000 dead inhabitants and the almost total destruction of the city. Aerial assistance from the Western Allies, which was sent from Italy and Great Britain, only reached the Polish capital with the greatest of difficulty, and with Soviet indifference was unable to change the course of events.[6]

The Warsaw Uprising was reflected in Bletchley Park's work. The centre read a signal referring to a German panzer corps which was transferred to the east via Warsaw at the end of July 1944 with the task of halting the Soviet divisions.[7] This signal would probably have been turned over to the Polish authorities in London by the British, who were opposed to the idea of the uprising and tried to restrain the Poles from any action which might affect good relations with the Soviets. It might have had some influence on the Poles' decision, delaying it for a few days, with important consequences, but it was only intercepted and read after the fighting had begun and thus came too late.

3

It appeared that the winter would bring nothing new in the west, when, quite unexpectedly, Hitler surprised everyone with an unforseen action. At about the same time as the Allies were breaking the *Wehrmacht*'s resistance in France and when, as ordered, the Germans were not retreating in time and were losing a great many soldiers and a great deal of equipment, the dictator revealed to his closest entourage that he was planning for the autumn an offensive in the west, which would break through the front and force his enemies to retreat in panic.[8] For some months past he had certainly been living in his own world of dreams and deception, but he still realized that he could not plan an offensive without soldiers. He perceived the need to divert twenty-five divisions to the west, but was unable to transfer them from the Eastern Front, and so he gave his Minister of Propaganda, Goebbels, wide powers to sweep the exhausted country for new recruits. He was assisted in this by Himmler, the head of the *SS*, who was nominated head of reserve forces in the interior. The age for conscription was reduced to sixteen and raised to sixty, potential soldiers were drawn from offices, factories, shops, schools, hospitals and even from prisons and concentration camps. Moreover, about three hundred thousand demoralized men who had managed to extricate themselves from the crushing defeats in France were sent to camps and formed into new units. Despite the continual bombing, Albert Speer succeeded in keeping the war industries on a sound footing, transferring factories underground and supplying the new divisions with the necessary equipment. At the beginning of November, Hitler's new army became reality. It consisted of eighteen hastily formed infantry divisions, in which the barely trained recruits were stiffened by front-line soldiers, four *SS* panzer divisions, in which the soldiers' average age was eighteen, and two parachute divisions. Marshal Göring promised anti-aircraft cover. Von Rundstedt, who several months previously had been sent into the wilderness, was appointed to command it. He had little say, however, since Hitler made all the plans and gave all the orders.[9]

As soon as the opportunity for attack appeared, the Chancellor immediately came to life. He was already in his new field headquarters in a concrete underground bunker near Bad Nauheim, to the north-west of Zeigenberg. He ordered *SS* Colonel Otto Skorzeny, the same officer who, in September of the previous year, had carried out the daring rescue of Mussolini, confined on the Gran Sasso mountain (see Chapter 9, p. 141), to report to him. Now a new mission awaited the Colonel, which was to crown all his previous exploits. In great secret Hitler issued him with orders to prepare with the utmost urgency a special English-speaking commando unit, which, in British and American uniforms, and driving captured enemy tanks and vehicles, would appear in the front line of the attacking German divisions. The unit's mission was to capture important bridges and create chaos amongst the enemy by masquerading as some of his own units, giving false information, putting up incorrect road signs and sowing panic by whispering propaganda about German successes.[10]

Just as the idea of using Skorzeny's men in Allied uniforms (contrary to international conventions) remained a secret, so all the preparations were made as unobtrusively as possible, for only complete surprise carried any chance of success, on which the German dictator was basing all his calculations. Above all it was necessary to select the most suitable point for the attack, where the enemy was weakest, and Hitler, once again guided by his intuition, made an excellent choice in the Ardennes. These low, but barren, mountains formed a natural obstacle and for that reason the American units in the area were weak and, when surprised, presented no serious problem. Furthermore, the attack needed to be prepared in such a way that the divisions were organized and brought up to the start line, and supplies arranged so that the enemy suspected nothing. Movement took place only at night without lights, led by motorcyclists, and only specifically involved commanders knew of the planned offensive.[11]

Independently of every security measure, which is used on the assumption that the enemy's conventional intelligence is operating, von Rundstedt also ordered total radio silence. Although the Germans continued to believe that their ciphers were unbreakable, suddenly, at the beginning of December the British monitoring stations ceased to intercept those *Enigma* signals which used very difficult keys and were restricted to Hitler and his senior commanders. The Allies were already so used to obtaining information about the Germans' most secret plans from their radio signals, that the mere fact of sudden radio silence should have aroused their vigilance; however, it did not. Perhaps this was the result of over-confidence bred from recent victories, perhaps weariness and approaching winter were the causes; in any case, Hitler achieved his surprise. Once again, as in previous years, fortune favoured the Germans, for when on 16 December, von Rundstedt's tanks moved, the weather in the Ardennes was so bad that all Allied aircraft were grounded. Within three days the Germans had advanced more than seventy kilometres and had reached Ciney to the south-east of Namur. The main target of the offensive was the Belgian port of Antwerp, through which the Allies were sending most of their supplies.[12]

Once the attack had begun the air waves immediately came to life and the monitoring stations began to intercept German signals and send them to Bletchley Park. This suggested to Allied Intelligence that von Rundstedt's complete radio blackout had been really meant for the Germans themselves. The secret of the impending offensive had to be kept, since conventional Allied Intelligence was operating everywhere and was just waiting for some slip or indiscretion.[13]

After three days the weather improved and once again the sky was filled with British and American aircraft. The Germans immediately suffered accordingly, and their advance lost its impetus. The initial shock passed, Eisenhower regrouped and put Allied forces, under Montgomery's command, to the north of the German attack; the American garrison at Bastogne defended bravely and this initially serious threat was averted. The Fifth German panzer division continued to advance until 23 December, but two days later Bletchley Park deciphered an urgent signal in which the German commanders, von Rundstedt, Model and Manteuffel, reported to Hitler that a further advance on Antwerp was impossible and that an attempt should be made to capture Liège and establish a line from there to

Aachen. Naturally, he rejected this argument, but the reality of the situation prevailed and in January the final German offensive eventually came to a standstill. Further serious operations ceased, although Hitler was planning a new offensive in Alsace; the front became static and the two worst winter months arrived. The Germans regrouped their divisions and once again there was a change of command: this hopeless post was entrusted to *Luftwaffe* Field Marshal Albert Kesselring. All these events and changes were passed on to the Allied Western commander by Bletchley Park.[14]

That was the situation in the west, but on the other side of the Third *Reich* even the harsh winter provided no real breathing space. On 12 January the last great Soviet offensive began.

4

General Heinz Guderian, who in the last months of the war was Head of the German General Staff, had prepared a plan for the defence of the country, about which he had several times tried to convince Hitler. The basis of the plan was the belief that the main danger was approaching from the east and that every available effort should be made to halt it. Above all the Eastern Front had to be shortened and the maximum amount of men and equipment pulled back to the German frontier so that the defence of the country, and primarily Berlin, could be possible. The plan envisaged an evacuation by sea of the Sixteenth and Eighteenth armies, which had been cut off in Courland. A certain amount of their equipment would be lost, but over a period of several weeks it would be possible to save about five hundred thousand men, and Grand Admiral Dönitz had confirmed that the fleet under his command would be able to effect such an operation.[15] The plan further envisaged that all German forces still in Italy, together with any reserves in the *Reich*, would be immediately transferred to Pomerania. They would be joined by the Sixth *SS* Panzer division, commanded by Sepp Dietrich, a fine fighting unit, which would be moved from the Ardennes regardless of the ensuing weakening of the defence in the west. This would allow the formation of a shock army of forty divisions and 1,500 tanks, with which Guderian would undertake an attack on the Soviet positions in order to create a defensive line on the pre-war Polish–German frontier where there were still some old fortifications. This would provide some chance of temporarily staving off the threat to Berlin.[16]

Guderian was a resolute and courageous man capable of opposing even Hitler himself; he also had a valuable ally in Dönitz, for whom the dictator had a high regard; he based his arguments on the excellent intelligence material supplied by Colonel Reinhard Gehlen, head of Military Intelligence in the East, but he achieved nothing. Hitler did not even want to listen to the General's arguments, he did not even look at the maps showing the situation on the Eastern Front and the balance of forces, he impatiently waved the generals aside when they attempted to describe the seriousness of the situation and left the room. He was interested only in offensive plans, which consumed the remains of his energy. He was not in the least concerned about defence.

Until mid-January 1945 the dictator stayed in his Western Field head-quarters near Bad Nauheim, but after receiving news of the Soviet offensive, he returned to Berlin and, together with his suite, moved into a spacious underground bunker beneath the *Reich* Chancellery. It was built on two levels: the upper one contained twelve rooms where the lesser members of the Chancellor's staff lived and worked, while the lower one contained twenty rooms occupied by the Chancellor himself, Bormann, Goebbels, an attendant *SS* doctor, and also offices and a small conference room. Naturally the bunker had no windows; it had been built in great haste in 1944 and the concrete walls were bare and cold, almost without decoration, which resulted in a constant atmosphere of depression and melancholy, irrespective of the inhabitants' moods.[17]

In just a deep shelter, completely isolated from the world, rarely seeing the sky and the sun, hearing only the whistling of falling bombs and feeling their detonations, the exhausted and barely living dictator, with trembling hands and a drooping head, tried to continue to run the dying country and lead the almost ruined army. For several months, while still in his East Prussian headquarters and later in the west, he had been behaving like a sleep-walker on the edge of a precipice, retaining his balance only by a miracle; now he lost all sense of reality. He constantly dreamt of attack and continually imagined that he controlled men and equipment, and so sent orders to non-existent armies and long-shattered divisions; he marked on his maps the progress of German attacks, which existed only in his imagination. The time of day ceased to have any significance: conferences lasted until morning and he would go to bed at daybreak. His entourage of senior officers and close associates very carefully tried to direct his attention to the reality which began just a few metres from the ceiling of his bunker, but their fear of the dictator's rage continued to be so strong that none of them dared to tell him this to his face. Guderian tried by giving technical lectures, hoping thus to achieve some sensible decisions, which would enable a more effective defence to be made, but Hitler did not listen to him at all and, usually after a few minutes, got up and went out. Finally, when the General undertook a new, this time political, initiative and came to an understanding with the Ministry of Foreign Affairs and later with Himmler on the armistice in the west, Hitler, on 21 March, immediately ordered him to cease all his duties and take a holiday for health reasons.[18]

The personal magnetism of the *Reich*'s most powerful man began to weaken, accompanied by the destruction of his health by stimulants, his strange lifestyle and the terrible mental pressure caused by the succession of defeats. Sometimes, however, there were moments when the dying embers of the legend suddenly burst into flame and attracted as they once had. In mid-March Albert Forster, the *Gauleiter* of Pomerania, arrived at Hitler's bunker; he was a hard and experienced man who viewed things realistically. He had come to present the hopelessness of the situation around Danzig and obtain the *Führer*'s permission to withdraw and abandon the city to the Russians, rather than to ask for help. After less than twenty minutes of conversation with Hitler this almost broken man emerged beaming: 'the *Führer* has promised me new divisions, Danzig will be saved!'[19]

However, such scenes were becoming very rare, the myth was dying, the iron will which had formerly destroyed any obstacle, began to weaken and crumble. This was clearly evident in an incident involving General Dietrich von Saucken. In March, as a direct result of Forster's intervention, the General received command of the still existing Second Army Group fighting around Danzig. He arrived at Hitler's headquarters in an elegant uniform, decorated with the Knight's Iron Cross with oak leaves, with his sword by his side and with a monocle in his eye. Instead of the Nazi salute, which was obligatory in the Army at that time, he gave a normal salute and lightly bowed. Everyone present held their breath, but Hitler said nothing and only nodded to Guderian to outline the situation on the Danzig sector of the front. When Guderian had finished, the dictator added a few comments of his own and made it quite clear that the General would be subordinate to the region's *Gauleiter*, Albert Forster. There was a slight pause followed by something quite unexpected. Von Saucken struck the map with his hand and, without taking out his monocle, said: 'I have no intention of obeying the Gauleiter's orders.' There was complete silence, which was broken by Guderian, who in a friendly way tried to change the General's attitude. He was joined by Bormann, but von Saucken repeated firmly: 'I have no intention of doing so.' Once again this was followed by silence, when suddenly Hitler said in a tired, toneless voice: 'Very well Saucken, you will be in full command.'[20]

It might have seemed that in such circumstances, when the fortunes of Germany continued to lie in the hands of a sick man, the Allies no longer had anything to fear and that the war in Europe was virtually over. Yet it was otherwise. In December 1944 the American press suggested that, despite the Allies' massive superiority, they might still have great difficulty in finally destroying the Third *Reich*. Hitler was a fanatic and would never surrender, he was also in the process of preparing a defensive redoubt in the Alps not far from Berchtesgaden, extending into Bavaria, Austria and northern Italy. Deep underground caverns were drilled out of the solid rock for factories, storehouses, living quarters, shelters and other facilities, while trains loaded with arms and supplies headed rapidly towards them. At the last minute Hitler, together with leading Nazis and top military leaders, would move there, surround himself with two hundred thousand *SS* veterans and defend 'The Alpine Redoubt' for months and even years. There was even a belief that the Germans might attack Switzerland to take over its underground defensive installations.[21]

At the same time throughout the whole of Germany a secret underground organization, called *Werwolf*, began to grow; it was organized by the *SS* and consisted mainly of youngsters in the *Hitlerjugend* (the Nazi equivalent of the boy scouts). After a short period of training, the members of *Werwolf* were to start operations on territory already occupied by the Allies, carrying out acts of sabotage and murdering occupation troops and German collaborators.[22]

At first such press remarks were ignored, but attitudes swiftly changed. Once more the mistake of insisting upon unconditional surrender appeared only too clearly. How much easier it was for Goebbels to incite the German people to resist to the end, painting for them a picture of their fate under an occupation by severe and brutal victors, who refused to enter into any negotiations. General Eisenhower took the whole matter very seriously and it was he who decided the lines of advance against Germany.

Information on these preparations by the Germans came from conventional intelligence, but it was not sufficently accurate and, furthermore, it was essential to know what Hitler himself intended to do. It was difficult to have agents amongst his closest staff, but it was still possible to read his radio messages. By now Bletchley Park had no trouble in breaking them, since it was fully in command of *Enigma* and *Geheimschreiber* ciphers. By reading signals sent from the underground bunker it was possible to follow the *Führer*'s movements, since after all he could be maintaining the illusion that he was in the capital, while simultaneously preparing in secret to escape south from the almost encircled city to his final defensive stronghold. By the last few months of the war British radio-intelligence experts had so much experience that they could establish from the tone of a deciphered signal whether or not it had originated from Hitler. When in mid-April they were faced with a signal declaring that 'Once again Bolshevism will suffer Asia's old fate, it will founder on the Capital of the *Reich*. Berlin stays German, Vienna will be German again and Europe will never be Russia', they had no doubts that this was the work of the madman who had begun the war.[23] He was in that case in Berlin and apparently intended to stay there until the end. Furthermore, from the signals which he sent and received, there was no indication of the existence of an 'Alpine Redoubt'. In fact it later transpired that it had been a Goebbels-inspired propaganda story, whose aim had been to encourage the Germans to continue fighting.

5

People in a hopeless situation grasp at the most unusual means to survival, and so it was with expiring Nazism. On 12 April President Roosevelt died and the German Minister of Propaganda, Goebbels, created as much fuss over this as if the war depended on some solitary duel between the leaders, one of whom had suddenly died before they could come to grips. What press there still was in Germany described the death as an exceptional event, the radio repeated it many times, treating it as a gift from God which would change the course of the war. The American-Soviet alliance would accordingly collapse and victory would now go to Germans. Whispered propaganda linked Roosevelt's death with the secret weapons which would any day enter action; soldiers manning defensive positions in the West passed on the tale that American divisions would join them and that together they would attack the Russians.

Meanwhile the Third *Reich* was in its death-throes, which were as evident on every front as they were in the underground bunker where Hitler and his staff had isolated themselves. Bletchley Park deciphered signals which indicated that right up to the very end the bunker was the scene of a power struggle, as though the country had a great future before it, instead of ruin and final total defeat. On 23 April a signal from Göring was deciphered in which the Deputy Chancellor, in the south of Germany, while reaffirming his loyalty, offered to assume complete control over the country within twenty-four hours, since Hitler no longer had freedom of action. No reply on that same day would be confirmation that the *Führer* accepted his proposal. The reaction was immediate: Göring was thrown out of the Party, stripped of all his duties and an order was issued for his arrest. The originator of this reply to Göring was Bormann, who thus, just before the final catastrophe, rid himself of yet another rival.[24]

The underground bunker came to life once more and those immured within witnessed the dictator's final outburst of optimism. On 26 April American and Soviet units met for the first time at Torgau, to the west of Elbe, and a misunderstanding arose between the commanders as to the boundaries of the zones of occupation. The bunker intercepted a report from a neutral radio station, which exaggerated the event. Hitler reacted to this rather insignificant incident as if struck by an electric current and his eyes lit up with their old fire. In great excitement he turned to his staff: 'There is a possibility that tomorrow our enemies will turn on each other. . . . Any day and at any time war might break out between the Bolsheviks and the Anglo-Saxons.'[25]

On the evening of the same day a small reconnaissance aircraft landed by the Brandenburger Tor; it was piloted by the famous Hanna Reitsch, the same woman who had carried out a test flight on a V–1 flying bomb. She brought with her the wounded new Commander of the *Luftwaffe*, General Robert von Greim, whom Hitler had appointed in place of Göring and whom he wished to inform of this in person. Hanna Reitsch, with whom the *Führer* had a sentimental relationship, offered to get him out of Berlin. Hitler refused. This was the last attempt made to persuade him to leave the encircled city.[26]

Meanwhile in the north, near Hamburg, Himmler, the head of the *SS*, had made secret contact with the representative of the Swedish Red Cross, Count Folke Bernadotte, with the intention of using him as an intermediary to begin discussions with the Western Allies on a ceasefire. In the underground bunker in Berlin, just as in Bletchley Park, the enemy's signals were read and events on his side of the front were studied carefully. Hitler was given a Reuter despatch describing Himmler's initiative. His fury was so great that not only did he relieve Himmler of all his duties and issue an order for his arrest, but he immediately carried out a short investigation and saw to it that the traitor's liaison officer, *SS* General Hermann Fegelein, who worked in the bunker, was shot on the spot.[27] The dictator's grasp, rapacious to the last, was no longer, however, able to reach Himmler himself, who continued to act on his own. The Western Allies rejected any idea of discussions with the head of the *SS*, who was responsible for countless crimes, but Himmler was not the least discomforted and began preparations to assume power and form a new government.[28]

Hitler passed the last two days of April peacefully. The whole bunker now trembled from the heavy artillery shells which were exploding on the *Reich* Chancellery, but the dictator no longer paid attention to anything outside. He had reconciled himself to his fate and knew that he now had to carry out his decision concerning his own life. He dictated his political will and married Eva Braun, who had arrived at the bunker a few days previously to share his last hours and fate.

In the afternoon of 30 April those in the bunker heard a single shot amidst the clamour of exploding shells.

6

All the offices, barracks and huts at Bletchley Park continued to work: the teleprinters carried on typing, the experts continued to pore over their texts, deciphering signals at top speed, but the most important and the most dramatic period of the war had ended.

The war still continued in the Far East and the atom bomb had not yet been dropped, but *Enigma* and all its secrets, successes, achievements and failures had played its part.

NOTES

1. Mrs Thompson, op. cit.
2. Winterbotham, op. cit., pp. 202–5.
3. Calvocoressi and Wint, op. cit., pp. 760–5.
4. Winterbotham, op. cit., pp. 210–11.
5. Ibid, p. 211.
6. Józef Garliński, *Poland, SOE and the Allies*, London, 1969, pp. 187–209.
7. Public Record Office, file DEFE 3/1, despatch CX/MSS/T264/50, 2 August 1944, 16.30.
8. Peter Elstop, *Hitler's Last Offensive*, London, 1971, pp. 4–6.
9. Ibid, pp. 7–16.
10. Ibid, pp. 19–23.
11. Ibid, p. 15.
12. Ibid, pp. 179–89. Also: Winterbotham, pp. 213–14.
13. Winterbotham, op. cit., p. 214.
14. Ibid, pp. 217–18. Also: Calvocoressi and Wint, op. cit., pp. 526–33.
15. Gerhard Boldt, *Hitler's Last Days*, London, 1973, pp. 50–3.
16. Ibid, pp. 76–7.
17. Fest, op. cit., p. 726.
18. Ibid, pp. 94–6.
19. Ibid, p. 729.
20. Boldt, op. cit., pp. 79–81.
21. Charles Whiting, *Werewolf*, London, 1972, pp. 138–9.
22. Ibid, p. 139.
23. Winterbotham, op. cit., p. 222.
24. Ibid, pp. 222–3. Also: Boldt, op. cit., pp. 138–9.
25. Boldt, op. cit., pp. 145–6.
26. Ibid, pp. 154–5.
27. Fest op. cit., p. 744.
28. Speer, op. cit., pp. 486–7.

Epilogue

IN THE SMALL SWISS TOWN of Zug, between Zürich and Lucerne, stands a modern factory, built by Boris Hagelin in 1952. It is called Crypto AG and has an attractive and interesting appearance, while not of an overpowering size. This is the only firm of its kind in the world producing secure cipher machines in all four ciphering fields: text, voice, data and facsimile. Thus its machines are in use in nearly one hundred countries, providing as they do maximum security.

To get inside the factory one has to receive an invitation and a pass, go through a security check and be accompanied the whole time by a representative of the management. Yet it is worth the effort, for the interior is quite fascinating.

First of all the guest is shown a colour film outlining the development of the factory and its most important facilities. The straightforward commentary, against a film background, provides an easy introduction and prepares one for subsequent impressions. After the film one is led through a series of rooms in which various complex parts of the machines are designed and produced. Almost every question is answered, but one needs to be a specialist to understand all the answers. Despite the secrecy in which these machines are produced, the visitor is free to express interest in many areas and observe a number of production stages.

The exhibition provides the next impressive moment. In a hall several storeys high and arranged on different levels linked by stairs, several dozen exhibits are displayed showing graphically progress in the field of cryptology. First of all one comes to the earliest Greek and Roman devices, which although primitive, are also ingeniously simple. These are followed by the Swedish gravestone (the Rök Stone) from the ninth century on which the Vikings enciphered the story of their hero, Vämod.

The Middle Ages are poorly represented, since at that time the sciences were all viewed alike and secret writing was equated with the occult, alchemy and metaphysics. They have only one exhibit, which is a reconstruction of an invention of 1430 made by Baptista Alberti, which looks like a circular clock in a small box.

188

The next exhibit is a printed text of 1621 containing a secret signal. It is based on 'steganography', which is the art of burying or concealing information in an ordinary text. A little further on are some cylindrical objects from the end of the eighteenth century, one of which, constructed in Sweden in 1786, was really the first cipher machine. Next to it is the first machine made by an Englishman, Charles Wheatstone, who used the case of a large clock, and which created a sensation in Paris in 1867 (see Chapter 1, p. 8). This department is completed by machines dating from the First World War, which were very much more complicated, although still manual.[1]

Moving on one comes to equipment designed after 1918. The name of Boris Hagelin dominates, since he improved an earlier design, based on revolving drums, and perfected several ideas which enabled the first electro-mechanical machines to be produced. He designed the whole range of machines, the 'C' series, the most successful of which was the *C–35* produced to the specification of the French Army. One can only stand in amazement before this little toy, which can be slipped into a pocket. From it the legendary *M–209* was developed, which was bought by the American Army and of which more than 140,000 were made. Next to it is a further brainchild of Hagelin's, which was used by the Germans and which has an amazing story: the *C–41* (see Chapter 9, pp 149–50).

A little further on we come to the first original *Enigma* which was built by Scherbius in 1920 and sold commercially. It had as yet no plug connections and looked unexceptional, while externally it was no different from other devices built around the same time. There were a great many such machines, all of them electro-mechanical and based on the drum principle, producing millions of combinations. Designers were working on both sides of the Atlantic, both in Europe and the United States, simultaneously achieving very similar results.

Despite the advent of the Second World War and its enormous demands, the cryptologists were unable to break through the barrier of the basic principles on which their machines were based. These continued to be electro-mechanical even in the initial period after the war. The supreme example of this type of machine was the small and extremely elegant *HX–61*, which looks like a good portable typewriter, with no visible keys. The number of possible combinations produced by this machine is so amazing that the brain can hardly comprehend it unaided. The expert describing it at one of the lectures gave an example: if one machine setting is represented by a small grain of sand, another setting by another grain, and so on, then the whole room would quickly fill up with sand, as would the whole town, the country and the entire earth . . . just to begin with.[2]

This, however, did not satisfy the human mind, so, during the sixties, there was a real revolution in cryptology. In a separate room, and arranged on different shelves, are machines symbolizing man's creative powers and continual striving for progress. These are the very latest cipher machines, which in a few seconds can carry out calculations which during the last war were considered inconceivable. Each one of these machines automatically identifies the sender which it is expecting; at night it needs no operator and sets itself using its own basic key, after reading the individual signal key. It immediately accepts an incoming message, deciphers it and types it out in the original language on thin strips of paper. Finally, it automatically confirms the receipt of the signal. This marvel works in exactly the same way when sending a top-secret signal.

The accompanying expert then takes the visitor to a separate shelf which holds the supreme example of recent high technology in this field: the *Cryptomatic HC–570*. The first thing one sees is an attractive casing not dissimilar to a large portable typewriter (57 cm wide, 54 cm deep, 23 cm high and weighing about 21 kg). On opening the covering hood with a special key and raising it, the impression that one is looking at a typewriter increases dramatically. In front there is a keyboard arranged identically to a normal typewriter: on the top row there are numbers and below letters in the sequence familiar to every typist. Above the keyboard, just as in any typewriter, there is a sheet of paper on which typed symbols appear. However on the right there is an additional keyboard, next to which is a device through which move two strips of paper covered in a pattern of punched holes. This marvellous machine has a memory and can be fed information either manually, using the keyboard, or by an opto-electric punched paper tape high-speed reader; a text of thirty-two characters can be automatically corrected; as they show up on a running text display before being processed, the operator has seven basic keys, which permit an infinite number of combinations. The keys can only be obtained by using a mechanical key, which remains in the sole possession of the person responsible for the security of the agency using the machine. This same key opens the covering hood and provides an additional means of security. A key for a particular message may be automatically produced and fed in by an internal random number generator. For on-line communications with a partner terminal, an optional telephone coupler is available. Naturally only the highest government agencies can use such an elaborate and expensive machine.[3]

Examining this splendid product of human ingenuity, the visitor who knows the secrets of the last war must turn back to the beginning of the exhibition and stop once more in front of the *Enigma*. How modest and unassuming this wooden box, with its drums, plugs and keyboard, looks against the marvellous modern machines. This contrast becomes even more vivid when one remembers that all its intricacies, which taxed the brains of the experts at the time, could now be solved by a computer within minutes.

But everything is relative. The almost unbelievably rapid technical progress which began while the fighting was at its height with both sides drawing on their last resources of energy and continued in the post-war period, in no way diminishes the value of the war's cryptological achievements. *Enigma*'s inconspicuous and modest case, lost amongst the exhibition's other fine items, remains a symbol of one of the greatest pre-war and wartime accomplishments. It was a silent victory, cloaked in the greatest secrecy, and until recently concealed in the deepest archives, and still only partly disclosed; and it was accomplished by almost unknown people. Their successes were not acknowledged by reports from the front, their names were not included in lists of decorated war heroes, their photographs were not emblazoned on the pages of special editions of wartime newspapers.

They moved through the six years of war like phantoms and as enigmatically as the name of the machine whose secret they succeeded in discovering.

NOTES

1. Stürzinger, 'Cipher Technique Today', op. cit.
2. Ibid, p. 14.
3. Crypto AG, a pamphlet describing *Cryptomatic HC–570*, Zug, 1978.

Appendix

I INTRODUCTION

In order to decipher signals enciphered on the *Enigma* machine, it was necessary to possess such a machine and also to know its settings (keys). The Germans believed that this cipher system, if correctly used, ensured complete security; they did, however, realize that in a war both the machine and its keys could fall into enemy hands. They did not anticipate that the application of new cryptanalytical methods exploiting some of the machine's own characteristics, and weak points of operating instructions as well as mistakes by the cipher clerks, would enable the cipher to be broken using only intercepted transmissions. Polish cryptanalysts made use of all these circumstances relatively early on and solved the *Enigma* cipher by the end of 1932. Nevertheless, German experts were very careful and throughout the pre-war period introduced changes and modifications, which were intended to improve the cipher. All of these changes were quite quickly spotted by the Poles.

To appreciate the Polish cryptanalysts' methods it is first necessary to understand how the *Enigma* worked and how it was set and used.

II A DESCRIPTION OF THE *ENIGMA* MACHINE

The *Enigma* cipher machine shown on the photograph (plate 23) was issued to the Navy, Army, Air Force and other para-military organizations (SD the Police) before and during the war.

The machine fits into a wooden box which measures $18 \times 28 \times 34$ cm. With the lid of the box open (see photograph), we can see on the machine's upper side a keyboard similar to a typewriter's with twenty-six keys corresponding to the twenty-six letters of the alphabet.

There are, however, no keys with numbers or punctuation. Behind the keyboard, there is another cover (also open on plate 23). This lid contains twenty-six round transparent windows with the letters of the alphabet arranged similarly to the keyboard. When this cover is closed there is an electric bulb (visible on the photograph) under each window. Pressing a key causes one of the bulbs to come on and illuminate the letter above it, which is never the same as that on the original key. This comes about by the fact that pressure on the key disconnects the bulb with the same letter and in its place connects up the battery. This can easily be followed on Figure 1, p. 21 which depicts the machine's internal connections, showing how pressure on the key Q disconnects the bulb Q. The fact that no letter may replace itself is one of the machine's characteristics and is called the principle of exclusivity.

The electro-mechanical enciphering mechanism lies at the back of the machine behind the bulbs. This mechanism consists of three rotors on a single shaft, which rotate each time a key is depressed, and of two fixed rotors on either side of the moving ones. The moving rotors are called enciphering rotors while the fixed one on the right is called the entry rotor and the one on the left the reflector. By means of a lever the reflector can be moved either towards or away from the enciphering rotors which allows them to be removed together with the shaft. The rotor can then be taken off the shaft and arranged in any desired order.

The enciphering rotors are linked to the keys by cogs and appropriate gearing. Pressure on any key causes the right hand rotor to make 1/26th of a complete revolution. After a full revolution, the middle rotor comes into play and lastly the left-hand rotor begins to rotate when the middle one has also made a complete revolution.

Therefore, after twenty-six letters have been typed the middle rotor carries out 1/26th of a revolution, and after $26 \times 26 = 676$ letters, the left-hand rotor likewise carries out 1/26th of a revolution. It is necessary to type $26 \times 26 \times 26 = 17{,}576$ letters for the left-hand rotor to make a complete revolution. This is due to the fact that the enciphering rotors have 17,576 different positions. Furthermore, the three rotors can be arranged on the shaft in 6 different combinations, which then gives us $6 \times 17{,}576 = 105{,}456$ different positions.

Figure 2, p. 24, shows enciphering rotors, composed of two discs made of insulating material. Each one has twenty-six electrical contacts spaced regularly around its circumference. On one side the contacts are protruding and spring-loaded, and on the other flush with the surface of the disc. The contacts of one disc are linked by insulated wire with the other disc's contacts in an irregular way. The twenty-six contacts of one disc can be connected to the twenty-six contacts of the other disc in 403 291 461 126 605 584 000 000 ways.

The enciphering rotor has a ring with the letters of the alphabet, or the numbers 1 to 26; usually the commercial version of the machine had a ring with letters and the military one had numbers arranged regularly around it. This ring can be rotated in relation to the rest of the rotor and, by means of a rachet, it can be fixed at the position corresponding to the required letter or number. In addition to the cog-wheel linking the rotor's movement to the keys, each enciphering rotor has another larger serrated disc for turning the rotor manually. When the metal cover is closed, part of this ring with one of the letters is visible in a little window above the illuminated letters, and next to the window is an aperture for the serrated disc which protrudes thus enabling the rotor to be turned with the lid closed. There are three such windows and apertures, one for each rotor. The enciphering rotors are marked with Roman numerals. Above one of the contacts is a small groove, from which the contacts are counted making it easier to assemble them in the factory.

The reflector which is situated on the left of the enciphering rotor has twenty-six spring-loaded contacts, which are irregularly linked in pairs among themselves.

The entry rotor which is to the right of the three enciphering rotors has twenty-six flat contacts which are linked to the keyboard by a sort of switchboard, known as the plug connections.

The front of the wooden box can be opened (see plate 23) and then all the plug connections are visible. They consist of twenty-six double sockets located on a plate situated in the front under the keyboard, as well as double leads with jack-plugs. The sockets are marked with letters of the alphabet and the sockets can be connected up with one another by means of the double leads. In Figure 1 socket W is connected up with socket E. After the letter W is typed out, electric current will flow not to contact no. 23 on the entry rotor (W is the 23rd letter of the alphabet), but to no. 5, since E is the 5th letter; conversely current will flow from letter E to contact no. 23 (W). The twenty-six sockets can have a maximum of 13 leads connected up, but different numbers of connections were used at different times, and the number varied from five to thirteen.

Current is generated by a 4.5-volt dry battery. It is situated in a space on the right-hand side of the rotors.

A block diagram of the *Enigma* machine is shown on Figure 3. Pressing a key causes an electric circuit to be made; the current from the battery flows through the key contacts, the plug connections, the entry rotor, the three enciphering rotors one after the other to the reflector and back again through the enciphering rotors, the entry rotor, the plug connections to the bulb and the battery.

The machine's construction contributes to one further feature; namely the principle of reciprocity. This means that when at a particular setting we press the letter A, for instance, and the letter M lights up, if on the same setting we press the letter M, then A will light up. The point of this is that with the same setting the machine can encipher and decipher without any additional adjustments.

The usual operating team consisted of two cipher clerks with one typing out the letters on the keyboard, and the other writing down the letters lighting up in the windows. Sometimes they were joined by a third, and then number two would read out the letters aloud and number three would write them down.

III THE METHOD OF ENCIPHERMENT

There are many ways of using the *Enigma* machine. Several times, both before and during the war, the Germans changed their procedures trying to improve them and make it harder to break the cipher. For example, the operating instructions of 8 July 1937 laid down the following procedure in which four elements of the daily key were given, in other words the machine setting which had to be adjusted: the order of rotors on the shaft, the setting of the rings, the basic encoding position, the plug connections.

Plate 6 shows the daily keys for 4 May. On the basis of that key the operator had to work through the following four stages: (1) remove the enciphering rotors, together with the shaft, and fit them on the shaft in the order indicated in the key, that is rotor II on the right, rotor III in the middle and rotor I on the left, then replace them together with the shaft. (2) set the ring on rotor I at position 16, the ring on rotor III at position 11 and II at position 13. (3) close the lid and, using the exposed serrated discs on the enciphering rotors set them as follows: 1 on the left hand one, 12 in the middle and 22 on the right; these numbers corresponded to the basic position. (4) using the plug leads connect up socket C with socket O, D with I, F with R, H with U, J with W, L with S and finally T with X.

The net recognition groups given in the table of daily keys were used to identify the particular radio net and were included in the cryptogram.

After setting the machine according to this daily key, the operator chose three letters at random, which became the telegram key. He then typed out these letters twice, six letters in all, and they appeared in the illuminated window. For example, for the telegram key XFR he obtained the letters h f i k l b for the double key encipherment; these he then included at the beginning of the signal. Then he altered the enciphering rotors so that the letters XFR appeared in the windows and set about enciphering the text, which he typed out after having included at the beginning the six letters of the telegram key and the net recognition group.

Deciphering was carried out by the same process in reverse. First of all the operator set the machine according to the current daily key, and starting at the basic position he typed out the six letters comprising the enciphered telegram key, in this case h f i k l b. Then the letters XFR, in other words the telegram key appeared twice in the windows. He then adjusted the rotor so that the letters XFR appeared in the windows and only then did he begin to decipher the message.

IV CHARACTERISTICS OF THE *ENIGMA* CIPHER FROM THE CRYPTANALYST'S POINT OF VIEW

The *Enigma* cipher possessed certain features which were used by the Polish analysts to break it; among these were some characteristics of the machine's actual construction and the method of operation laid down by the German Cipher Office. Also helpful were mistakes made by the cipher clerks and the incorrect drafting of signals.

In the description of the machine it was stated that the middle rotor made 1/26th of a revolution for every complete revolution of the right-hand rotor, in other words after 26 letters had been typed. It followed therefore, that after the six letters which were necessary to encipher the telegram key twice in 21 cases out of 26, that is about 81 per cent, the middle rotor did not move nor did the left-hand rotor change its position. It follows from this that, together with the reflector, they could be treated as a single stationary rotor. This fact was extremely useful in finding the internal connections of the right-hand rotor.

The order of the rotors on the shaft could be altered; German procedures required such a change every so often, as a result of which different rotors moved into the right-hand position and the method developed for finding out the right-hand rotor's connections ensured that the connections of all the rotors could be worked out.

The rotors can be arranged in 17,576 different positions. This means that after 17,576 letters have been typed every possible combination has been used, and insofar as the keys have not been changed, all three enciphering rotors will have returned to their original positions. Thus the Germans reckoned that not more than 20,000 letters should be enciphered on the same machine setting for the cipher to be secure. This was stated by General Fellgiebel at a briefing session in April 1943. If the position of the right-hand rotor could be established, which was possible (most of the right-hand rotor positions could be mathematically rejected),then with messages beginning with the word ANX, and there were many such messages, all that remained to be done was to work through $26 \times 26 = 676$ positions, which did not require a great deal of time to find the basic position and ring setting. During the war the Germans included in their operating procedures instructions to include at the beginning and end of each message a word having no connection with the text in order that the cipher clerks should avoid using stereotyped beginnings of messages, address groups and endings.

The description of the machine mentioned two features of its construction: the principles of reciprocity and exclusivity, which were both used by the Polish cryptanalysts to help them solve *Enigma*. The principle of reciprocity together with the double encipherment of the telegram key at the same basic position formed the basis for the development of a number of methods both for discovering the machine's internal connections and reconstructing the keys.

Up to 1938 the basic encoding position was fixed in advance for a certain period for all users of a particular net and they all enciphered the message keys on the same setting. Knowledge of the basic position was necessary only to decipher the message keys, but the Polish analysts worked out a method of deciphering the keys from the beginnings of the messages; therefore it was unnecessary to know the basic encoding position. In 1938 the Germans changed the method of encipherment; the operator chose a basic position at random and wrote it at the beginning of the message, and then he carried out the double-key encipherment. The double-key encipherment was only changed to single encipherment during the war. Double encipherment had been a very great mistake, which the Poles had exploited to the full.

The operators made quite a number of mistakes of which the Poles did not fail to take advantage. Amongst these was for instance, their liking for telegram keys such as AAA, or three other identical letters. This was soon forbidden, but then they chose letters next to each other on the keyboard, and this was also quickly forbidden. Such characteristic keys were a great help in finding the telegram keys, but after they were discontinued, the Poles devised a new method based specifically on the fact that repeated or adjacent letters could be eliminated.

An interesting example was the solution of the SD code, which was used for encoding signals before they were enciphered, which in turn made it possible to discover the connections of the fourth and fifth enciphering rotors. After the introduction of *Enigma* for the *SD* ciphers, the Poles were unable to read its signals even when they had broken the daily and telegram keys. It was assumed, therefore, that the *SD* must be using some special method, until in one of the signals the word EINZ (one) was noticed amidst the deciphered letters, which were otherwise quite incomprehensible. It was then obvious that the operator had received the text with the number '1' in clear. Since the machine had no numbers, he had sent it as a word. It was clear that the rest of the message was in code. The Poles then rapidly solved this comparatively easy code, which, however, had further consequences. When in 1938 the Germans added fourth and fifth rotors to *Enigma* and changed the method of enciphering telegram keys, the *SD* introduced the additional rotors, but continued to encipher telegram keys with the same basic encoding position. This mistake led to the discovery of the connections of the fourth and fifth rotors.

V RECONSTRUCTING THE MACHINE'S INTERNAL CONNECTIONS

A mathematical permutation theory was used to reconstruct the rotors' internal connections. This theory had been enlarged by the Polish cryptanalysts and Rejewski had formulated a new theorem about the product of the transpositions, which was of great importance in the breaking of *Enigma*.

The *Enigma* cipher is a substitution cipher, in other words the machine changes plaintext letters into other letters, and mathematically this change is called a permutation, while a transposition is a specific type of permutation. For example, if the plaintext letter a is enciphered as b, the letter b as c, and c as a, then this permutation can be written: (a b c) or; (c a b) and it is called a cycle. Two letter cycles are called transpositions. For instance the cycle (w e) where the letter w becomes the letter e, and e becomes w is a transposition.

The plug connections given on plate 6 are a transposition; the connections of socket C with socket O make a transposition (C O). The permutation representing these connections, called S, will look as follows:

$$S = (CO) (DI) (FR) (HU) (JW) (LS) (TX) (A) (B) (E) (G) (K) (M) (N)$$
$$(P) (Q) (V) (Y) (Z)$$

This permutation consists of seven two-letter and twelve single letter cycles since the plug connection for these letters have not been made.

The flow of current through the enciphering rotor also creates a permutation. Thus for instance rotor II has the following connections (in the top line the flat contacts are represented by letters corresponding to their numbers and so respectively are the spring-loaded contacts in the bottom row – thus a is linked to contact u etc):

$$\begin{pmatrix} a\ b\ c\ d\ e\ f\ g\ h\ i\ j\ k\ l\ m\ n\ o\ p\ q\ r\ s\ t\ u\ v\ w\ x\ y\ z \\ u\ v\ w\ z\ l\ q\ p\ x\ h\ f\ s\ r\ j\ d\ c\ n\ k\ e\ y\ i\ g\ t\ m\ o\ b\ a \end{pmatrix}$$

This permutation can be designated by the letter M and written down in cyclical form:

$$M = (b\ v\ t\ i\ h\ x\ o\ c\ w\ m\ j\ f\ q\ k\ s\ y) (a\ u\ g\ p\ n\ d\ z) (l\ r\ e)$$

The permutation M consists of three cycles: one sixteen-letter, one seven and one three.

This permutation M, as well as the permutations representing the internal connections of the remaining enciphering rotors, the reflector and the keyboard connections with the entry rotor constituted the machine's secret. The course of the current from the keyboard to the bulb can be expressed as an equation consisting of the product of the permutations. If we use the letter A to denote the permutations effected by the machine on depressing any key, then it will consist of the product of the permutations, where each one corresponds to the flow of current through the mechanism in each block (Figure 3, p. 31) and also of the permutation, which we shall call P, representing 1/26th of the drum's complete revolution, which takes place after the key is pressed. Permutation P consists of a single twenty-six letter cycle replacing each letter by the one following it:

$$P = (a\ b\ c\ d\ e\ f\ g\ h\ i\ j\ k\ l\ m\ n\ o\ p\ q\ r\ s\ t\ u\ v\ w\ x\ y\ z)$$

We call the permutation, created by the plug connections S, the permutation representing the connections between the keys and entry rotor H, the rotors (going from left to right) L, M, N and the reflector permutation R. Then permutation A, as well as the permutations expressing the next five depressing of keys called B, C, D, E and F will look as follows:

$$A = S\ H\ P\ N\ P^{-1}\ M\ L\ R\ L^{-1}\ M^{-1}\ P\ N^{-1}\ P^{-1}\ H^{-1}\ S^{-1}$$
$$B = S\ H\ P^2\ N\ P^{-2}\ M\ L\ R\ L^{-1}\ M^{-1}\ P^2\ N^{-1}\ P^{-2}\ H^{-1}\ S^{-1}$$
$$C = S\ H\ P^3\ N\ P^{-3}\ M\ L\ R\ L^{-1}\ M^{-1}\ P^3\ N^{-1}\ P^{-3}\ H^{-1}\ S^{-1}$$
$$D = S\ H\ P^4\ N\ P^{-4}\ M\ L\ R\ L^{-1}\ M^{-1}\ P^4\ N^{-1}\ P^{-4}\ H^{-1}\ S^{-1}$$
$$E = S\ H\ P^5\ N\ P^{-5}\ M\ L\ R\ L^{-1}\ M^{-1}\ P^5\ N^{-1}\ P^{-5}\ H^{-1}\ S^{-1}$$
$$F = S\ H\ P^6\ N\ P^{-6}\ M\ L\ R\ L^{-1}\ M^{-1}\ P^6\ N^{-1}\ P^{-6}\ H^{-1}\ S^{-1}$$

If we assume that the middle and left-hand rotors have not moved which is quite likely, since in twenty-one cases of twenty-six they remain stationary, it is possible to treat both these rotors and the reflector as one stationary unit Q. The equations will be now:

$$A = S \ H \ P \ N \ P^{-1} \ Q \ P \ N^{-1} \ P^{-1} \ H^{-1} \ S^{-1}$$
$$B = S \ H \ P^2 \ N \ P^{-2} \ Q \ P^2 \ N^{-1} \ P^{-2} \ H^{-1} \ S^{-1}$$
$$C = S \ H \ P^3 \ N \ P^{-3} \ Q \ P^3 \ N^{-1} \ P^{-3} \ H^{-1} \ S^{-1}$$
$$D = S \ H \ P^4 \ N \ P^{-4} \ Q \ P^4 \ N^{-1} \ P^{-4} \ H^{-1} \ S^{-1}$$
$$E = S \ H \ P^5 \ N \ P^{-5} \ W \ P^5 \ N^{-1} \ P^{-5} \ H^{-1} \ S^{-1}$$
$$F = S \ H \ P^6 \ N \ P^{-6} \ Q \ P^6 \ N^{-1} \ P^{-6} \ H^{-1} \ S^{-1}$$

In the above equations the left-hand side is known and on the right side only P is known. In order to find out the rotors' internal connections this series of six equations must be solved, which is exceptionally difficult. Things were made much easier when a copy of all keys for a two-month period were obtained from the French Intelligence; and so for this period the plug connections were known, in other words the permutation S and from all material it was possible to find out the permutations A, B, C, D, E and F, by a method discussed in the following section. These equations could be solved by using Rejewski's theorem of the product of transposition: if two permutations are composed solely of transpositions, then their product will include an equal number of cycles of the same length.

The solution of these equations gave the internal connections of the rotors as well as of the reflector. In order to find out H (the connections between the entry rotor and the keyboard) a method was developed based on knowledge of the daily keys for a two-month period.

It was not difficult to find during this two-month period for which the daily keys were known two days in which the order of the rotors on the shaft was the same and in which the right-hand rotor was in the same position, in other words when for the right-hand rotor the difference between the basic position and ring setting was the same. For each of these two days six equations A, B, C, D, E, and F had to be written, these equations will be different for each day as the plugboard connections S are different as well as the permutation R but P and N will be the same. From these twelve equations H can be calculated. This is a difficult and lengthy task and the result is surprising because permutation H equals identity. This means that the key with letter A is connected to the first contact of the entry rotor, letter B to second, C to third and so on.

Knowledge of all internal connection of the *Enigma* enabled a replica of the German machine to be built.

VI BREAKING THE TELEGRAM KEYS

For the first few years after the machine's introduction the Germans enciphered telegram keys using the method previously described. Every signal on a particular net had its telegram key enciphered twice with the same daily key, in other words with the same machine setting and basic encoding position, which, together with the details of the daily key, were not known to the decipherer. Despite this and without a more detailed knowledge of the machine, it was possible to break these keys. It was also helpful that the German cipher clerks at that time often used stereotyped keys, such as AAA, SSS, QWE, and so on. This made life somewhat easier for them and prevented mistakes, since it was much simpler, for instance, to type out the same letter six times, or even three adjacent ones, than three letters on different parts of the keyboard. Eventually this sort of key was prohibited, but too late, for the Polish analysts had used this type of characteristic key to decipher the telegram keys, which also helped to solve the equations described in the previous section.

Let us assume that the analysts had sixty-five signals with the following first six letters which are a doubly enciphered key:

1. auq amn	14. ind jhu	27. pvj feg	40. sjm spo	53. wtm rao
2. bnh chl	15. jwf mic	28. qga lyb	41. sjm spo	54. wtm rao
3. bct cgj	16. jwf mic	29. qga lyb	42. sjm spo	55. wtm rao
4. cik bzt	17. khb xjv	30. rjl wpx	43. sug smf	56. wki rkk
5. ddb vdv	18. khb xjv	31. rjl wpx	44. sug smf	57. xrs gnm
6. ejp ips	19. ldr hde	32. rjl wpx	45. tmn eby	58. xrs gnm
7. fbr kle	20. ldr hde	33. rjl wpx	46. tmn eby	59. xoi guk
8. gpb zsv	21. maw uxp	34. rfc wqq	47. taa exb	60. xyw gcp
9. hno thd	22. maw uxp	35. syx scv	48. use nwh	61. ypc osq
10. hno thd	23. nxd qtu	36. syx scv	49. vii poh	62. ypc osq
11. hxv tti	24. nxd qtu	37. syx scv	50. vii poh	63. zzy yra
12. ikg jkf	25. nlu qfz	38. syx scv	51. vqz pvr	64. zef yoc
13. ikg jkf	26. obu dlz	39. syx scv	52. vqz pvr	65. zsj ywg

For clarity we have omitted the prefix and net recognition groups, and we have presented the six letters in groups of three letters, the first of which represented the first encipherment of the key, and the second the second encipherment. In other words the plaintext of both groups was the same, and thus the first letter represented the same letter of the key as did the fourth, the second as the fifth and the third the same as the sixth.

Closer analysis of the beginning of these signals shows that if they have the same first letter, for example the second and third ones have the letter b, then the fourth letters will be same. In our example the fourth letter in each message is the letter c. Furthermore, it is clear from the signals shown here that many have identical beginnings, for instance the ninth and tenth, twelfth and thirteenth etc. Since in a twenty-six letter alphabet there are $26 \times 26 \times 26 = 17{,}576$ three-letter combinations, it follows that signals with identical beginnings should be rare, and since this is not the case and there were frequent repetitions in the daily batch of intercepted transmissions, it is clear that the cipher clerks were, for one reason or another, using keys as already described (AAA, SSS etc.).

In the first signal the first and fourth letters are identical. This is the letter a; so the cipher clerk had selected a letter unknown to the cryptanalyst, which twice produced the same ciphertext letter, in other words there had to be a single-letter cycle (a). On the basis of Rejewski's theorem that there has to be another single-letter cycle, it turns out to be the (s) cycle in example 35. From the principle of reciprocity it follows that the first letter of the first signal key is the letter s, and in signal 35 the letter a.

Proceeding in a similar way with the third and fourth signals, we observe that in the third one the first letter is b, which at the fourth letter becomes c, while in the fourth signal c becomes b. We have thus a two-letter cycle (bc). Another two-letter cycle is formed by the first and fourth letters (rw), of 30th and 55th signals.

Examining the signals, in which letters of the previous cycles do not appear, and beginning with 5 where d becomes v, we see that in number 49 v becomes p, that in 27 p becomes f and so on, until we come to number 61 where y becomes o and finally in number 26 o becomes the first letter of the cycle d, thus closing the cycle which then looks as follows: (d v p f k x g z y o). Similarly we can arrive at another ten-letter cycle starting from the letter e, which has not so far figured in any cycle. We now produce the following cycle: (e i j m u n g l h t). Typing out a letter in a cycle always causes a letter from a cycle of similar length to light up.

The change from the first letters at the beginning of each signal to the fourth is the product of the permutations for A and for D as described on page 198. This change gives us the six previously discussed cycles, namely: AD = (a) (s) (bc) (rw) (dvpfkxgzyo) (eijmunqlht). Proceeding similarly with the second and fifth letter we obtain the product BE. BE = (blfqveoum) (hjpswizrn) (axt) (cgy) (d) (k), while from the third and sixth letters we obtain the product CF. CF = (abviktjgfcqny) (duzrehlxwpsmo).

In order to read the keys of all the signals the cycle must be arranged in the following manner, assuming that signals 35–39 have the letters AAA as their key:

```
a    bc      dvpfkgzyo
s    rw      iethlnumj
axt     b l f q v e o u m d
ygc     j n h r z i w s p k
        a b v i k t j g f c q n y
        x l h e r z u d o m s p w
```

The key of the first signal, which, after the first encipherment was auq, will be SSS, since the letter S comes under the letter a in the single-letter cycle, in the re-arranged BE cycles u is above S, and in the CF cycles q is also above S. Proceeding in a similar fashion with the remaining signals we obtain the following keys:

auq amn	:	SSS	khb zjv	:	LLL	taa exb	:	PYX
bnh chl	:	RFV	ldr hde	:	KKK	use nwh	:	ZUI
bct cgj	:	RTZ	maw uxp	:	YYY	vii poh	:	EEE
cik bzt	:	WER	nxd qtu	:	GGG	vqz pvr	:	ERT
ddb vdv	:	IKL	nlu qfz	:	GHJ	wtm rao	:	CCC
ejp ips	:	VBN	obu diz	:	JJJ	wki rkk	:	CDE
fbr kle	:	HJK	pvj feg	:	TZU	xrs gnm	:	QQQ
gpb zsv	:	NML	qga lyb	:	XXX	xio guk	:	QWE
hno thd	:	FFF	rjl wph	:	BBB	zyw gcp	:	QAY
hxv tti	:	FGH	rfc wqq	:	BNM	tpc esq	:	MMM
ikg jkf	:	DDD	syx sow	:	AAA	zzy yra	:	UVW
ind jhu	:	DFG	sjm spo	:	ABC	zef yoc	:	UIO
jwf mic	:	OOO	sug smf	:	ASD	zsj ywg	:	UUU ·
			tmn eby	:	PPP			

This table shows not only the deciphered telegram keys but also six full enciphered alphabets and their plain texts:

A = (as) (br) (cw) (di) (ev) (fh) (gn) (jo) (kl) (my) (pt) (gx) (uz)
B = (ay) (by) (ct) (dk) (ei) (fn) (gx) (hl) (mp) (ow) (gr) (su) (vz)
C = (ax) (bl) (cm) (dg) (ei) (fo) (hv) (ju) (kr) (np) (gs) (tz) (wy)
D = (as) (bw) (cr) (dj) (ep) (ft) (gq) (hk) (cv) (lx) (mo) (nz) (uy)
E = (ac) (bp) (dk) (ez) (fh) (gt) (io) (jl) (ms) (nq) (rv) (uw) (xy)
F = (aw) (bx) (co) (df) (ek) (gu) (hi) (jz) (lv) (mg) (ns) (py) (rt)

From these six alphabets permutations were obtained and used to solve the arrangement of equations described in the previous section (see pp. 196–8).

In 1933 the Germans forbade their cipher clerks to use characteristic keys, but in the meantime other methods were developed to discover the telegram keys.

In 1938 the method for enciphering telegram keys was again changed. Henceforth the basic encoding position was to be altered for each signal and so the above methods no longer applied, therefore new methods were developed.

VII RECONSTRUCTING THE DAILY KEYS

Possession of a duplicate cipher machine as well as the ability to reconstruct telegram keys was not enough to be able to read a whole signal. It was essential to devise methods of setting the machine, in other words to reconstruct the daily keys. A number of such methods were developed; on the one hand the Germans were changing their operating procedures, and this had to be taken into account, while on the other hand the Poles were constantly trying to improve their own techniques. There were simple methods and complicated methods, manual and mechanical, cheap ones and expensive ones. Only some of them will be described to show how specific elements of the key could be reconstructed.

The method for discovering which of the rotors on the shaft was on the right was based on the concept that if any two sentences, each of about one hundred letters in length, were written one under the other, then in German the result on average would be eight columns with the same letters recurring e.g.

$$w \ e \ l \ c \ h \ e \ r \ldots\ldots$$
$$l \ \emptyset \ t \ z \ t \ \emptyset \ n \ \cdot \cdot \cdot \cdot \cdot$$

This feature remained also when both sentences were enciphered using the same or similar key (i.e. two identical first letters). However, these same two sentences enciphered on two different keys produced a ciphertext of more or less similar frequency and with only four columns having equal letters. With an adequate supply of intercepted signals usually a dozen or so pairs of signals appeared whose two first letters were the same and only the third letter was different. After writing out both signals in a pair, so that the letter enciphered with the same rotor setting come under each other, one could find out at what juncture the centre rotor moved and also which rotor was on the right. The arrangement of the remaining rotors could be found by the grille method, which also gave the plug connections.

The grille method exploits the fact that within the first six letters, that is the twice enciphered key, usually neither the left hand nor the centre rotor move and that, furthermore, the plug connections change only a few of the letters (with six connections they leave fourteen letters unchanged).

We must now consider the equations for A, B and C discussed on page 198 and calculate in each one Q, which will be the same in all three. Omitting the permutations of S, we arrive at the following three expressions:

$$PN^{-1}P^{-1}APNP^{-1}$$
$$P^2N^{-1}P^{-2}BP^2NP^{-2}$$
$$P^3N^{-1}P^{-3}CP^3NP^{-3}$$

In these expressions the permutations, P, N, A, B and C are known and since the permutation S does not change all the letters, it is reasonable to expect that in the permutations A, B and C several transpositions will remain unchanged. The above expressions will now no longer be equal to one another nor equal to Q but some transpositions will be repeated. Although N rotor's internal connections are known, its position is not, but there can only be twenty-six different positions, consequently converting the N permutation in succession through P^{-1}, P^{-2}, P^{-3} ... P^{-25}, we arrive at all the permutations corresponding to N rotor's successive positions. Next we must carry out further conversions, one by one transposing A, B and C through the previously calculated permutations. Eventually the transpositions will be repeated. These are the transpositions which were not altered by the S permutation and belong to the Q permutation.

In practice the recurring transpositions were sought by means of a grille (slotted *sheet*) on which are written out permanently the N permutations changed to the power of P, while under the sheets are further sheets with the permutations of A, B and C which are moved in relation to the other sheets.

In order to find out the position of the remaining two rotors $26 \times 26 = 676$ attempts had to be made and each one consisted of typing out the first six letters of a signal with the left hand and middle rotor in every possible position, until eventually the same three letters, which were already known as a result of the methods for discovering the telegram keys were obtained.

It was necessary to establish whether, while depressing the first three keys, the middle rotor had moved, and secondly, whether it moved when the typing continued for if there was any movement it provided information on the setting of the right-hand rotor's ring. The setting of the rings of the middle and left-hand rotors could be obtained by means of trial and error.

Using the grille it was possible to work out not only the plug connection, but also the ring settings and these would be valid for a month, since before the war that was how often they were changed.

As many slotted sheets had to be prepared as there were rotors. In the event of the rotor order not being known, each sheet had to be used in succession until the right one was found giving the order of the rotor on the shaft. In order to avoid every day having to work through on the machine every possible combination so as to establish the position of the middle and left-hand rotors, a catalogue of all the possible permutations of the product $LMPM^{-1} L^{-1}$ of which there are $6 \times 26 \times 26 = 4,056$, was compiled.

The grille system has been described in quite great detail, since in certain circumstances it was used almost up to the outbreak of the war. It was also the first method which provided the elements of the daily key and is a good illustration of how these elements could be established. Therefore the remaining methods, or rather some of them, will be described very much more briefly.

Another means of establishing the order and position of the rotors as well as the plug connections was a filing system covering the numbers and cycle length of every possible position of the rotors, which, using three of them was 105,456. In the examples for AD, BE and CF the permutation S influences only the letters within the cycle, leaving the overall cycle unchanged. It sufficed, therefore, to compare the products of AD, BE and CF on a given day with similar products in the filing system in order to establish the required elements of the daily key.

In order to speed up the filing system a special machine called a cyclometer (see Figure 4, p. 34) was built. It consisted of two replicas of *Enigma* linked together, but without a keyboard and with only the rotors and different connections to bulbs, a number of which lit up corresponding to the double length of a cycle in a particular position.

The final two elements of the daily key, that is the basic encoding position and the ring settings, could be established more easily using the beginning of a signal. It was noticed that a great many signals began with the word ANX. The thing to do, therefore, was to take a signal and in all positions of the rotors try and see if any of the two first letters of the cryptogram produced the letters ANX. Most of the right-hand rotor's positions could be rejected mathematically, which greatly cut down on the labour required. It was only during the war that the Germans introduced instructions that a random word should be used before the text of a message.

On 15 September 1938 the Germans introduced into the Army and Air Force a new enciphering system, which meant that the previous methods were no longer applicable. Later, on 15 December, they added rotors IV and V. Therefore new ways to adapt to this had to be worked out. This was speedily done. One completely mechanical method was ready as early as November 1938 and used a machine called a *Bombe*. A second method, based on the *perforated sheets*, was not ready for quite some time. As has already been mentioned, it was thanks to the *SD* ciphers that the internal connections of rotors IV and V were quite easily established.

The new method of enciphering changed from the previous practice of retaining the same basic encoding position for the whole day to a system whereby each signal possessed its own basic position, chosen at random by the encipherer, and on which, as before, the telegram key was enciphered twice. It was only during the war that double-key encipherment was reduced to single encipherment. At the beginning of a signal the encipherer wrote out three three-letter groups, of which the first was the random basic position in clear, followed by the double-key encipherment. Although the products AD, BE and CF no longer existed, there continued to be a relationship between the first and fourth, second and fifth and third and sixth letters of the key and both methods exploited this relationship. If, for example, the first three groups of letters representing a telegram's key were: GKD WAV WHA then it was known that GKD represented the basic encoding position, while the first letter of the key became W after the first encipherment and also after the second. This arose from the fact that here there was a single-letter cycle (a constant point of permutation). A situation in which a letter of a key was transposed into the same letter after both encipherments was called 'female' by the British. If we now assume that the letter W was not changed by the plug connections then we must work through every position of the machine for W and see whether within three letters we obtain the same letter. If this occurs, it is necessary to ascertain whether this position is the right one, for there can be false ones. Thus further 'female' situations had to be found in other keys, and usually two further ones provided enough information to avoid a false reading.

Of course, instead of typing out and checking after every three letters to see whether three pairs of similar letters have become the same letter in each pair, it is possible to build a machine which will run through all the positions automatically and very much faster and which will stop at the right place. The AVA firm built six such machines; one for each rotor arrangement (Figure 5, p. 36) and was called *Bombe*.

The *perforated sheets* method produced results irrespective of the plug connections. It was also based on 'female' situations and the idea was that, if in a certain position we encipher the whole alphabet from a to z, then we obtain some permutation of A; if on the other hand we again encipher it three positions further on, then we obtain another permutation D. If we write out the permutation D under the permutation A, it transpires that one or more similar letters coincide one above the other, for instance:

$$A = I \ J \ WA \ D \ T \ldots$$
$$D = Z \ A \ WS \ MT \ldots$$

in which the letters W and T fall in the same place.

We can thus work through all 17,575 possible positions including them in the first class, if they are 'female', and the rest in the second. The ratio of first-class positions to second-class ones numbers on average 2:3.

For each position of rotor N a sheet of paper was prepared containing 26 by 26 squares corresponding to all the positions of rotor L and M. The squares representing 'female' positions were perforated, while the remainder were not. Each rotor sequence required twenty-six sheets. If on a given day, for instance, there were six 'female' pairs in the telegram keys, then six suitable sheets had to be selected from the series.

These were then placed on top of each other and specially aligned. So that parts of each sheet did not slide out of sight during the process, a sheet in practice had 51 by 51 squares, as seen on Figure 6, p. 40. Applying cyclically six sheets from the series of twenty-six, after a time a hole appeared through all six sheets. From the position of these sheets the sequence of rotors could be obtained, as well as the ring setting, and by comparing the letters of the key with those on the machine, so could the permutation of S, in other words the whole daily key.

After the Germans had increased the number of rotors to five, sixty sets of sheets each set comprising twenty-six sheets, were required.

Select Bibliography

ARCHIVAL SOURCES

1. *Archives*
Bundesarchiv-Militärarchiv, Freiburg, West Germany.
Instytut Polski i Muzeum im. gen. Sikorskiego (General Sikorski Historical Institute), London: Enigma machine.
Public Record Office, London: Intelligence from enemy radio communications, file DEFE/3.

2. *Unpublished documents, reports and statements*
Bonatz, Heinz, his opinion on the book, *The Ultra Secret*, Mainaschaff, 5 Nov. 1974.
Besprechung bei Chief H.N.W. von 15. bis 17. April 1943. National Archives and Record Service, Washington, document no. T-312–R-604.
Calvocoressi Peter, an interview, London, 8 Feb. 1979.
Chapman, John W. M., German Military and Civilian Cryptographic Services, University of Sussex, Brighton, 1978.
Danilewicz, Leonard Stanisław, 'AVA', description of the operations of the firm set up in Warsaw by his brother Ludomir (in Polish), Penrhos, 28 Feb. 1975.
Entzifferung deutschen Marinecodes, Berlin, 18 Aug. 1943, Seekriegsleitung: Abteilung Funkaufklärung, Kriegstagebücher, 1939–1945.
Evans, P. W. (aide to the American Military Attaché in Berlin), report on Enigma of 2 July 1931. Archives and Record Service, Washington, document No. 4131–B–2.
Garby-Czerniawski, Roman, recorded interview, London, 13 July 1978.
German instruction how to operate Enigma of 1937. Bundesarchiv-Militärarchiv, Freiburg.
Golombek, Harry, recorded interview, London, 21 Dec. 1977.
Good, Jack, Post-production script of *The Secret War* (producer Brian Johnson), project No. 06246/2036, London, 1977.
The Greatest Secret of the Second World War (transcript in German of a documentary programme on *Enigma*), Radio Hesse, Frankfurt-am-Main, 1975.
Hepp, Leo, recorded interview, Ulm, 19 Sept. 1977.
Hüttenhein, Erich, (a) Erfolge und Misserfolge der deutschen Chiffrierdienste im Zweiten Weltkrieg, paper presented at the conference 'Moderne Technologien und ihre Konsequenzen für die Kriegführung: das Beispiel der Funkaufklärung', Bonn, 15 Nov. 1978. (b) Recorded interview, Bonn, 26 Sept. 1977.

Select Bibliography

Intelligence from enemy radio communications (Enigma), *Public Record Office*, London, file DEFE 3/1, ZTP 1–936, 1941, documents No. 383, 384, 389, 395, 422, 589, 770, 902, 920; despatch XL 4251–4500 dated 31 July 1944 and 2 August 1944; despatch CX/MSS/T264/50.

Jacobs, Walter, Cipher Machines and Mathematics, American University, Washington.

Johnson, Brian, interview, London, 2 June 1978.

Kurz, Hans Rudolf, recorded interview, Bern, 22 Sept. 1977.

Langer, Gwido, (a) Reminiscences (in Polish), England, 1946. (b) Report for 1939–40 (in Polish), appendix: France, Paris, 12 May 1940.

Lisicki, Tadeusz, (a) Enigma, history and methods of breaking the German mechanical cipher Enigma (in Polish), London, September 1975. (b) Polish methods for the reconstruction of the Enigma setting the daily keys and German efforts to combat these methods, London, 1973.

Mayer, Stefan, (a) Authorized conversation with the author, London, 9 May 1977. (b) The breaking up of the German ciphering machine Enigma by the cryptological section in the 2nd Department of the Polish Armed Forces General Staff, London, May 1974. (c) Supplement to the paper of May 1974 (Enigma), London, December 1974.

Meyer, Walter, Remarks on Enigma, Thun (Switzerland), 8 July 1978.

Möller, Johannes (Germany), recorded interview, Cologne, 27 Sept. 1977.

Pawlica, Józef, interview, London, 16 June 1978.

Rejewski, Marian, (a) Appendix to a memorandum by G. Langer drawn up in France, 1941 (in Polish). (b) Reminiscences of my work in the cipher office of the Second Bureau of the General Staff in 1930–1945, Bydgoszcz, 1967 (in Polish).

Riste, Olav, The Norwegian Government in Exile and the Allies, 1940–1945, a lecture given during a Conference on Governments Exiled in London during the Second World War, London, October 1977.

Rohwer, Jürgen (Germany) (a) Diagram prepared in December 1976 for a lecture at the American Historical Association. (b) Interview, London, 5 July 1977. (c) Interview, London, 7 July 1978.

Różycka, Maria Barbara, Curriculum Vitae of Jerzy Różycki, Warsaw.

Schnieper Xavier, recorded interview, Lucerne 18 Sept. 1977.

Stand der englische Entzifferung, Berlin, 8.11.1940. Seekriegsleitung: Abteilung Funkaufklärung, Kriegstagebücher, 1939–1945.

Stengers, J. (Brussels), interview, London, 27 July 1978.

Stürzinger, Oskar (Switzerland) (a) Cipher Technique Today, paper from a series of seminars entitled 'Electronic War', Winter term 1976/77, Swiss Federal Institute of Technology, 17. Nov. 1976. (b) Historical Highlights on Mechanized Cipher System, extract from a speech held at the Swiss Federal Institute of Technology, Department of Military Science, Zürich, May 1960. (c) 'Maschinelle Chiffrierverfahren', paper presented on 10 Feb. 1960 at a Colloqium of Military Science in Switzerland (d) Interview, London, 23 July 1977. (e) Interview, London, 28 July 1977. (f) Recorded interview, Zug, 22 Sept. 1977.

Thompson, Ruth, recorded interview, Oxford, 9 Dec. 1977.

Welchman, Gordon, transcript *The Secret War – Enigma*, Project No. 06246/2–36, London, 1976.

Werther, Waldemar (during the war co-worker of Cipher Office of *OKL*), 'Die Entwicklung der Deutschen Funkschlüsselmachinen: die Enigma', paper presented at the conference 'Moderne Technologien und ihre Konsequencen für die Kriegführung: das Beispiel der Funkaufklärung', Stuttgart, 17 Nov. 1978.
Winterbotham, Frederick W. Transcript, *The Secret War*, Enigma, Project No. 06246/2–36, BBC, London, 1976.
Woolard, William, Post-production script of *The Secret War*, Enigma, Project No. 06246/2–36, London, 1977.

3. *Letters to the author*
Batey, Mavis (Oxford), 12 Feb. 1979, 18 Feb. 1979.
Bell, Ernst L. III (New Hampshire, USA), 18 April 1978.
Bonatz, Heinz (Mainaschaff, W. Germany), 16 Sept. 1978.
Braquenié, Corneille (Paris), 6 Feb. 1979, 26 Feb. 1979.
Calvocoressi, Peter (Woburn Sands), 16 Feb. 1979.
Chapman, John W. M. (Brighton), 28 Jan. 1978, 15 Feb. 1978, 11 May 1978.
Finch, Margaret (Basingstoke), 20 Feb. 1979, 23 Feb. 1979.
Fitzgerald, Penelope (London), 17 Feb. 1979.
Hepp, Leo (Ulm, W. Germany), 11 Aug. 1977, 4 Nov. 1977, 8 Feb. 1978.
Hoffmann, Karl Otto (Löhne, W. Germany) 19 Aug. 1977, 8 Sept. 1977, 8 Feb. 1978.
Hüttenhein, Erich (Bonn, W. Germany), 14 Aug. 1977.
Jacobs, Geoffrey (London), 24 Oct. 1978.
Johnson, Brian (London), 18 Jan. 1979.
Jones, Reginald V. (Aberdeen), 10 Jan. 1979, 18 Jan. 1979.
Kurtz, Hans Rudolf (Bern, Switzerland), 22 July 1977, 11 Aug. 1977.
Meckel, Hans (Hamburg), 3 Sept. 1977, 22 July 1978.
Meyer, Walter (Thun, Switzerland), 8 July 1978, 3 Aug. 1978, 28 Feb. 1979.
Möller, Johannes (Köln, W. Germany), 8 Aug. 1977.
Rings, Werner (Brissage, Switzerland), 2 July 1977.
Pünter, Otto (Bern, Switzerland), 10 Jan. 1978.
Rohwer, Jürgen (Stuttgart, W. Germany), 25 July 1977, 18 Aug. 1977, 25 Aug. 1977, 7 Oct. 1977, 26 Oct. 1977, 20 Jan. 1978, 22 Feb. 1979.
Stürzinger, Oskar (Zug, Switzerland), July 1977, 19 June 1978, 4 July 1978, 11 Oct. 1978, 25 Oct. 1978, 6 Nov. 1978, 29 Nov. 1978.
Vanwelkenhuyzen, J. (Brussels, Belgium), 9 Nov. 1977.
Winterbotham, Frederick W. (Devon), 14 Dec. 1978, 18 Jan. 1979.

4. *Other letters*
Chapman, John W. M. (Brighton) to Tadeusz Lisicki, 28 Apr. 1978.
Danilewicz, Leonard Stanisław (Penrhos, Wales) to Tadeusz Lisicki, 12 Jan. 1975, 28 Feb. 1975, 7 June 1975, 11 Aug. 1975, 26 Oct. 1975.
Mayer, Stefan (London) to Colonel Gustave Bertrand, 9 May 1976.
Rejewski, Marian (Warsaw) to T. Lisicki, 9 Aug. 1974, 11 Aug. 1974, 10 Sept. 1974, 1 Nov. 1974, 13 Jan. 1975, 20 Jan. 1975, 9 Feb. 1975, 28 Mar. 1975, 24 Aug. 1975, 14 Sept. 1975, 9 Nov. 1975, 18 Jan. 1976, 19 May 1976, 25 May 1976.

Select Bibliography

BOOKS AND ARTICLES

Accoce, Pierre and Quet, Pierre, *La Guerre a été gagnée en Suisse*, Librairie Académique, Perrin, Paris, 1966.
Alcazar, Angel, an article about his remarks in *The Daily Telegraph*, London, 23 Sept. 1978.
Astley, Joan Bright, *The Inner Circle*, Hutchinson, London, 1973.
Beesly, Patrick, *Very Special Intelligence*, Hamish Hamilton, London, 1977.
Bekker, Cajus, *Hitler's Naval War*, Purnell, London, 1974.
Bell, Ernst L. III, *An Initial View of Ultra as an American Weapon*, T.S.U. Press, New Hampshire, 1977.
Bertrand, Gustave, *Enigma*, Plon, Paris, 1973.
Bielewicz, Julian A., *Secret Language*, Communicating in Codes and Ciphers, Jupiter Books, London, 1976.
Boldt, Gerhard, *Hitler's Last Days*, Arthur Barker, London, 1973.
Bonatz, Heinz, *Die Deutsche Marine-Funkaufklärung, 1914–1945*, Wehr und Wissen, Darmstadt, 1970.
Bonjour, Edgar, *Geschichte der Schweizerischen Neutralität*, Basle and Stuttgart, 1970.
Bregman, Aleksander, *Najlepszy sojusznik Hitlera* (Hitler's Best Ally), 4th edn., Orbis, London, 1974.
Brissant, André, *Canaris* Weidenfeld and Nicolson, London, 1973.
Broome, Jack, *Make another Signal*, Kimber, London, 1973.
Buchheit, Gert, *Die deutsche Geheimdienst*, München, 1976.
Calvocoressi, Peter, 'The Secrets of Enigma', three radio talks, *The Listener*, London, 20 Jan. 1977, 27 Jan. 1977, 3 Feb. 1977.
Calvocoressi, Peter and Wint, Guy, *Total War*, Penguin, London, 1972.
Cave, Brown Anthony, *Bodyguard of Lies*, Harper and Row, New York, 1975.
Chapman, Guy, *Why France Collapsed*, Cassell, London 1968.
Clark, Ronald W., *The Man who Broke Purple*, Weidenfeld and Nicolson, London, 1977.
Collier, Basil, *The War in the Far East, 1941–1945*, London, 1969.
Collier, Richard, *Eagle Day*, New York, 1966.
Colvin, Ian, *Canaris, Chief of Intelligence*, Mann, Maidstone, 1973.
Costello, John and Hughes, Terry, *The Battle of the Atlantic*, Collins, London, 1977.
Davies, Norman, *White Eagle, Red Star*, Macdonald, London, 1972.
Deavours, C. A. and Reeds, James, 'The Enigma', *Cryptologia*, Switzerland, Oct. 1977.
Deighton, Len, *Fighter*, Cape, London, 1977.
Dulles, Allen, *The Craft of Intelligence*, Harper and Row, New York, Evaston and London, 1963.
Elstop, Peter, *Hitler's Last Offensive*, Secker and Warburg, London, 1971.
Farago, Ladislas, *The Game of the Foxes*, Hodder and Stoughton, London, 1972.
Fest, Joachim C., *Hitler*, Weidenfeld and Nicolson, London, 1977.
Fitzgerald, Penelope, *The Knox Brothers*, Macmillan, London, 1977.
Fitzgibbon, Constantine, *Secret Intelligence in the 20th Century*, Hart Davis, MacGibbon, London, 1976.

Foote, Alexander, *Handbook for Spies,* Museum Press, 2nd edn., London, 1964.

Fricke, W. F., *Agenten funken nach Moskau,* Kreuzlingen, 1954.

Friendly, Alfred, 'Confessions of a Code Breaker', *The Washington Post,* 27 Oct. 1974.

Garliński, Józef, *Hitler's Last Weapons,* Friedmann, London, 1978.
Poland, SOE and the Allies, George Allen and Unwin, London, 1969.

Haldane, R. A., *The Hidden World,* Hale, London, 1976.

Hinsley, F. H., *British Intelligence in the Second World War,* Vol. I, H.M.S.O., London, 1979.

Hoffmann, Karl Otto, *Die Geschichte der Luftnachrichtentruppe,* Vowickel Verlag, Neckargemünd, 1965/68/73.

Höhne, Heinz, *Codeword: Director,* Secker and Warburg, London, 1971.

Iwanowski, Wincenty, 'Tajemnica Enigmy', *Wojskowy Przegląd Historyczny,* Warsaw, Dec. 1977.

Johnson, Brian, *The Secret War,* BBC, London, 1978.

Joll, James, *Europe since 1870,* Weidenfeld and Nicolson, London, 1973.

Jones, Reginald, *Most Secret War,* Hamish Hamilton, London, 1978.

Kahn, David, *The Codebreakers,* Macmillan, New York, 1967.
Hitler's Spies, Hodder and Stoughton, London, 1978.

Kennedy, Ludovic, *Pursuit* (The Chase and Sinking of the Bismarck), Fontana, London, 1975.

Kesselring, Albert, *The Memoirs,* Kimber, London, 1974.

Kimche, Jon, *Spying for Peace,* Weidenfeld and Nicolson, London, 1961.

Kozaczuk, Władysław, *Bitwa o tajemnice,* 2nd edn., Książka i wiedza, Warsaw, 1969. *Wojna w eterze,* Wydawnictwa Radia i Telewizji, Warsaw, 1977.

Kurz, Hans Rudolf, *Nachrichtenzentrum Schweiz,* Frauenfeld and Stuttgart, 1972.

Lewin, Ronald, *Ultra Goes to War,* Hutchinson, London, 1978.

Masterman, John C., *The Double-Cross System in the War of 1939 to 1945,* Sphere, London, 1973.

Matt, Alphons, *Zwischen allen Fronten,* Verlag Huber, Frauenfeld and Stuttgart, 1969.

Middlebrook, Martin, *Convoy,* Penguin, London, 1978.

Montagu, Ewen, *Beyond Top Secret U,* Davies, London, 1977.

Navarre, Henri, *Le Service Renseignements, 1871–1944,* Plon, Paris, 1978.

Norman, Bruce, *Secret Warfare,* David and Charles, Newton Abbot, 1973.

Paillole, Paul, *Services Spéciaux (1935–1945),* Robert Laffont, Paris, 1975.

Perrault, Gilles, *The Secrets of D-Day,* Corgi, London, 1966.

Piszczkowski, Tadeusz, *Plebiscyt i powstania na Górnym Śląsku,* London, 1972.

Polonsky, Antony, *Politics in Independent Poland, 1921–1939,* Clarendon Press, Oxford, 1972.

Pünter, Otto, *Der Anschluss fand nicht statt,* Verlag Hallweg, Bern and Stuttgart, 1976.

Radó, Sándor, *Codename Dora,* Abelard, London, 1977.

Randal, Brian, 'The Colossus', The University of Newcastle upon Tyne, 1976. 'The History of Digital Computers', The University of Newcastle upon Tyne, 1974.

Renauld, P. 'La machine a chiffrer "Enigma" ', *Bulletin trimestrial de l'Addociation des Amis de l'Ecole Superieure de Guerre,* No. 78 (2e trimestre), France, 1978.

Rings, Werner, *Schweiz im Krieg, 1933–1945,* Ex Libris Verlag, Zürich, 1974.

Rohwer, Jürgen, *The Critical Convoy Battles of March 1943,* Allen, London, 1977.

Select Bibliography

'Special Intelligence und die Geleitzugsteuerung im Herbst 1941', *Marine-Rundschau*, International, Bonn-Duisdorf, Nov. 1978.

Royce, Hans, Zimmermann, Erich and Jacobsen, Hans-Adolf, *20. Juli 1944*, Berto-Verlag, Bonn, 1961.

Ryan, Cornelius, *The Longest Day*, Fawcett, New York, 1960.

Roskill, Stephan W. *The War at Sea, 1939–1945*, Stationary Office, London, 1954–1961.

Schellenberg, Walter, *The Schellenberg Memoirs*, Deutsch, London, 1956.

Schramm, Wilhelm von, *Verrat im Zweiten Weltkrieg*, Düsseldorf-Wien, 1967.

Seale, Patrick and McConville, Maureen, *Philby: the Long Road to Moscow*, Hamish Hamilton, London, 1973.

Sims, Edward H., *The Fighting Pilots*, Cassell, London.

Smith, Peter C., *Convoy PQ 18, Arctic Victory*, New English Library, London, 1977.

Speer, Albert, *Inside the Third Reich*, Weidenfeld and Nicolson, London, 1970.

Ścieżyński, Mieczysław, *Radiotelegrafia jako źródło wiadomości o nieprzyjacielu*, Przemyśl, 1928.

Tabata, Masanori, 'Was World War II Code Deciphered? "Enigma" still Puzzle', *The Japan Times*, Tokyo, 27 Aug. 1977.

Thompson, R. W., *Generalissimo Churchill*, Hodder and Stoughton, London, 1973.

Whaley, Barton, *Codeword Barbarossa*, MIT Press, Cambridge, Massachusetts and London, 1973.

Whiting, Charles, *Spymasters,* Dutton, London, 1976.

Werewolf, Corgi, London, 1972.

Wildhagen, Kark Heinz and others, *Erich Fellgiebel*, Im Selbstverlag, Hannover, 1970.

Williams, Neville, *Chronology of the Modern World, 1763–1965*, Penguin, London, 1975.

Winterbotham, Frederick W., *The Ultra Secret*, Futura, London, 1975.

Woytak, Richard A., 'The Origins of the Ultra-Secret Code in Poland, 1937–1938', *The Polish Review*, No. 3, Vol. XXIII, New York, 1978.

PERIODICALS

Basler Nachrichten (daily), Basle.

Bulletin de l'Amicale des Anciens Membres des Services Speciaux de la Defence Nationale (quarterly), France.

Bulletin trimestrial de l'Association des Amis de l'Ecole Superieure de Guerre (appears three times p.a.), France.

Cryptologia (quarterly), Switzerland.

The Daily Telegraph, London.

East European Quarterly, Colorado.

Frankfurter Rundschau (weekly), Frankfurt-am-Main.

The Guardian (daily), London.

Horizont (weekly), East Berlin.

The Japan Times (weekly), Tokyo.

The Listener (weekly), London.

Marine-Rundschau, International (monthly), Bonn-Duisdorf.
New Scientist (weekly), London.
Newsletter of the American Committee of the History of the Second World War (monthly), USA.
The New York Times (daily), New York.
The Observer (weekly), London.
The Polish Review (quarterly), New York.
Polska (monthly), Warsaw.
Przegląd Telekomunikacyjny (monthly), Warsaw.
Przegląd Wojskowo-Historyczny (quarterly), Warsaw.
Skrzydła (monthly), London.
Der Spiegel (weekly), West Germany.
The Sunday Times (weekly), London.
The Times (daily), London.
The Washington Post (weekly), Washington.

Index

Aachen 181
Abyssinia 67
Adcock, Frank 49
Africa 74, 78, 129, 137
Alamein 131
Albert, see Radó 108
Alberti, Baptista 7, 188
Alborg 86
Alcazar, Angel 143
Aleuten 177
Alexander, C. H. 49
Algeria 130, 133
Algiers 132
Alsace 3, 181
America 8, 135
Amsterdam 7
Anders, Władysaw 14, 141
Ankara 151
Anna 115
Antwerp 180
Anzio 141, 142
Ardennes 179, 181
Argentina 71
Arnhem 177
Arras 57
Arth 109
Ascension Island 137
Asché, see Schmidt 16, 17, 23, 26, 35, 39, 49, 76, 125
Asia 129, 184
Astley, Joan vii, xviii
Athens 97
Atlantic 1, 46, 73, 74, 78, 79, 89, 91, 92, 94, 95, 96, 98, 125, 130, 136, 137, 138, 143, 145, 153, 184, 189
Auschwitz x
Australia 126, 176
Austria 4, 35, 109, 151, 183

Babbage, Charles 49
Bad Nauheim 179, 182

Badoglio, Petro 141
Baldegg, Mayer von 109, 111, 116
Balkans 145, 151, 156, 159
Baltic Sea 4, 77, 78, 79, 95, 139, 166
Barry, Stuart Milner 49
Basel 15, 26, 110
Bastogne 180
Batey, Mavis viii, xviii
Bavaria 69, 183
Bay of Biscay 77
Bayeux 165
Bazna, Elyesa 151
Beaverbrook, Lord 84
Beck, Ludwig 104, 105, 168, 171
Bedfordshire 52
Belgium 15, 61, 67, 71, 77, 83, 100, 103, 107, 128, 156, 157, 164, 165, 166, 177
Belgrade 7
Bell, Ernest xviii, 127
Bennet, Susan xviii
Berchtesgaden 163, 183
Bergen 96,
Berghof 170
Berlin 5, 9, 12, 66, 67, 69, 70, 71, 73, 79, 82, 84, 97, 100, 103, 105, 106, 111, 114, 116, 118, 124, 130, 140, 144, 159, 167, 169, 171, 173, 181, 182, 184, 186
Bermuda 137
Bern 15, 109, 110, 116, 117, 175
Bernadette, Folke 186
Bertrand, Gustave vi, 13, 14, 15, 16, 17, 19, 20, 22, 23, 26, 35, 38, 42, 43, 45, 49, 56, 57, 61, 132, 133
Bevan, John Henry 158
Bevin, Ernest 17
Bill 115 117
Birch, Frank 49,
Bismarck, Otto von 5
Black Sea 68, 78, 159
Bletchley Park vi, ix, xii, xiii, xiv, xvii, xx, 48, 50, 51, 52, 53, 54, 55, 57, 58, 59, 60, 61, 62,

64, 71, 73, 77, 78, 79, 82, 85, 86, 87, 88, 89,
  91, 92, 93, 94, 95, 96, 97, 98, 99, 116, 117,
  118, 120, 126, 127, 128, 129, 130, 133, 137,
  138, 139, 140, 142, 145, 146, 147, 148, 149,
  157, 163, 164, 165, 167, 168, 174, 176, 178,
  180, 181, 184, 185, 186
Blizna 167
Blomberg, Werner von 105
Bock, Fedor von 61
Böhm-Tettlebach, Hans 105
Bolek, see Bertrand 38
Bolivia 71
Bolli, Margrit 108, 109
Bon Encontre 62
Bonatz, Heinz xviii
Bormann, Martin 115, 182, 183, 185
Boulogne 160
Boxmoor 133
Bradley, Omar 160
Brand, Quintin 84
Braquenié, Corneille vii, xviii
Braquenié, Henri vi 46
Brauchitsch, Walter von 61, 62
Braun, Eva 186
Braun, Wernher von 166
Brazil 71
Brest 72, 95, 97, 156
Brisbane 176
Britain ix, 17, 52, 60, 86, 110, 121, 133, 135,
  138, 156, 157, 161, 164, 166
British Empire 71, 111, 126, 143, 151, 176
British Isles 51, 82, 83, 88, 89, 90, 103, 115,
  125, 133, 144, 162, 164
Brittany 156
Broadhurst, S. W. 148,
Brooks, Anthony xviii
Bros, Josip 74
Bruno xi, 56, 57, 58, 59, 60, 61
Brussels 101, 103
Brutus, see Czerniawski 163
Brześć 56
Bucharest 56
Buckinghamshire 50
Budkiewicz, Jerzy xviii
Bug 56
Bulgaria 70, 71, 74, 151, 159, 160
Burma 126, 176
Bussche, Axel von 169

Cadix, see Fouzes xi, 132
Caen 164

Cairo 129, 130
Calais 156, 160
Calvocoressi, Peter xviii, 49, 79
Cambridge 48, 49, 50, 147
Canada 101, 138
Canaris, Wilhelm viii, 65, 66, 69, 104, 105,
  115, 171
Cape Matapan 129
Cape Town 137
Captain Kent, see Sukulov-Gurevich 101,
  103, 108
Carlo 109
Casablanca 131
Central Europe 144, 162
Ceylon 176
Chamberlain, Neville 46, 60
Chapman, John W. M. xvii, 153
Chatham 52
Cherbourg 165
Chiang Kai-shek 176
Chicksands 52
Chile 71
China 71, 176
Churchill, Winston vii, 51, 55, 60, 61, 62, 63,
  73, 82, 84, 85, 88, 89, 90, 105, 116, 125, 126,
  129, 130, 131, 143, 144, 145, 150, 151, 152,
  156, 177
Cicero, see Bazna 152, 156
Ciężki, Maksymilian 2, 18, 19, 38, 42
Ciney 180
Clark, Mark 142
Clark, *Nobby* 49
Columbia 71
Cooper, *Josh* 49
Copenhagen 15
Courn Wood 138
Courland 181
Cracow 18
Crankshaw, Edward 49
Crete 70
Crypto, see Denniston 38
Cunningham, Andrew 129
Czechoslovakia 15, 106,

Daladier, Edouard 46
Danilewicz, Ludomir 2, 3
Danilov, Anton 101
Danzig, *see* Gdańsk 4, 50, 183
Davidson 54
Delhi 176
Denham, Henry 96

Denmark 15, 60, 67, 77, 83, 86, 88, 96, 101, 103, 166
Denmark Strait 95, 96
Denning, Norman 91
Denniston, Alastair 38, 42, 43, 44, 45, 49, 50, 53, 129
Denniston, Robin xviii
Dietrich, Sep 181
Director, see Peresypkin 108
Dodecanese 70
Dohnanyi, Hans von 106
Dollis Hill 147, 148
Dominican Republic 71
Dora, see Radó 108, 113
Dover 10, 62, 83, 156
Dowding, Hugh 84, 85, 86, 87, 88
Dönitz, Karl 74, 76, 78, 80, 91, 92, 98, 130, 136, 139, 181
Dulles, Allen 110, 117, 175
Dunderdale, Wilfred 45
Dunkirk 62, 159

East Africa 3
East Europe 4, 144
East Prussia 72, 100, 151, 170, 182
Ecuador 71
Egypt 71
Eisenhower, Dwight D. 130, 159, 180, 184
Elbe 185
England 1, 50, 53, 82, 83, 84, 86, 87, 88, 133, 156, 159, 160
English Channel 77, 83
Estonia 68
Ethiopia 71
Eton 48
Europe 2, 4, 7, 8, 57, 62, 74, 79, 100, 101, 103, 124, 128, 129, 130, 136, 143, 144, 151, 155, 156, 158, 159, 170, 183, 184, 189

Falaise 165
Far East 79, 126, 143, 151, 155, 158, 176, 186
Farnborough 168
Faroe Islands 96
Fellgiebel, Erich vii, 30, 33, 66, 68, 76, 105, 170, 171, 172, 173
Ferdinand (Fernand) 115
Ferté, la 62
Finch, Margaret vii, xviii
Finland 68, 70
Fitzgerald, Penelope vii, xviii

Fitzgibbon, Constantine 118, 173
Flowerdown 52
Flowers, T. H. 147, 148
Fogelein, Hermann 186
Foot, Michael R. D. xvii
Foote, Alexander 108, 117
Forster, Albert 183
Fouzes vi, 132
France vi, xi, xii, 3, 6, 13, 15, 17, 39, 43, 47, 51, 53, 57, 61, 62, 63, 67, 70, 71, 72, 77, 82, 83, 84, 89, 97, 100, 101, 103, 105, 107, 109, 110, 113, 114, 124, 125, 126, 127, 130, 131, 132, 133, 144, 145, 151, 156, 160, 163, 164, 165, 166, 170, 172, 177, 178, 179
Freetown 137
Freisler, Roland 171
French Riviera 177
Fricke, Kurt 138
Friedman, William F. vi, 10, 23, 122, 123, 124, 125
Fritsch, Werner von 105

Galway 90
Gamelin, Maurice 57, 62
Garby-Czerniawski, Roman xviii, 162, 163
Garliński, Józef x
Garnett, Richard xviii
Gaulle, Charles de 17, 109, 110, 117, 130
Gällivere 73
Gdańsk 4, 5, 50
Gdynia 94, 95, 96
Gehlen, Reinhard 181
Gehrs, Erwin 102
Geneva 107, 108
Germany xiv, 3, 14, 18, 46, 52, 54, 65, 71, 89, 101, 103, 106, 107, 108, 109, 110, 112, 115, 116, 123, 125, 126, 131, 133, 141, 156, 162, 163, 169, 170, 184, 185
Gersdorf, Rudolf-Christoph 169
Gibralter 96, 97, 130, 133, 162
Gilbert, *see* Trepper 101
Gisevius, Haus Bernd 175
Goebbels, Joseph 71, 131, 158, 166, 179, 182, 184, 185
Goerdeler, Carl 105, 170, 171
Gollnow, Herbert 102
Golombek, Harry vii, xviii, 49
Good, I. J. 49
Good, Jack 147
Göring, Hermann 69, 82, 83, 85, 86, 87, 88, 102, 103, 105, 155, 169, 170, 179, 185, 186,

Gort, Lord 62
Gottenhafen, *see* Gdynia 94
Göttingen 19
Gran Sasso 141, 179
Grand Chef, see Trepper 101
Great Britain xiv, 6, 51, 62, 63, 67, 70, 82, 83,
  84, 85, 89, 90, 91, 92, 100, 101, 103, 107,
  114, 115, 125, 126, 130, 132, 133, 136, 145,
  161, 162, 172, 178
Greece 67, 70, 71, 140, 144, 160
Greene, Tom 47
Greenland 95, 96
Greim, Robert von 186
Gretz-Armainvillers 56
Grey, Travis de 49
Gripenstierna 8
Guderian, Heinz 157, 181, 182, 183
Gustaw III 8
Guzzoni 140

Hagelin, Boris vi, xi, xii, 67, 113, 123, 124,
  134, 149, 150, 188, 189
Hague 90
Halder, Franz 61, 105, 113, 168
Halifax 143
Hamburg 95, 186
Hamburger, Ursula Maria 108
Hamel, Edmond-Charles 108
Hamel, Olga 108
Harnack, Arvid 102, 103, 114
Hase, Paul von 171
Hausamann, Hans vii, 110, 111
Hawaii 121
Hebrides 89, 93
Heilman, Horst 102
Helldorf, Wolf Heinrich von 106
Hennessy, Peter xviii
Henniger, Hans 102
Henrys, Paul 17
Hepp, Leo xviii, 173
Heydrich, Reinhard 65
Himmler, Heinrich 167, 169, 170, 179, 182,
  186
Hitler, Adolf 12, 13, 29, 32, 35, 37, 39, 46,
  50, 52, 53, 57, 60, 61, 62, 65, 66, 67, 69, 72,
  76, 82, 83, 85, 89, 90, 91, 94, 95, 97, 100,
  102, 103, 104, 105, 106, 107, 108, 110, 111,
  112, 114, 115, 116, 119, 121, 125, 130, 131,
  140, 141, 146, 151, 152, 155, 157, 163, 164,
  165, 166, 167, 168, 169, 170, 171, 172, 173,
  178, 179, 180, 181, 182, 183, 184, 185, 186

Hoffmann, Karl Otto xviii, 173
Holland 61, 77, 89, 101, 103, 107, 156, 157,
  166, 177
Hong Kong 176
Hoover, Herbert 26
Huelva 140
Humphreys 54
Hungary 151
Hüttenhein, Erich xviii, 69, 173

Iceland 93, 95, 96, 137
India 176
Indian Ocean 73, 78, 90
Ireland 71, 78, 90, 137, 161
Italy 52, 68, 70, 107, 109, 110, 124, 127, 130,
  131, 140, 141, 143, 178, 181, 183

Jacobs, Geoffrey xviii
Japan 71, 111, 112, 122, 123, 124, 125, 131,
  151
Jenkins, Roy 49, 131, 151
Johnson, Brian vii, xviii
Jones, Eric 54
Jones, Reginald V. ix, x, xvii, 50, 51
Jutland 49

Kabacki Woods 41
Kahn, David 146
Kaiser, Henry 135, 136
Kandy 176
Keitel, Wilhelm 66, 163
Kennedy, Ludovic 80
Kent 86
Kesselring, Albert 83, 88, 130, 140, 141, 142,
  181
Kiel 9, 95, 96
Kiermisz, Józef xviii
Kishinev 122
Kleist-Schwenzin, Ewald von 105
Kluge, Günter von 165, 177
Knatchbull-Hughessen, Hugh 151
Knox, Alfred Dillwyn vi, 42, 43, 44, 45, 48,
  49, 50, 51, 138
Koch, Hugo Alexander 9
Kołomyja 27
König, see Stelmann 15
Königsberg 66
Kreutlingen 109
Kristiansand 72
Krupp 94
Krzeslawice 18

Index

Kuckoff, Adam 102
Kummerow, Hans-Heinrich 102
Kurile Islands 151
Kursk 150
Kurz, Hans Rudolf vii, xviii, 113, 117, 173

Land, Emory S. 135
Langer, Gwido vi, 18, 19, 38, 42, 43, 44, 45, 56, 58, 64, 132, 133
Lausanne 108
Leber, Julius 170
Le Havre 157
Leigh-Mallory, Trafford 84
Leipzig 105
Lemoine 15
Lemp, Fritz 89, 90, 93
Leon, Herbert 50
Lever, Mavis 51
Lewin, Ronald xviii
Lida 27
Liège 180
Lisicki, Tadeusz vi, vii, xvii, 133, 153
Lofoten Islands 93
London x, 7, 43, 44, 45, 49, 50, 56, 57, 58, 61, 79, 84, 85, 88, 89, 105, 109, 128, 129, 130, 133, 152, 166, 167, 168, 174, 177
Lorraine 3
Lothian, Lord 126
Luc, see Langer 38
Lucerne 15, 108, 109, 110, 111, 115, 188
Lucy, see Roessler 109
Lugano 110
Lütjens, Günter 96, 97
Luxemburg 77, 166, 167

MacFarlan vi, 57, 59, 60
Madrid 69, 143
Makarov, Mikhail 101
Malaysia 176
Manchu Kuo 71
Manier 15
Manteuffel, Hasso von 180
Margival 164
Maria, see Radó 108
Marseilles 103, 132
Marshall, George 145
Marstrand 96
Masson, Roger 110
Mayer, Stefan xvii 42, 43, 46
McCarty, Desmond 49
Meckel, Hans xviii

Medhurst, Charles 54
Mediterranean 52, 70, 74, 78, 79, 90, 128, 129, 131, 133, 145, 160
Menzies, Stewart vi, 46, 53, 54, 130
Metz 57
Mexico 46, 71
Meyer, Walter xviii
Michie, Donald 147
Midlands 84, 86
Midway 176, 177
Mihailovic, Draza 74
Mikado 121
Model, Walther 180
Möller, Johannes xviii, 9, 10, 173
Molotov, Vyacheslav 111
Monte Cassono 141
Montevideo 77
Montgomery, Bernard Law 129, 130, 140, 160, 180
Montpellier 132
Montreux 15
Moravec, František 38
Morocco 130, 131
Moscow 42, 100, 101, 103, 108, 109, 110, 111, 112, 113, 114, 115, 117, 118, 146, 150, 152, 158, 174, 177
Mountbatten, Louis 176
Muggeridge, Malcolm 118
Mulhouse 57
Munich (München) 35, 46, 66, 106
Münster 66
Murmansk 74
Mürren 15
Mussolini, Benito 35, 46, 140, 141, 143, 179

Namur 180
Naples 141, 142
Napoleon 17, 83
Narvik 73
Navarre, Henri 14, 15
Near East 52
Neuengamme x
Neurath, Konstantin von 105
Newfoundland 137
Newman, Max 147, 148
New York xviii, 123
New Zealand 176
Nîmes 132
Nimitz, Chester 176, 177
Normandy 156, 157, 163, 164, 165

North Africa xiv, 68, 70, 127, 128, 130, 132, 143, 147, 155
North America 78
North Atlantic 136, 138, 139
North Sea 77, 92
Northern England 84, 86
Northern Italy 141
Norway xiii, 60, 67, 72, 73, 77, 83, 86, 88, 93, 96, 97, 103, 106, 107, 156, 159
Nova Scotia 143

Oberndorf 69
Oder 166
Olga 113, 115, 117
Oran 132
Orselina 109
Oster, Hans 105, 173
Oxford 42, 49, 50

Pacific Ocean 90, 121, 122, 129, 136, 176
Pakbo see Pünter 109, 113
Palermo 140
Palestine 100
Palluth, Antoni 3, 19
Pantelleria 140
Papen, Franz von 151, 152
Paris 7, 8, 15, 38, 41, 42, 45, 56, 60, 61, 62, 69, 72, 103, 157, 159, 177, 189
Park, Keith 84
Pas de Calais xiii, 85, 157, 160, 163, 164
Patton, George 140, 159, 160, 164
Pau 132
Pawlica, Józef xviii
Pearl Harbor 121
Peenemünde 166, 167, 168
Penrhos 10
Peresypkin, Ivan 108
Perruche 15
Persia 71
Peru 71
Pétain, Philippe 63, 132
Petit Chef, see Sukulov-Gurevich 101
Petsamo 159
Philby, Kim 146
Pilatus 111
Pinky, see MacFarlan 57
Pisa 151
Ploesti 74, 159
Pokorny, Franciszek 18
Poland xvii, xx, 2, 3, 4, 5, 16, 17, 18, 19, 26, 38, 39, 41, 45, 49, 51, 56, 58, 66, 68, 70, 71

74, 83, 84, 91, 100, 103, 106, 107, 111, 117, 125, 126, 133, 144, 151, 162, 163, 166, 167, 168, 177
Pomerania 3, 4, 18, 181, 183
Pontresina 109
Portsmouth 157
Portugal 71, 110, 133
Potsdam-Marstall 69, 70
Poznań 3, 4, 5, 18, 19, 24
Prague 15, 103
Prussia 4
Przemyśl 10
Pünter, Otto vii, xviii, 109, 110, 111, 114, 117
Pyrenees 57
Pyry 41, 43, 48, 56, 59

Quebec 143, 144, 145, 150, 156

Radó, Sándor vi, 107, 108, 109, 110, 111, 112, 113, 114, 117, 118
Raeder, Erich 73, 83, 94, 95, 105, 138
Ramsey, Bertram 62
Raoul, see Moravec 38
Rapallo 6
Reichenau, Walter von 61
Reichwein, Adolf 170
Reile, Oskar 162
Reitsch, Hanna 185, 186
Rejewski, Marian vi, xvii, 19, 23, 25, 37, 44, 133, 198, 199
Rex, see Stelmann 15, 26
Rhineland 3, 35
Ribbentrop, Joachim von 111, 152
Riga 4
Rigi 111
Rimini 151
Rings, Werner xviii
Rock, Margaret 51
Roessler, Olga 108
Roessler, Rudolf vi, xiii, 108, 109, 111, 113, 114, 115, 116, 117, 118, 119, 146, 173
Röhm, Ernst 69, 104
Rohwer, Jürgen vii, xviii, 75, 173
Romania 53, 56, 71, 74, 103, 122, 157, 159, Rome 140, 141, 142
Rommel, Erwin 68, 129, 130, 141, 155, 156, 157, 164, 165, 166, 171
Roosevelt, Franklin vii, 117, 121, 125, 126, 131, 135, 143, 144, 145, 150, 151, 185
Równe 27

Index

Różycka, Maria Barbara xviii
Różycki, Jerzy vi, 19, 133
Rundstedt, Gerd von 62, 151, 157, 163, 164
  165, 166, 179, 180
Russia, *see* Soviet Russia

Saalwächter, Alfred 73
Sachsenhausen 152
Salerno 141, 142
Salter 117
Sandwich, see Menzies 42, 43
Sardinia 140
Saucken, Dietrich von 183
Saul, Richard 84
Saunders, Malcolm 54
Scapa Flow 66, 95, 96
Scarborough 52
Schacht, Hjalmer 106
Schaffhausen 110
Scheidt, Wilhelm 173
Scheliba, Rudolf von 102
Schellenberg, Walter 152
Scherbius, Arthur 9, 10, 11, 20, 28, 189
Schlabrendorff, Fabian von 169
Schleicher, Kurt von 104
Schlesser, Guy 15
Schmidt, Hans-Thilo 14
Schneider, Christian 109
Schnieper, Xavier xviii, 108, 111, 117, 119
Schramm, Wilhelm von 173
Schulze-Boysen, Harro vii, 101, 102, 103,
  114, 173
Schwannenfeld, Schwerin von 171
Scotland 1, 84, 86, 171
Sedan 61
Sedlacek, Karel 111
Seville 69
Siam 71
Siberia 113
Sicily 70, 140, 142
Sikorski, Władysław 162
Silesia 3, 4
Simpson, see Sedlacek 111
Singapore 126
Skorzeny, Otto 141, 150, 179
Slim, William 176
Sofia 74
Soissons 164
Sonia, see Hamburger 108
Sorge, Richard 112
South America 78

South Norway 86
South-east Asia 176
South-east England 84
Southern Sweden 96, 168
Soviet Russia (Russia) xii, 4, 6, 13, 17, 18, 68,
  100, 103, 107, 111, 112, 116, 144, 151, 152,
  156, 162, 169, 173, 184
Soviet Union 57, 67, 102, 109, 111, 115, 121,
  122, 144, 146, 150, 162, 173, 177
Spain 68, 70, 71, 97, 109, 133, 158, 162
Speer, Albert 71, 179
Speerle, Hugo 83, 88
Spondlemühle 15
St Gallen 110
Stachiewicz, Wacław 41
Stalin, Joseph vii, 53, 59, 103, 106, 111, 112,
  113, 114, 116, 118, 144, 150, 151, 156, 158,
  159, 162, 178
Stalingrad 118, 120, 131
Stanmore 85, 86, 133
Starogard 18
Station X, *see* Bletchley Park 50
Stavanger 86
Stauffenberg, Claus Schenk von vii, 169, 170,
  171
Stefan 115
Stelmann, *see* Lemoine 15
Stengers, J. xviii
Stieff, Helmuth 169, 171
Stimson, Henry 122
Stockholm 67, 96, 103, 124
Strachey, Oliver 49
Strasbourg 57
Stülpnagel, Karl-Heinrich 104, 156, 171
Stummel 138
Stumpff 83
Stürzinger, Oscar xvii
Stuttgart xviii, 132
Sudetenland 38, 46, 105
Suez Canal 130
Sukulov-Gurevich, Victor 101
Sweden vi, 73, 96, 124, 134, 149, 156, 168,
  185, 189
Switzerland xiii, xvii, xviii, 15, 71, 77, 106,
  107, 108, 109, 110, 111, 112, 113, 114, 115,
  116, 117, 118, 128, 134, 173, 174, 184

Tobata, Masanori 123
Taormina 140
Teddy 115
Teheran vii, 150, 152, 156, 158, 177

Tempelhof 12
Thames 86
Thiele, Fritz 68, 69, 152, 171
Third *Reich* xiii, 33, 39, 71, 90, 100, 101, 103, 106, 110, 125, 128, 161, 172, 174, 181, 183, 185
Thompson, Ruth xvii
Tiltman, J. H. 49
Tito, see Bros 74
Tizard, Henry 126
Todt, Fritz 71
Tokyo 79, 122, 126
Torgau 185
Toulon 130
Toulouse 62, 164
Tourville 61
Tovey, John 96, 97
Travis, Edward 129
Traxl, Alfred 102
Trepper, Leopold 100, 101, 103, 108, 112, 114
Trescow, Henning von 169
Tunis 130
Turing, Alan vi, 49, 58, 59, 147
Türkel, Siegfried 9
Turkey 71, 152
Turnow 15
Twinn, Peter 49, 51

Ukraine 102
Ulm 164
United Kingdom 54, 83
United States xii, 10, 17, 48, 67, 71, 74, 89, 91, 106, 107, 114, 115, 121, 122, 124, 125, 126, 127, 130, 136, 137, 138, 143, 145, 151, 156, 160, 163, 169, 172, 175, 176, 189
Uruguay 71
Uzès 132

Vansittart, Robert 105
Vanvelkenhuyzen, J. xviii
Vatican 71, 109
Venezuela 71
Versailles 4, 5, 6, 9, 13, 18, 28, 32, 35, 65, 66, 69, 77, 90
Verviers 15

Vichy 131
Vienna 9, 184
Vietinghoff, Heinrich 142
Vignolles vi, 56
Vinnica 102
Vistula 178
Volga 118

Wallner, Franz 111
Warsaw 2, 3, 7, 10, 16, 18, 19, 22, 25, 26, 38, 41, 42, 43, 56, 58, 59, 167, 178
Washington xii, 46, 77, 122, 124, 126, 130, 131, 145, 178
Wasserburg 69
Welchman, Gordon 49, 147
Wenzel, Johann 100
Western Europe 70, 112
West Indies 126
Wether 115, 117
Weygand, Maxime 17, 62
Wheatstone, Charles 8, 189
Wiesäcker, Ernst von 105
Wilde, Oscar xx
Wilhelmshaven 74
Wilmersdorf 9
Wilson, Angus 49
Wilson, Woodrow 4
Winn, Rodger 137
Winterbotham, Frederick W. vi, vii, xviii, 52, 53, 54, 55, 118, 127, 176
Winterinck, Anton 103
Witzleben, Erwin von 105, 171
Wyatt, Inzer 176
Wynn-Williams 147

Yamamoto, Isoroku 177
Yamamoto, Masaharu 123
Yardley, Herbert 122
Yefremov, Mikhail 101
Yugoslavia 71, 73, 107, 144, 151

Zeigenburg 179
Zimmermann, Arthur 46, 49
Zug 134, 188
Zürich 15, 110, 188
Zygalski, Henryk vi, 19, 37, 42, 43, 45, 133